IMAGES
of America

KNIGHTSTOWN

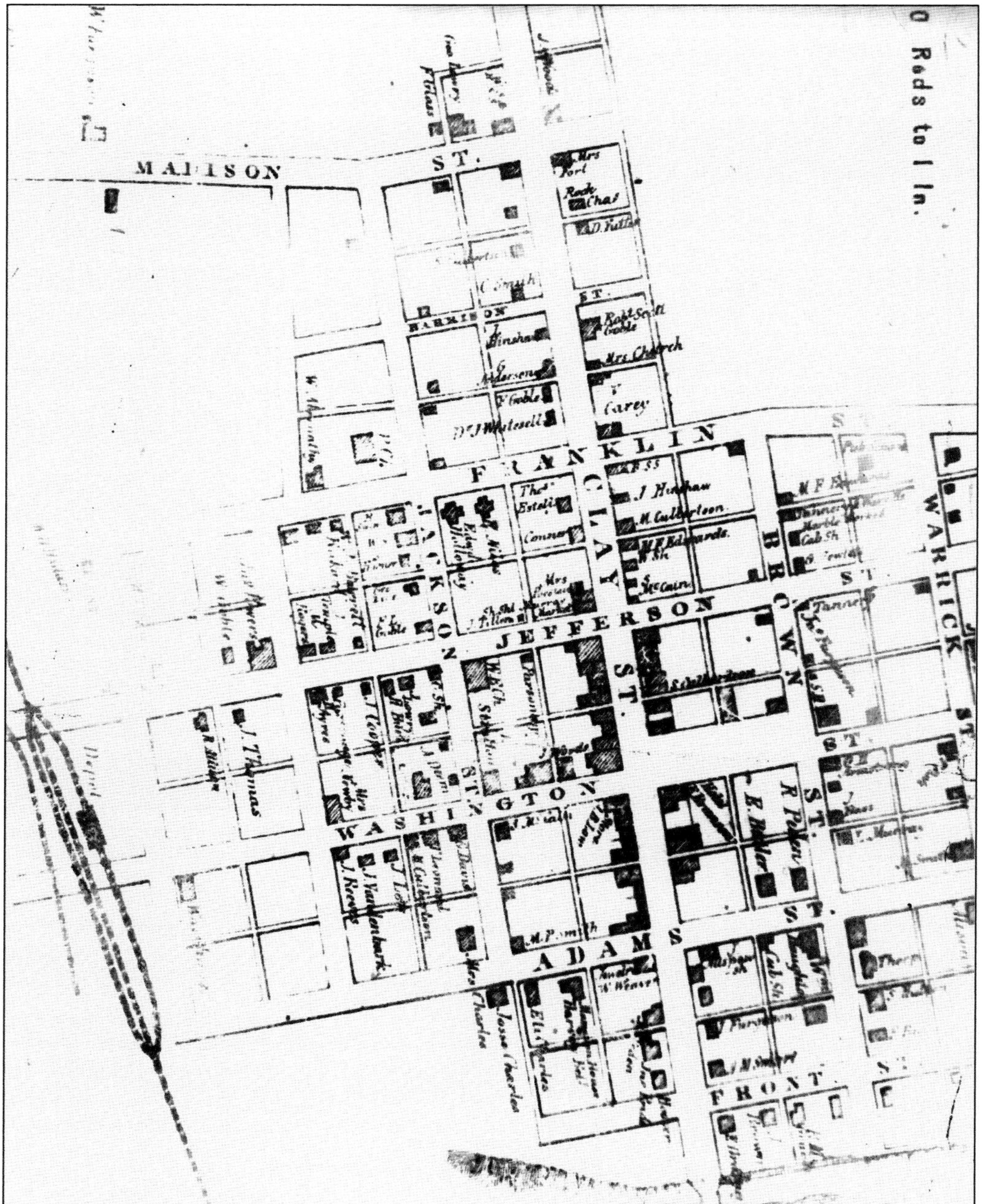

Knightstown has not changed much since it was platted by Jonathan Knight in 1827, when it contained 12 blocks and 85 lots. The central portion of town still features streets as they are shown in this vintage map. (Courtesy of Historic Knightstown, Inc.)

On the Cover: Knightstown featured several small, family-owned grocery stores in the early 1900s. In the market pictured here, employees and a customer look relaxed amid the wide variety of items for sale. (Courtesy of Historic Knightstown, Inc.)

IMAGES
of America

KNIGHTSTOWN

Karen Pyle Trent

ARCADIA
PUBLISHING

ISBN 978-0-7385-7823-1

Published by Arcadia Publishing
Charleston SC, Chicago IL, Portsmouth NH, San Francisco CA

Printed in the United States of America

Library of Congress Control Number: 2009943874

For all general information contact Arcadia Publishing at:
Telephone 843-853-2070
Fax 843-853-0044
E-mail sales@arcadiapublishing.com
For customer service and orders:
Toll-Free 1-888-313-2665

Visit us on the Internet at www.arcadiapublishing.com

To my dad

Contents

Acknowledgments

I owe my passion for local history to Dolly McCormack, who introduced me to Knightstown's story and the importance of preserving it. Dolly understands as much about Knightstown's past as anyone I know, and I found her enthusiasm and knowledge contagious. I also am grateful to longtime Knightstown residents Peg Mayhill, Carol Duncan, and Mary Craven, who is a descendent of Knightstown founder Waitstill M. Cary. Peg, Carol, and Mary brought Knightstown history to life for me with their remembrances and stories of the town in another era.

The task of putting together this project has been made so much easier by the existence of a small but significant treasure called Historic Knightstown, Inc. (HKI). Originally started by a group of Knightstown citizens in an effort to save the 1876 Knightstown Academy, the organization now oversees a local history museum on the west side of Knightstown's Public Square that safeguards a wealth of vintage photographs, documents, and memorabilia. HKI members Bob and Carolyn Myers, David Steele, and Joann Smith have been invaluable in allowing me access to the museum and answering my many questions. Former Knightstown resident Ed Knight and his "KHS Class of '57" Web site also have been a helpful and entertaining resource.

I would like to thank my editor, Anna Wilson, for her patience, as well as the *Banner* publisher, Eric Cox, for his support in helping me with the museum's collection of vintage photographs. Unless otherwise noted, images in this book were graciously provided by Historic Knightstown, Inc.

And finally, my family would say that my interest in Knightstown history is not a passion, it is an obsession. (They are probably right.) But I appreciate my husband, Mike, and daughters, Emily and Sarah, just the same for listening to my constant chatter about everything old and joining me occasionally on my fact-finding adventures.

INTRODUCTION

When former Ohioan Waitstill M. Cary discovered that the soon-to-be-built National Road would cut across his farm in what is now Henry County, Indiana, he conceived the idea of a town to be located where the National Road and the Big Blue River would meet. He then hired Jonathan Knight, one of the National Road engineers, in 1827 to plat out the town that he then named Knight's Town.

The construction of the National Road brought Knightstown to life, and for years it continued to feed the tiny town's success, as it served as a connection between the East Coast and the developing West. The building of America's first federally funded road brought thousands of people into new towns such as Knightstown, and with them came the need for goods, services, and homes for the new inhabitants.

Knightstown's early prosperity can be seen in its grand homes and significant architecture. Many outstanding examples of late-19th-century houses still exist, and they add to the charm of Knightstown's tree-lined neighborhoods. The town's remaining churches, commercial buildings, and educational facilities (including the National Register–listed Knightstown Academy) provide a strong reminder of what life in Knightstown was like in its earlier years.

Knightstown's ties to the road and to transportation have continued over the years. In the early 1900s, for example, miles of track were laid to accommodate the interurban—an electrically powered rail line that connected Richmond and Indianapolis in east-central Indiana—and ran right down the middle of Clay Street (later renamed Main Street) in downtown Knightstown. Several vehicles also were manufactured in Knightstown, including the Leader around 1910 and the Galahad hearse by the Knightstown Funeral Car Company in the 1930s.

Some buildings in Knightstown continue to make history. One example is Knightstown's Hoosier Gym, which was constructed in 1922. Interest in the old building was revived when it was chosen as the site to film the 1986 Oscar-nominated movie *Hoosiers*. Still full of charm, the gym now is used as a community center and is visited by thousands of tourists every year.

Though existing structures and neighborhoods continue to provide memories for locals and visitors alike, Knightstown is also remembered for buildings and experiences that no longer exist. Buildings such as the Alhambra, which was located on the east side of the Public Square, and the Hotel Jack on Main Street are gone, but the memories they provided certainly are not. And though the Indiana Soldiers' and Sailors' Children's Home, which had served Indiana children since 1865, still stands, it currently is used by the Indiana National Guard since its closing by the state in early 2009.

Knightstown certainly owes its existence to advancement through the building of a simple highway—the National Road. It also in part owes its decline to the construction of another—Interstate 70. The Henry County portion of the interstate was completed just north of Knightstown in the 1970s and pulled much of the traffic and visitors away from the small towns that had thrived on the National Road for more than a century. Renewed interest in the historic National Road and the road's designation as a National Scenic Byway have increased tourism traffic. Recovery has been gradual, but it continues. Fortunately many quality images remain that can document Knightstown's journey.

One

The Journey Begins

Though Knightstown was platted in 1827, it was not officially incorporated until 1837. Its main street is the National Road, which in Knightstown has also been known as U.S. 40, Clay Street, and Main Street. The Public Square, a block-long area with a center strip, was set aside on Washington Street just north of the main road through town. In 1827, Waitstill M. Cary offered lots for sale, and on August 11 of that year an advertisement ran in the Richmond, Indiana, newspaper titled "Sale of Lots in Knight's Town." In part, it described some of the selling points of the Knightstown area, "There are already erected, and now in operation, in the vicinity of this place, two saw and two grist mills and a carding machine." It was signed by Waitstill M. Cary and Jeremiah Grover.

Much of life in early Knightstown revolved around necessities. An inventory of businesses around the Public Square in the 1800s might have included grocers, dry goods, lumber, boots and shoes, buggies, and hardware. With the addition of Interstate 70 and major chain stores in the 20th century, residents now have access to the essentials elsewhere, and Knightstown businesses featuring the basics have all but disappeared.

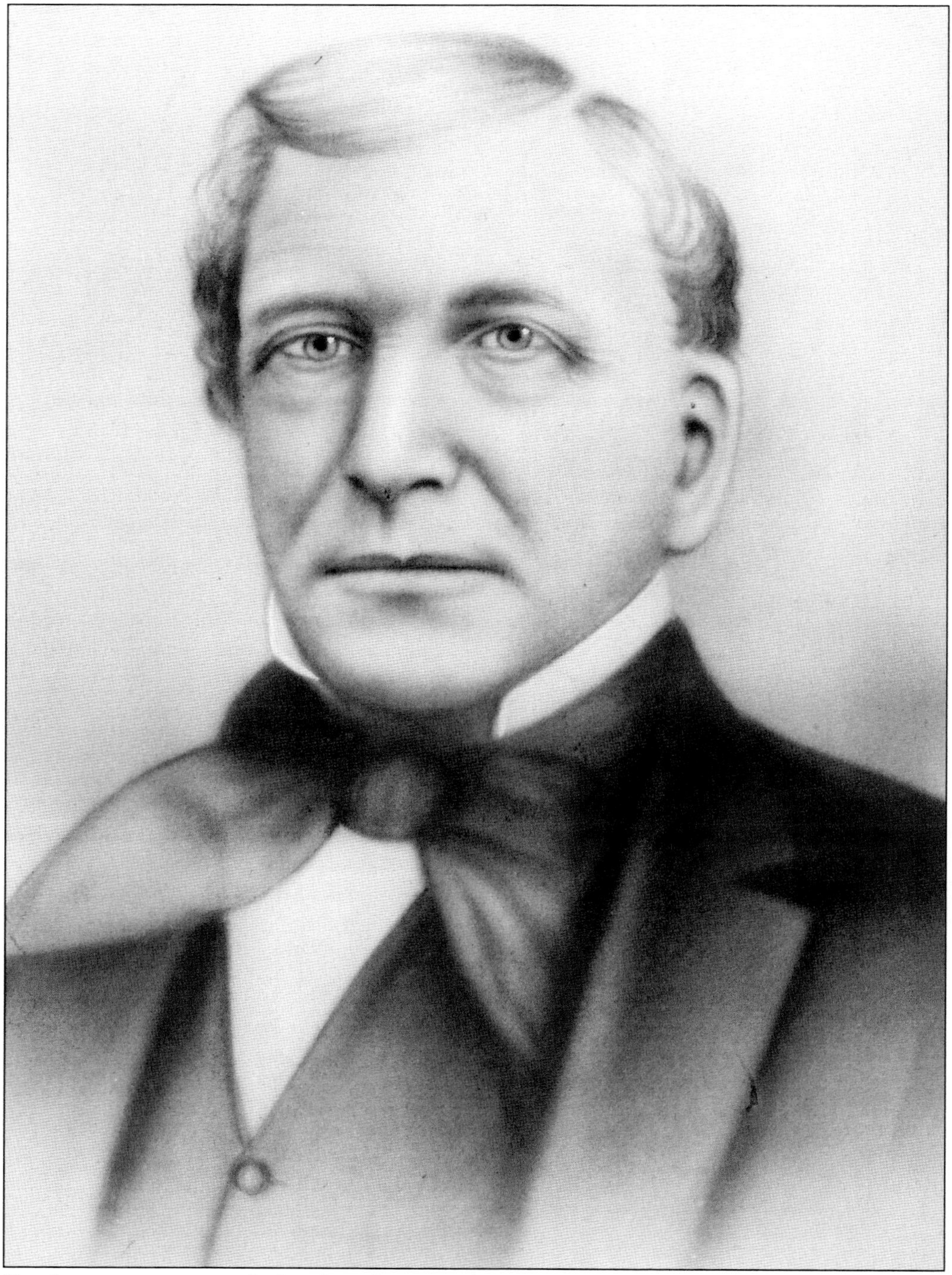

Knightstown was named after Jonathan Knight, a Pennsylvanian who was one of the chief engineers who surveyed and laid out the nation's first federally funded highway, the National Road. A versatile man with no formal education beyond primary school, Knight was a talented mathematician, inventor, politician, farmer, and family man. He was hired by landowner Waitstill M. Cary to plat the new town in 1827. Knight also platted the nearby town of Raysville. Born on November 22, 1787, Knight ironically died on his birthday in 1858. He was 71 years old.

Waitstill Munson Cary (at right) founded Knightstown on his farmland near where the National Road crosses the Big Blue River in east-central Indiana. Born in New Jersey in 1785, Cary married Nancy Rock on July 9, 1805. He spent several years near Cincinnati and Springfield, Ohio, before moving to the tiny village of West Liberty, Indiana, in June 1825 and then into nearby Knightstown a few years later. A hatter by trade, Cary chose to raise his family—a wife, one son, and six daughters—in the first house built in Knightstown and run a tavern next door. Cary's dwelling at the corner of the National Road and the Public Square is long gone, but it is commemorated by a stone and plaque (below) that mark the spot. Cary died in Knightstown in June 1863. (At right, courtesy of Mary Craven.)

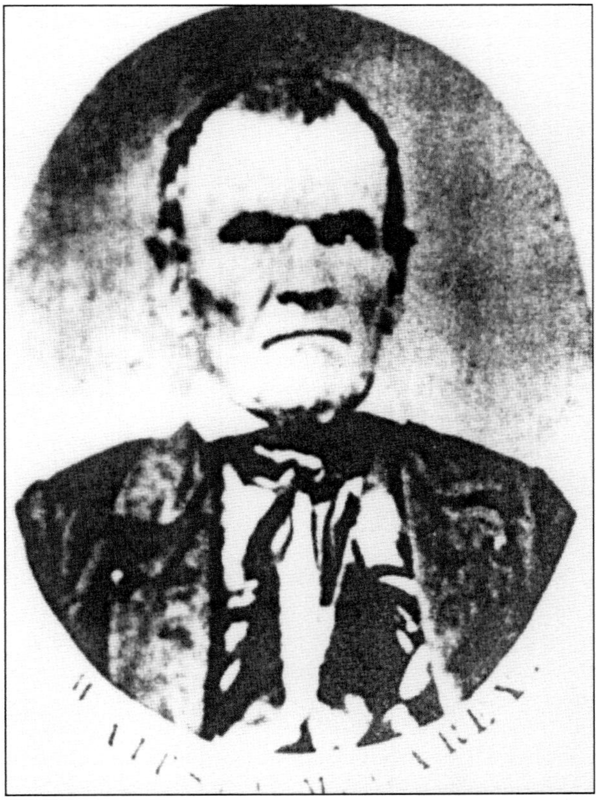

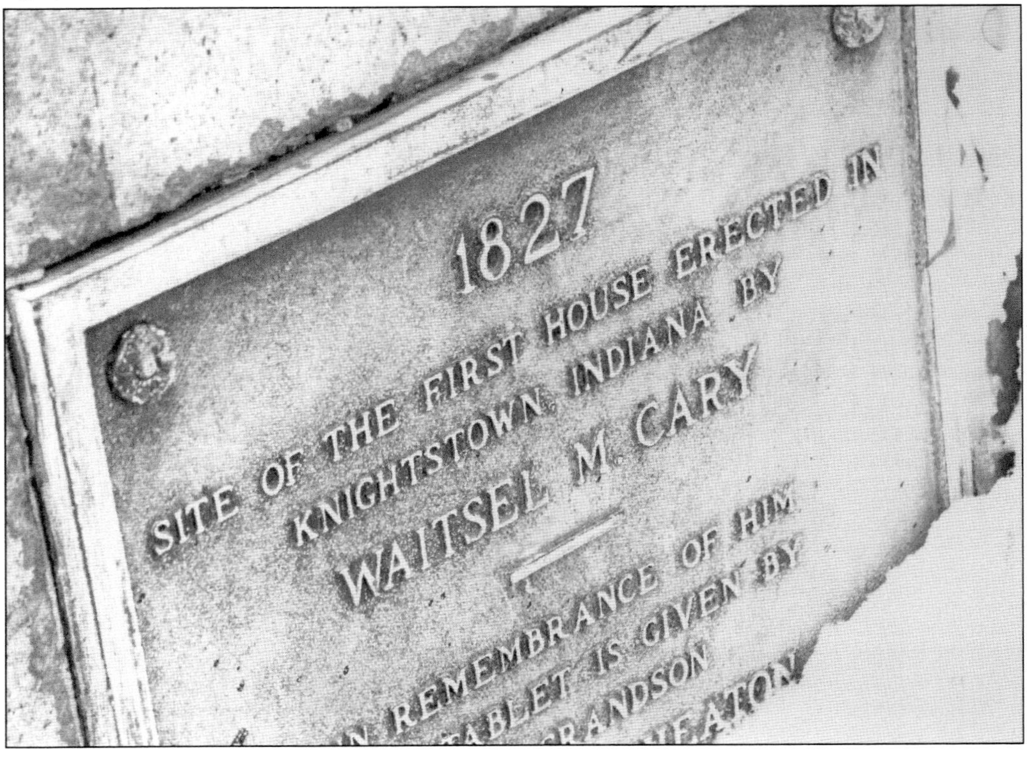

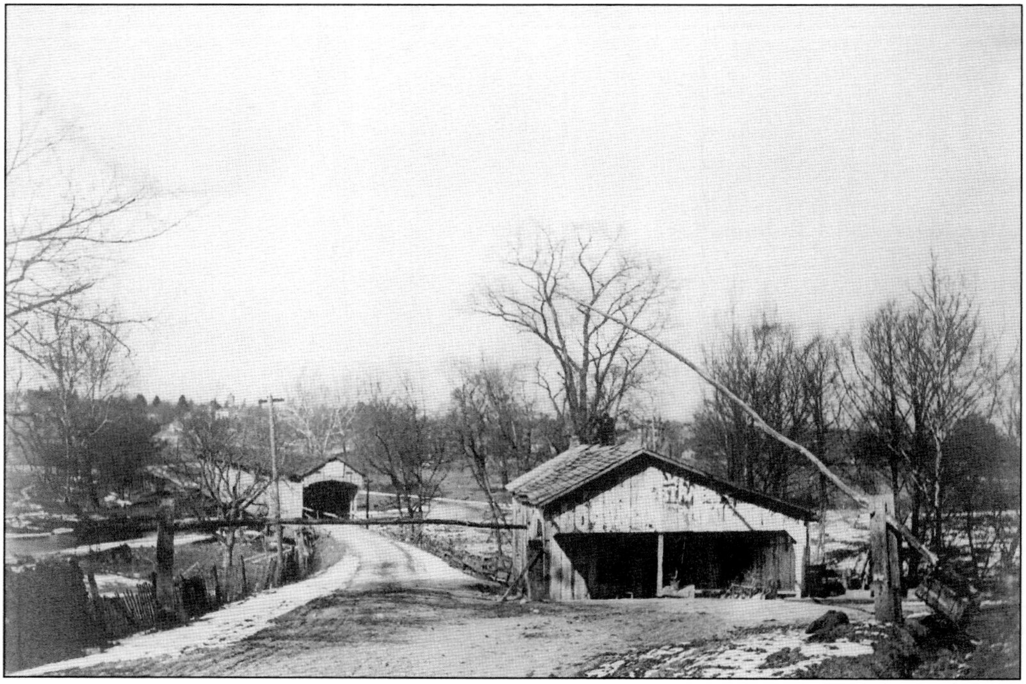

Before taxes were implemented to raise funds for road maintenance, tollgates often were used to collect money for road improvements. This tollgate (above), which was located on the path between Knightstown and the Indiana Soldiers' and Sailors' Children's Home just south of town, featured a bar that lifted up and down across the road to let travelers who had paid pass through. Another shot of the same tollgate around 1906 (below) shows more activity as a horse-drawn wagon passes under the toll bar travelling south toward the Children's Home in northern Rush County. A covered bridge is visible in the background.

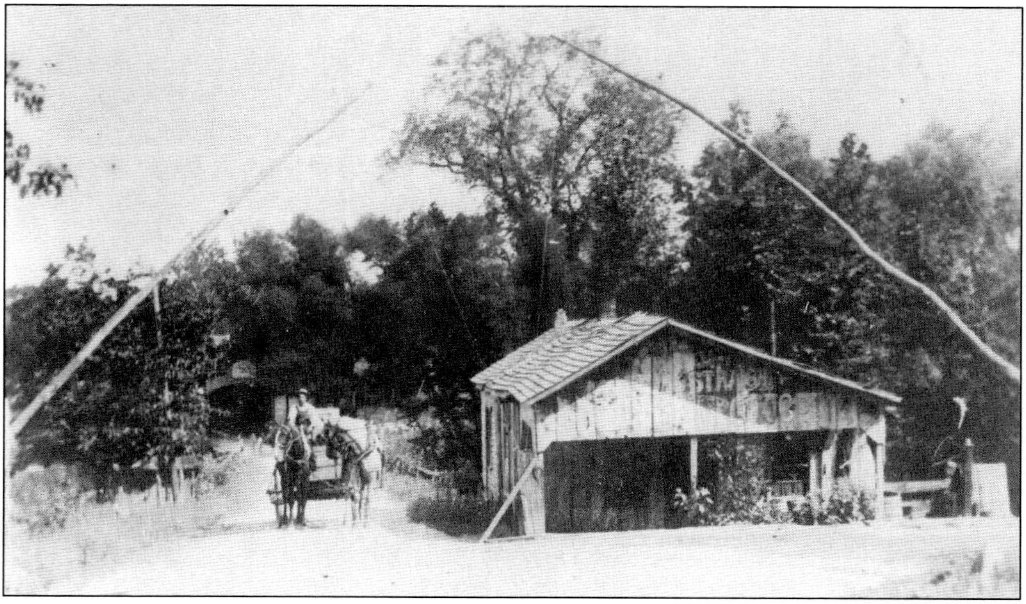

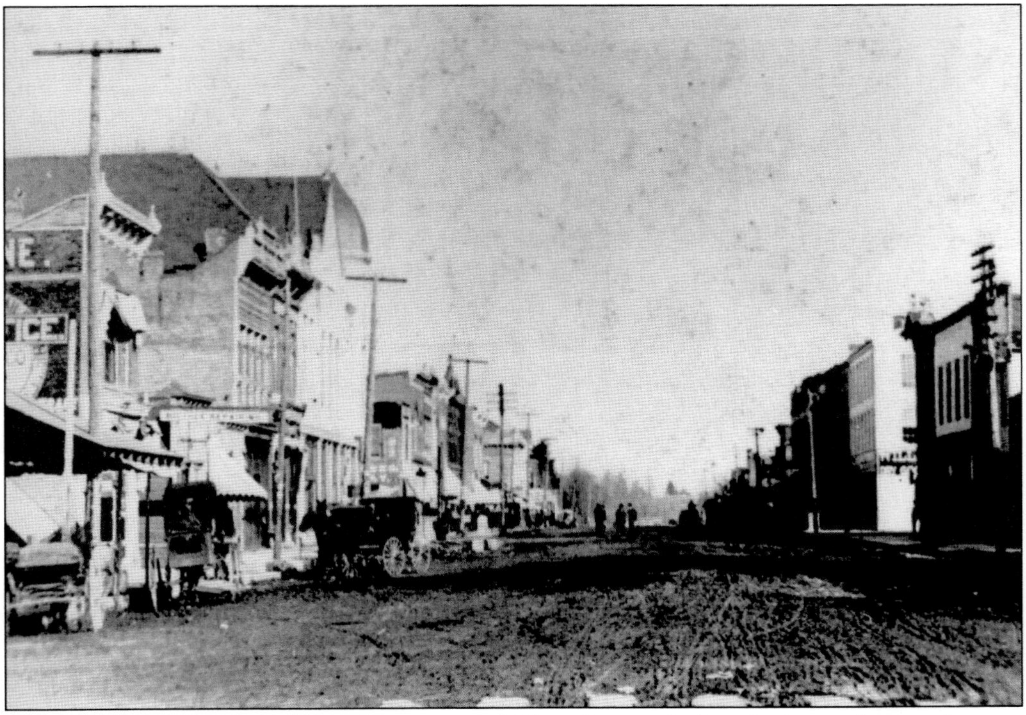

Looking east down Clay Street—later renamed Main Street—before the interurban tracks were placed in the early 1900s shows that the main street already was becoming a bustling area for business. Notice the Knightstown Sun newspaper office to the left and the stepping stones across the dirt road at the bottom of the photograph.

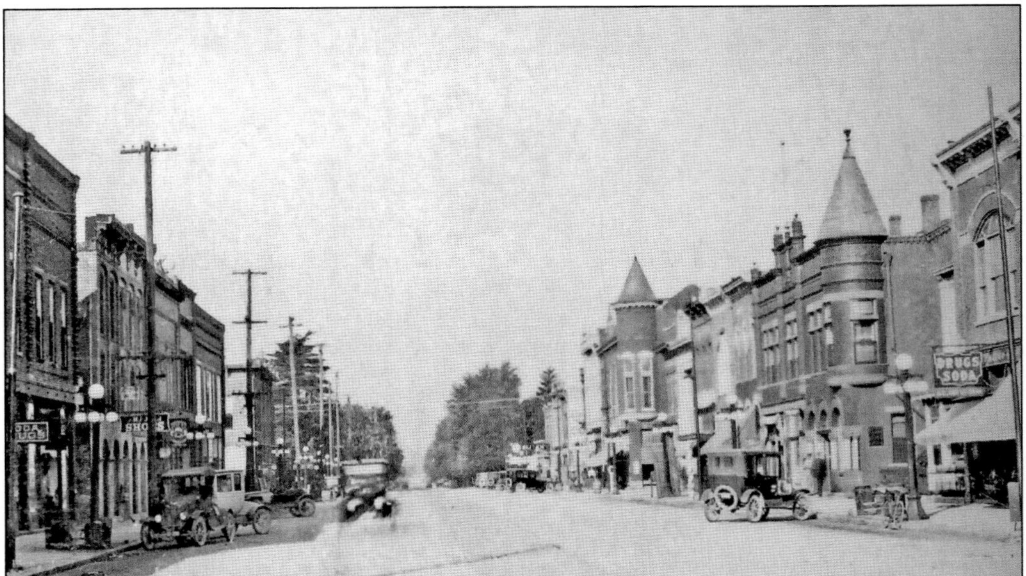

A later view of Clay Street toward the west shows several drugstores, a shoe store, a jeweler, and a veterinarian's office. The main street originally featured mostly residential structures, but they soon disappeared in favor of commercial buildings. Though businesses eventually spilled onto Clay Street, the commercial character of the Public Square continued to prosper.

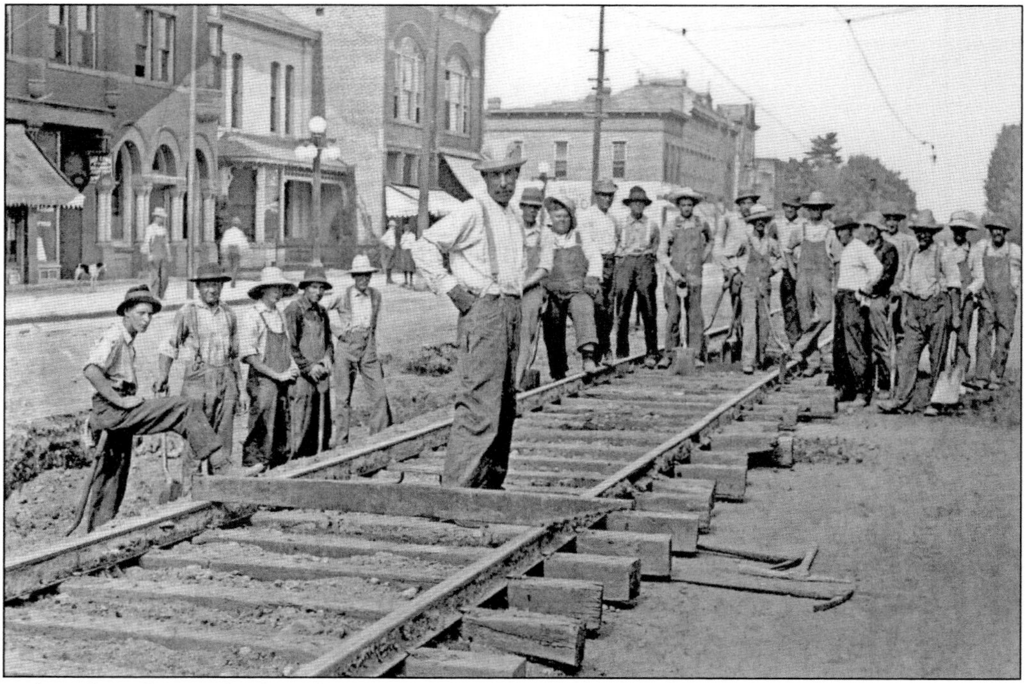

Miles of track were laid in the early 1900s to accommodate the interurban, a rail line that connected Richmond and Indianapolis in east-central Indiana and many of the smaller towns in between. Here workers take a break while working on a section of track down the middle of Clay Street in the heart of Knightstown.

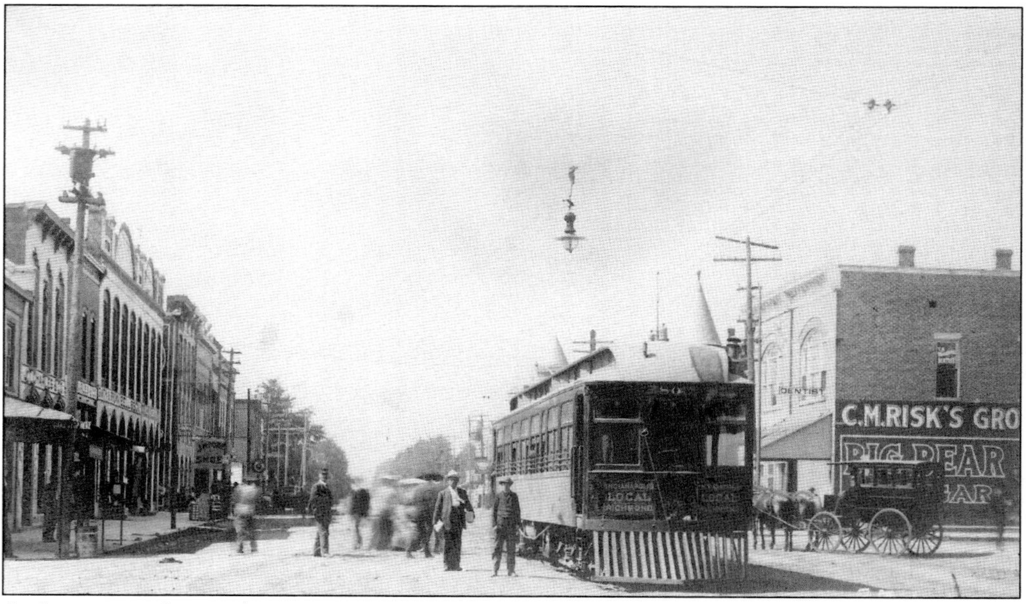

A glance west down Clay Street around 1908 contrasts old and new, as a horse and buggy pauses next to a modern, electric interurban car near the Public Square. The Terre Haute, Indianapolis and Eastern Interurban Line connected Knightstown, Dunreith, Spiceland, and New Castle. Bell's Hall is the arched building on the left; the C. M. Risk's Grocery is on the right.

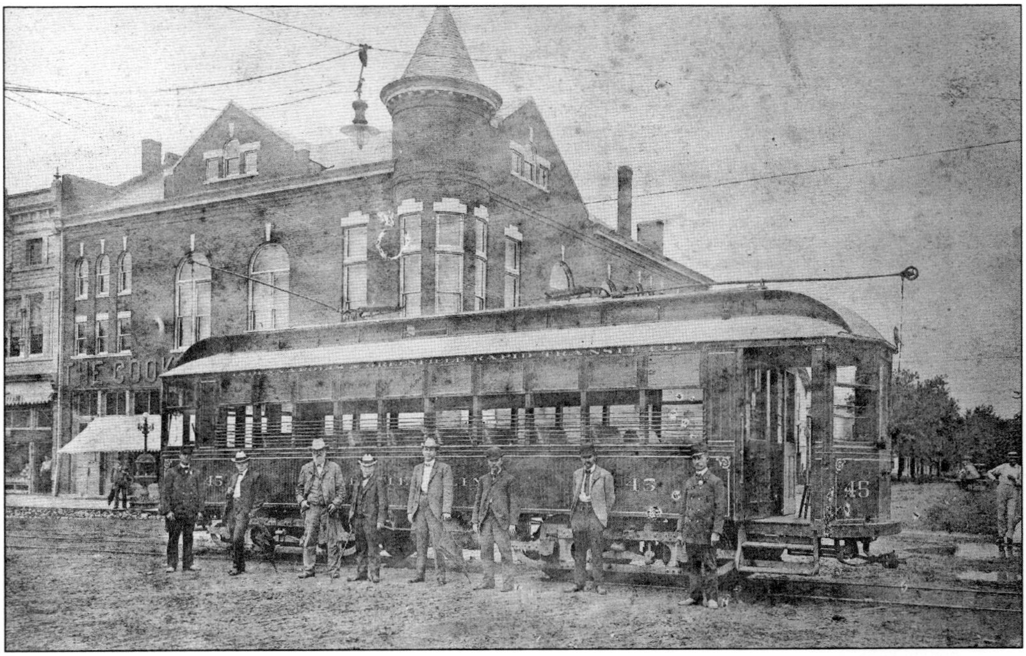

The interurban might have had the most significant effect on smaller towns such as Knightstown by providing faster, more convenient transportation to larger cities. The men standing here in front of the interurban car on Knightstown's main street could have used the service for goods and services related to their businesses. Interurban service was available to Knightstown from 1903 until 1938.

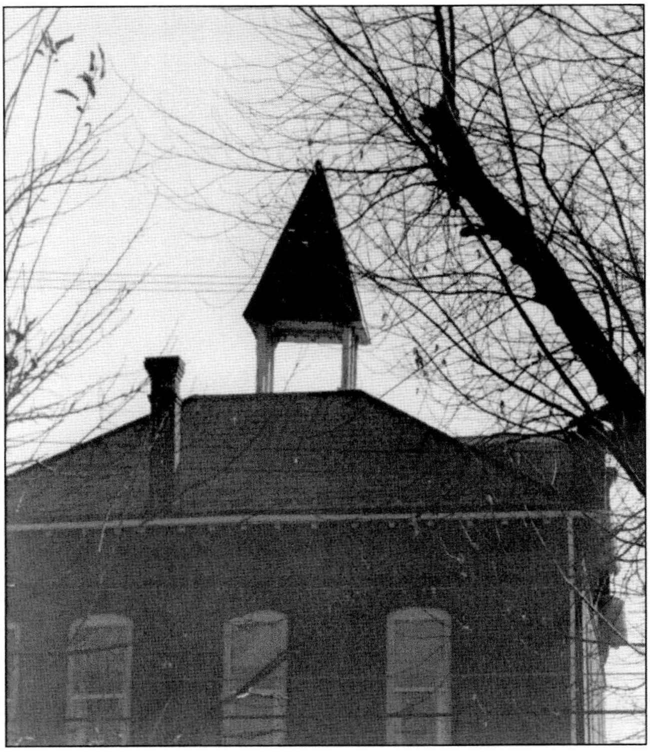

Knightstown's Romanesque Revival town hall is seen here. The hall was built in 1892 and served as the center of town business for many years. After town activities moved to more modern quarters, the hall was used as an antique store for a time and as apartments.

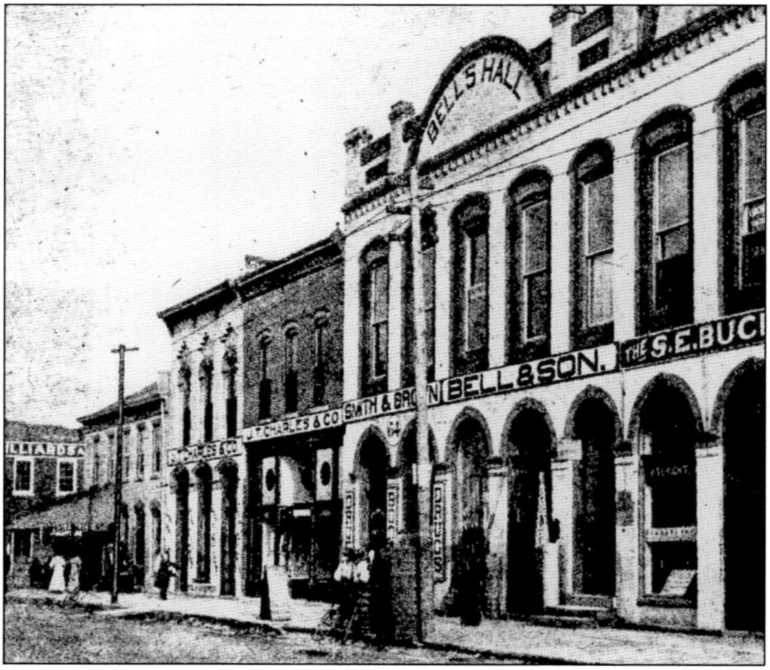

Bell's Hall was located on the second floor of this building and was at the center of Knightstown's entertainment scene in the 1800s. Weekly dances, concerts by musicians such as Knightstown's Silver Cornet Band, and even basketball games were available at Bell's Hall. At the time of this photograph, a drugstore was located on the first floor, and a billiards hall was in the next block to the left.

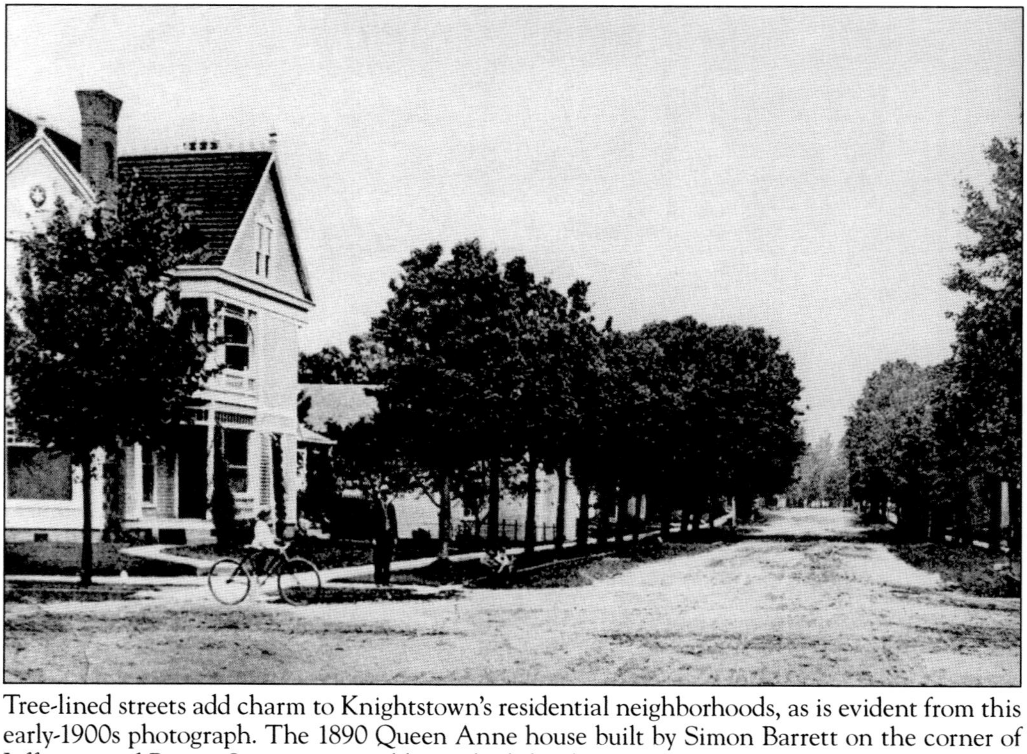

Tree-lined streets add charm to Knightstown's residential neighborhoods, as is evident from this early-1900s photograph. The 1890 Queen Anne house built by Simon Barrett on the corner of Jefferson and Brown Streets is viewable on the left side.

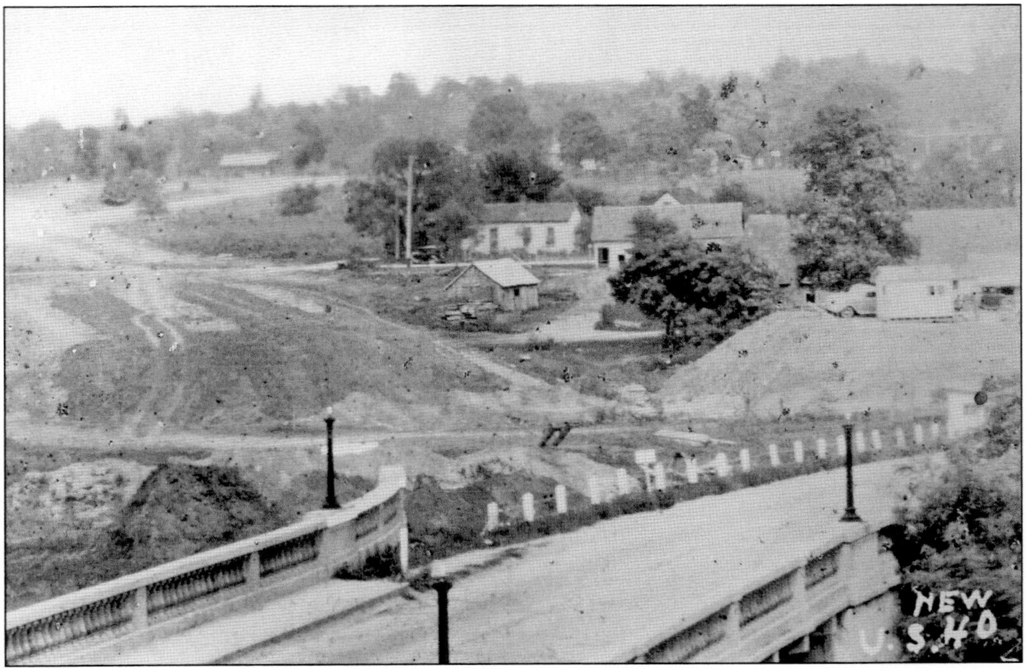

Work is completed on the National Road bridge over the Big Blue River (above) on Knightstown's east side. Before construction of the new concrete bridge, the National Road ran through nearby Raysville. With the building of the bridge, U.S. Highway 40 was rerouted just north of Raysville. The 1890 Sale Barn can be seen to the right in the photograph, which is still is used today. Later the bridge (below), which was constructed around 1920, became an avenue for automobiles traveling along U.S. Highway 40. Horse-and-wagon traffic, however, was still common at this time, as the use of horses and automobiles overlapped.

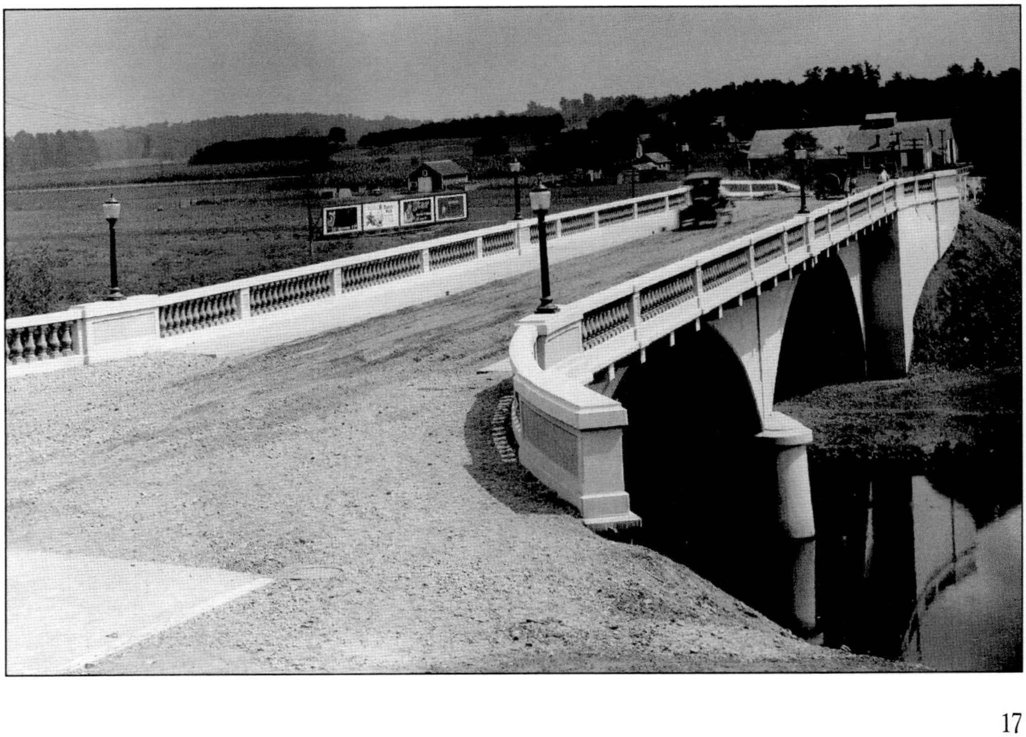

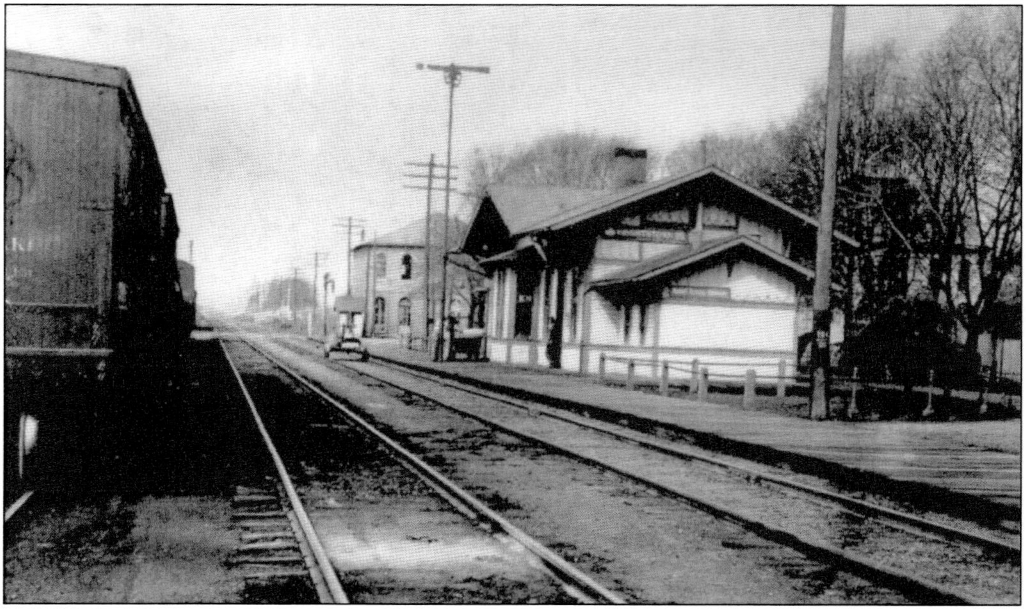

The Pennsylvania Railroad's (PRR) freight depot (above) saw a lot of action. For more than a century, the PRR delivered mail, freight, and passengers to Knightstown. The passenger depot (below) is shown about 1920. It was located between Jefferson and Washington Streets and faced south. Passengers used the steps to the left in the photograph to reach the elevated tracks. The Pennsylvania Railroad carried Pres. Abraham Lincoln's body through Knightstown on Monday, May 1, 1865, on its way to Springfield, Illinois, following his assassination in Washington, D.C. The PRR stopped running through Knightstown in 1981.

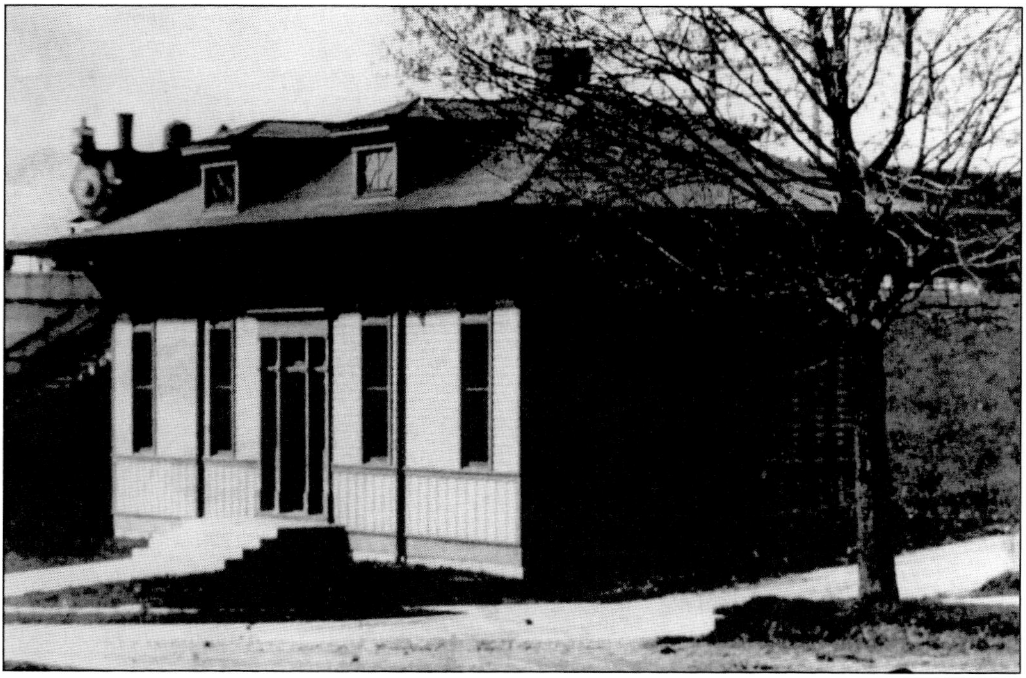

It is rather obvious that the pumping station was built in 1894. It probably was relatively new when this undated photograph was taken; fresh landscaping and a neat picket fence are noticeable out front. Located just west of Knightstown on the National Road, the pumping station still exists, though now it is painted white.

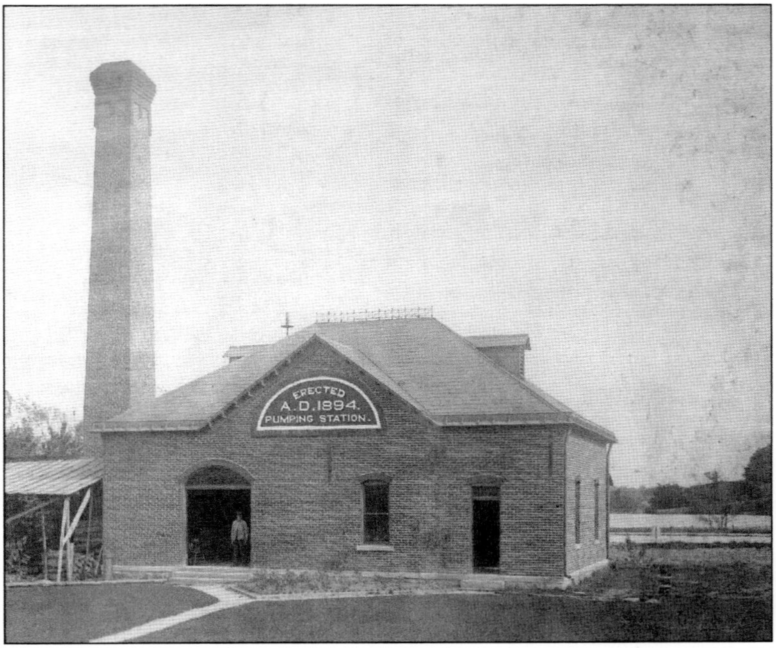

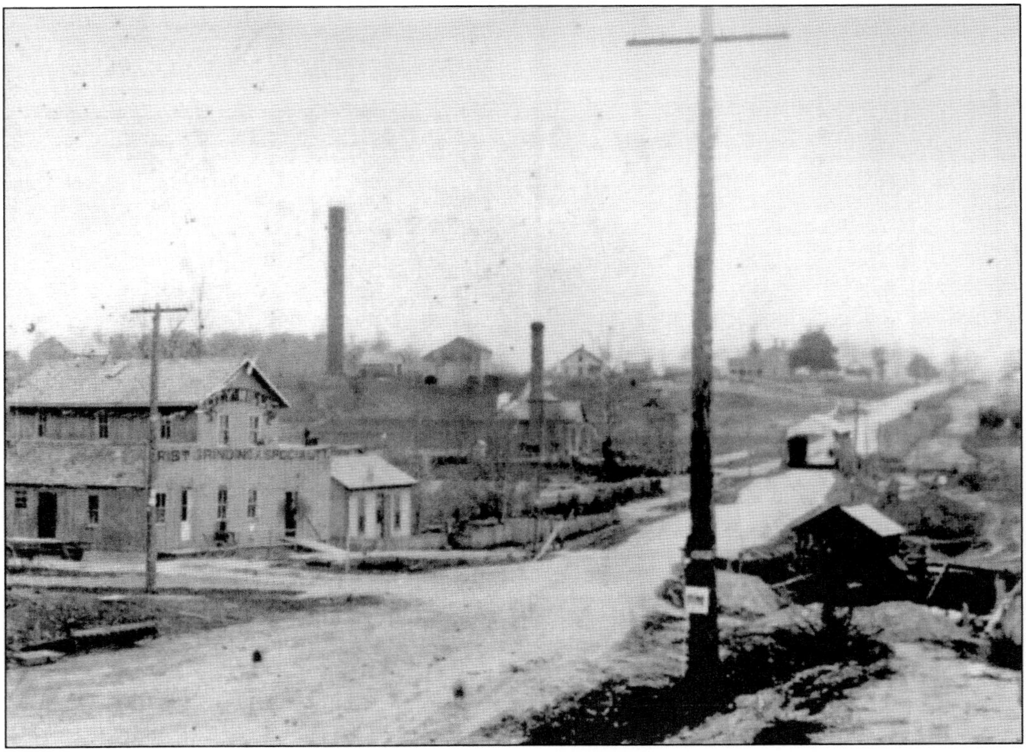

Looking west, the 1894 pumping station can be seen just past the City Mill. The covered bridge enabled passage over Montgomery Creek on the National Road. Today the new Knightstown Community High School is located just up the road on the left, and the covered bridge is gone in favor of a more modern structure.

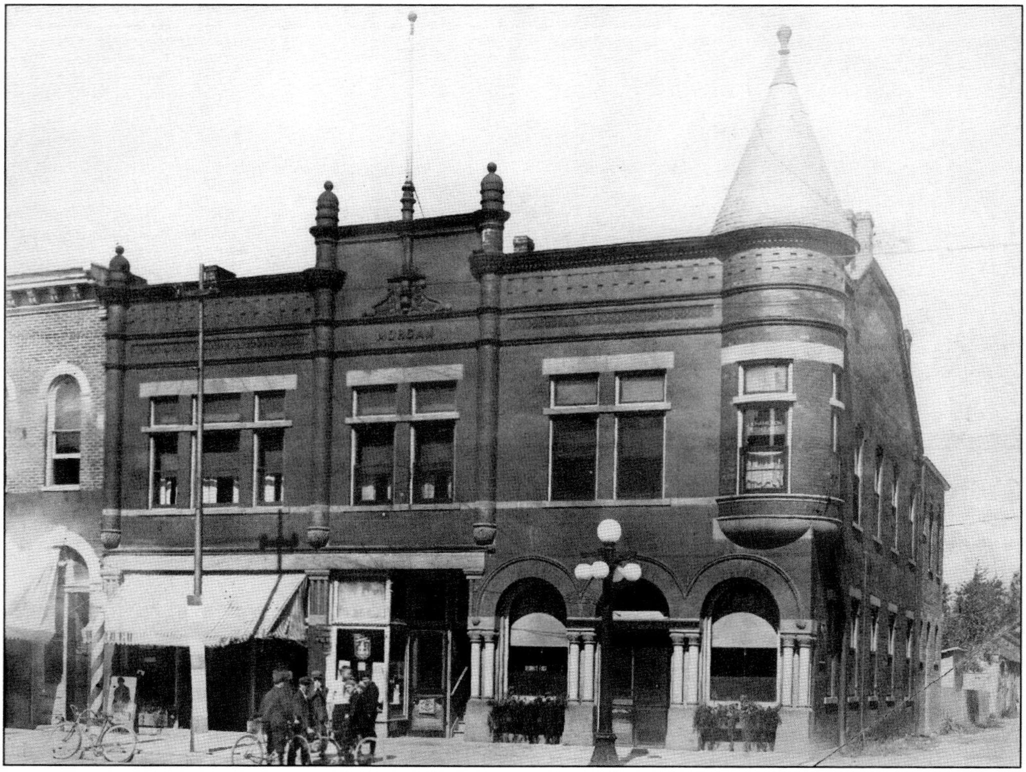

The Morgan Building was added to Knightstown's main street in 1865 by Robert Woods, where it was—and still is—a prominent fixture. The Romanesque Revival building later was remodeled and named for banker Charles D. Morgan and was home to the First National Bank, which was founded by Woods. In this *c.* 1905 photograph, another popular mode of transportation is shown in front of the Morgan Building—the bicycle.

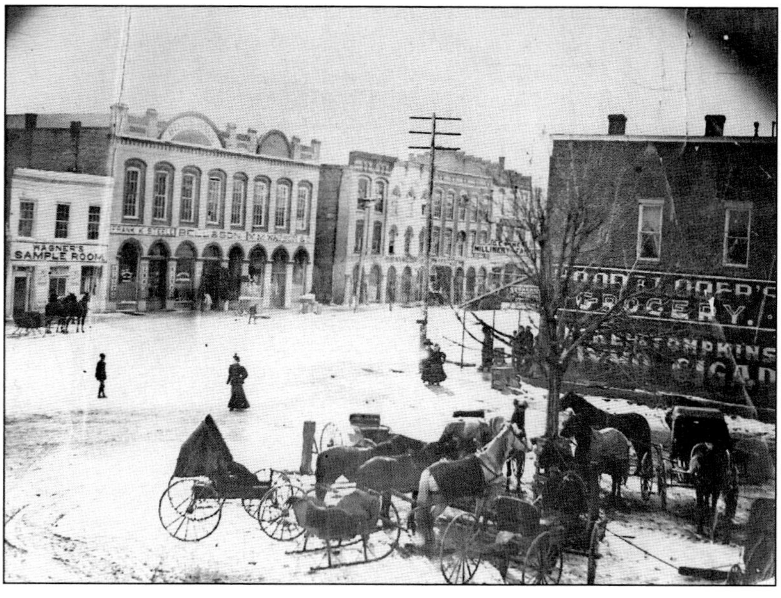

Horses and buggies were a familiar scene on Knightstown's Public Square in the 1800s. Streets at that time were unpaved (in other words dirt), which made for some messy travel during rain and snow. This corner, at Clay and Washington Streets, was a busy spot. Notice that Bell's Hall was located across the road on Clay Street.

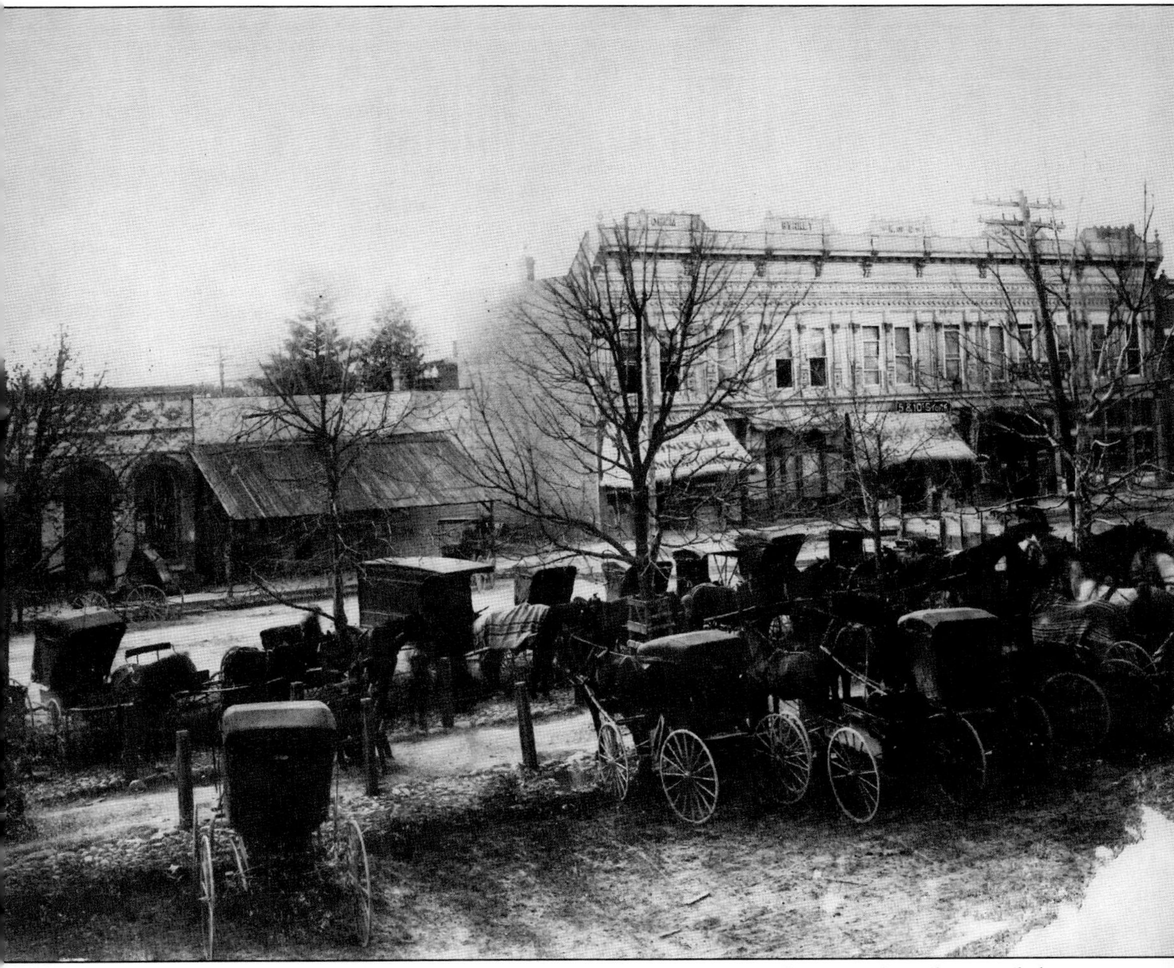

In the 1800s, horses and buggies created their own parking spaces and were tethered around the center of Knightstown's Public Square. Businesses on the square have come and gone over the years, as they often have been a reflection of the times. In 1884, for example, businesses on the Public Square included establishments such as a buggy shop, blacksmith, and livery barn. Later, as society progressed, these made way for gas stations, auto sales, and farm implements. Today the square is home to a tanning/video store, an insurance agency, and a catering business. The signs on the top edge of the building in the background of this photograph seem to indicate the businesses that were located below. From left to right, the first three are "Deem," "Byrket," and "K of P" (Knights of Pythias most likely); unfortunately the remaining two are obscured by the trees.

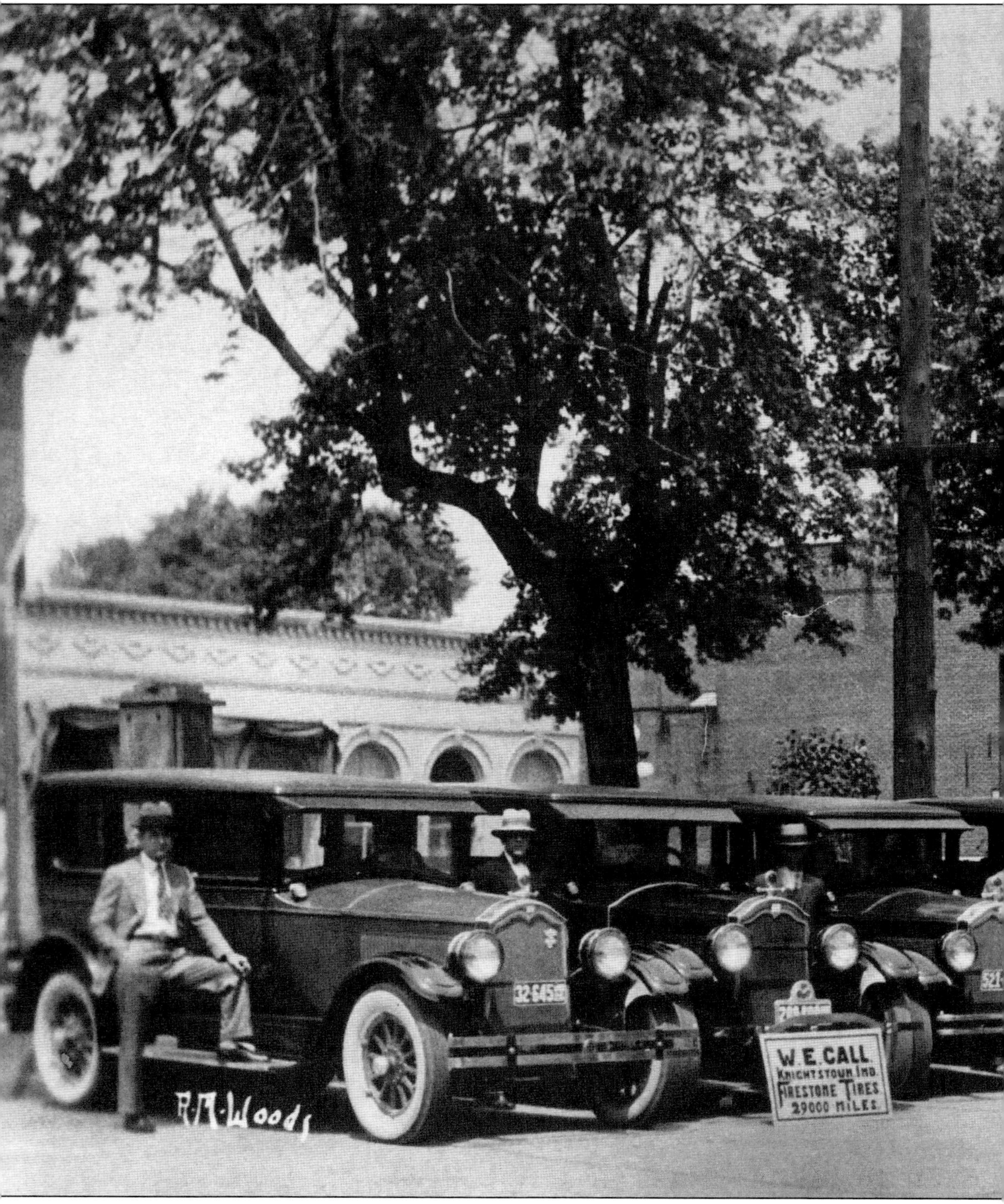

Fortunately for historians, Knightstown's Public Square has always been a popular spot for photographs. In this example, a group of dressed-up gentlemen are showing off a row of cars, perhaps as an advertisement for tires or a car show. The sign reads, "W. E. Call, Knightstown, Ind., Firestone Tires, 29,000 Miles." Knightstown comes by its interest in cars naturally. For a town of its size, Knightstown has had its share of vehicles to show off. Buggy and automobile

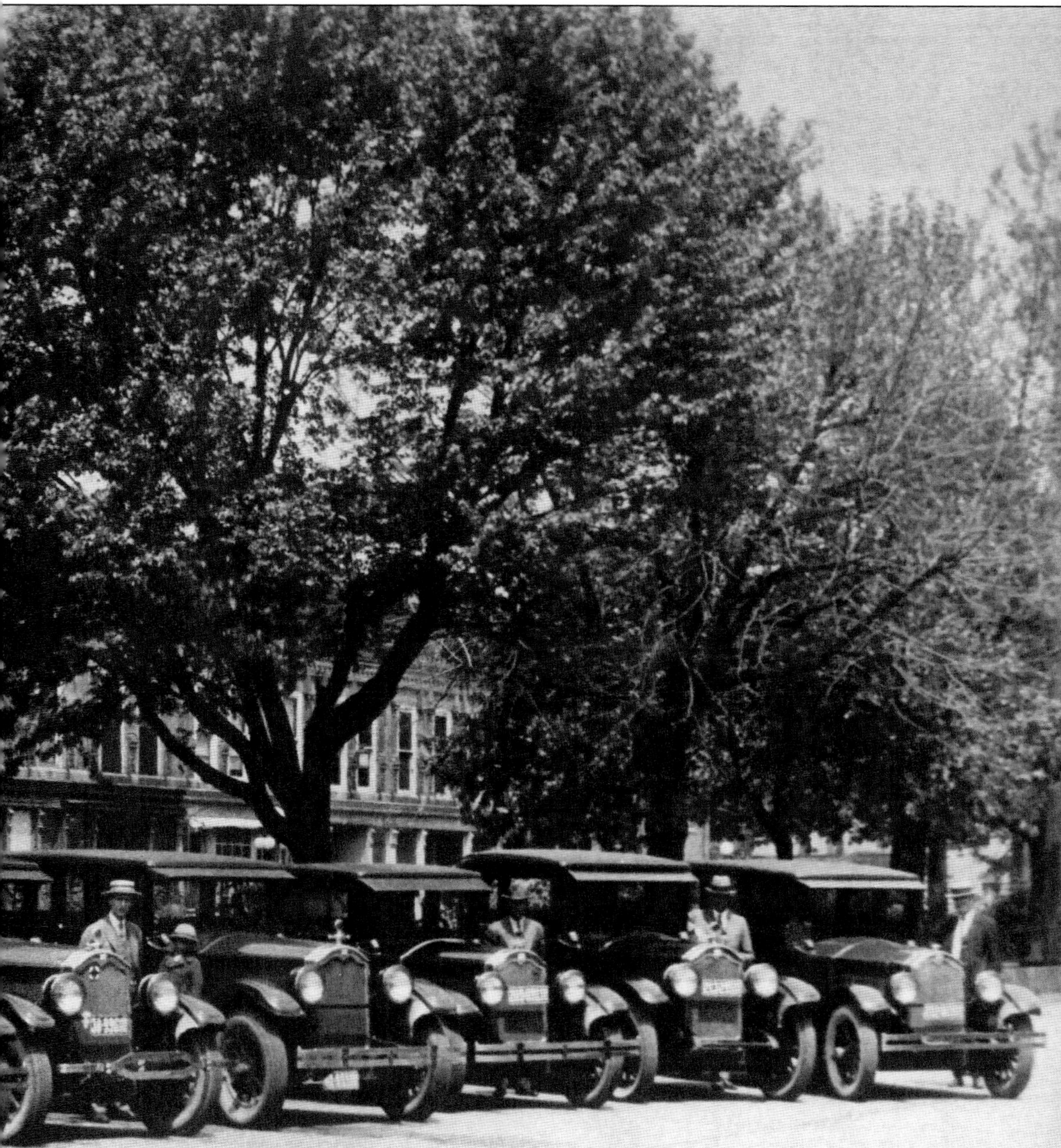

manufacturers in the early 1900s included the Knightstown Buggy Company, the Knightstown Body Company, the Knightstown Funeral Company, and the Columbia Electric Company, which produced the Leader. In fact, both the Knightstown Body Company (the Silver Knightstown) and the Knightstown Funeral Car Company (the Galahad) manufactured hearses, and these rivals were in business for much of the same time.

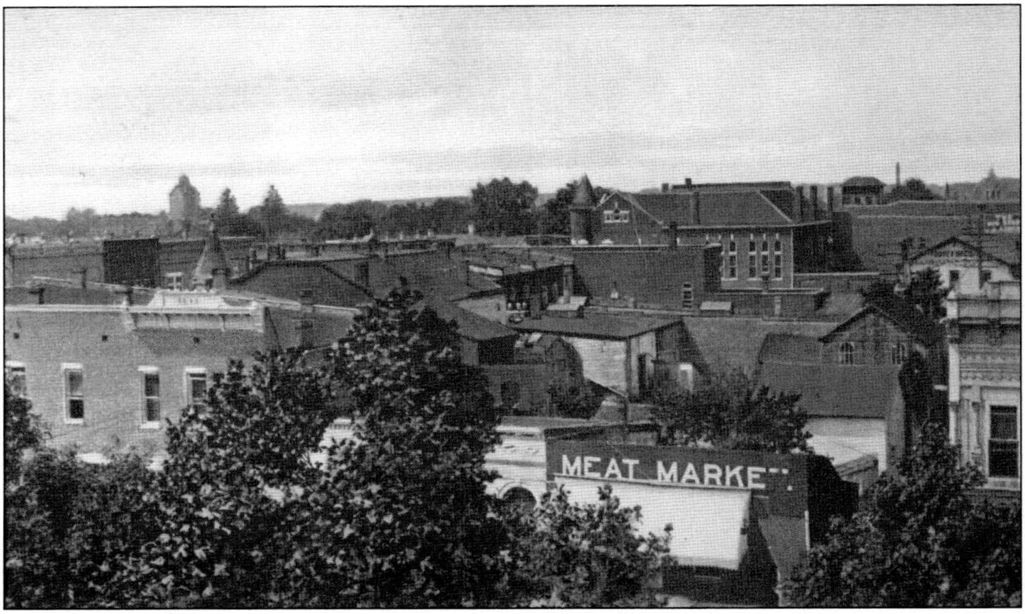

A meat market sign (above), which might have belonged to Graves Meat Market or to the Walling and Son establishment, can be seen peeking over the treetops on the Public Square. According to the *1884 Manufacturing and Mercantile Resources and Industries of the Principle Places in Wayne, Henry, Delaware, and Randolph Counties, Indiana*, the Walling and Son "slaughter house is one of the best equipped in the state. Two assistants are employed and a steam engine and boiler are used in the manufacture of sausage and for dressing meats. They dispose of about 250 head of fat cattle and 150 head of sheep annually, and about 300 hogs are slaughtered during the cold season." Shoppers on the Public Square could also pick up a variety of groceries and produce, which these men are displaying here (below).

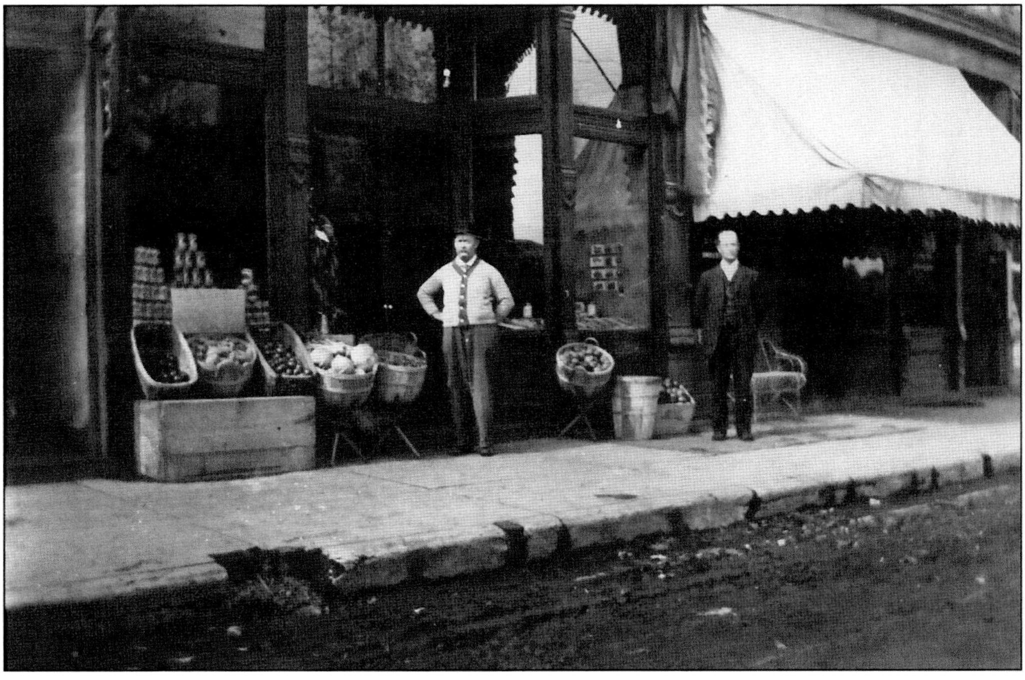

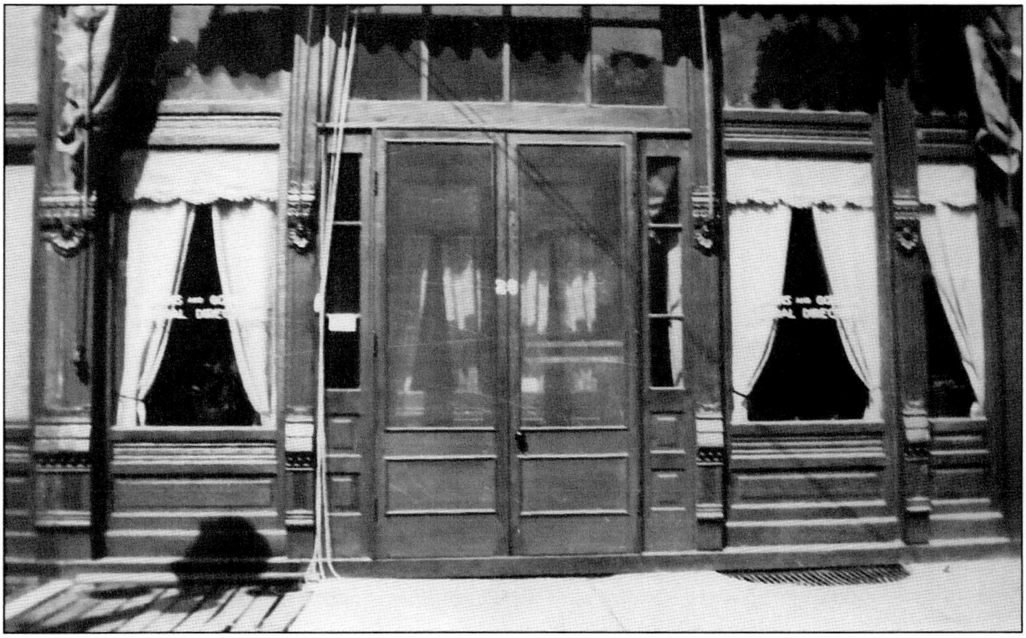

There is no telling how many people have walked through these doors to a building on Washington Street on the west side of the Public Square. In this c. 1930 photograph, the space was occupied by Hoskins and Gordon Funeral Directors. Later "Rags" Walters ran his upholstery business from this spot.

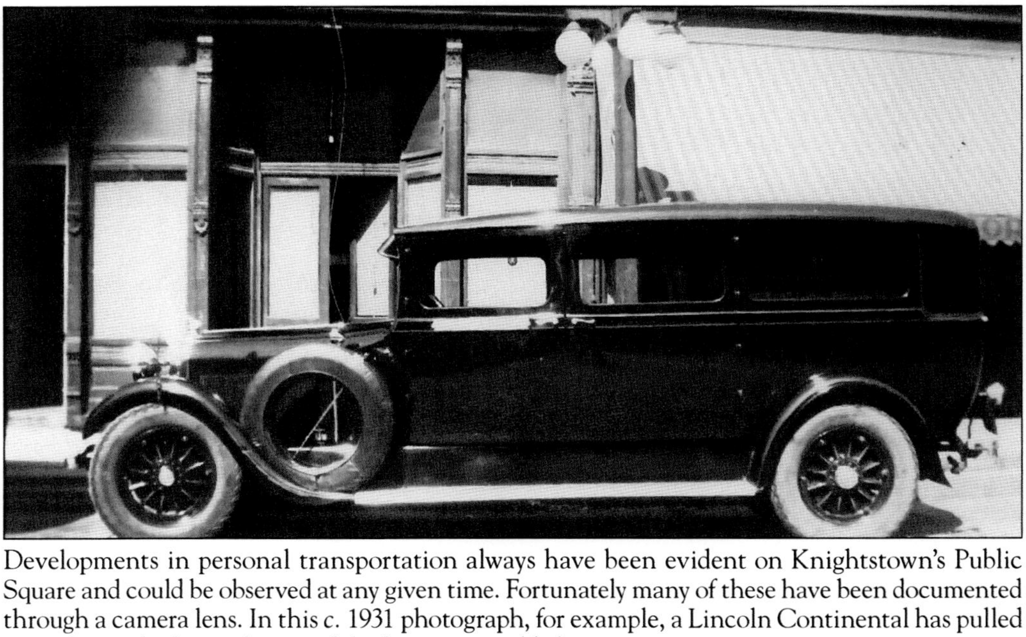

Developments in personal transportation always have been evident on Knightstown's Public Square and could be observed at any given time. Fortunately many of these have been documented through a camera lens. In this c. 1931 photograph, for example, a Lincoln Continental has pulled up and is parked outside one of the business establishments.

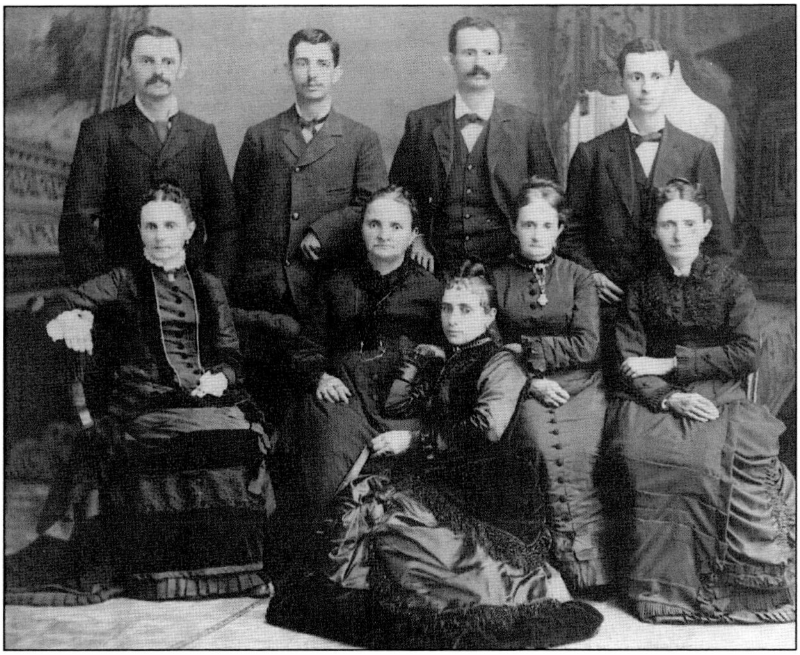

This photograph is believed to be of the Weil family, prominent business owners in Knightstown in the 1800s. Three of the brothers pictured here owned stores on Main Street in Knightstown.

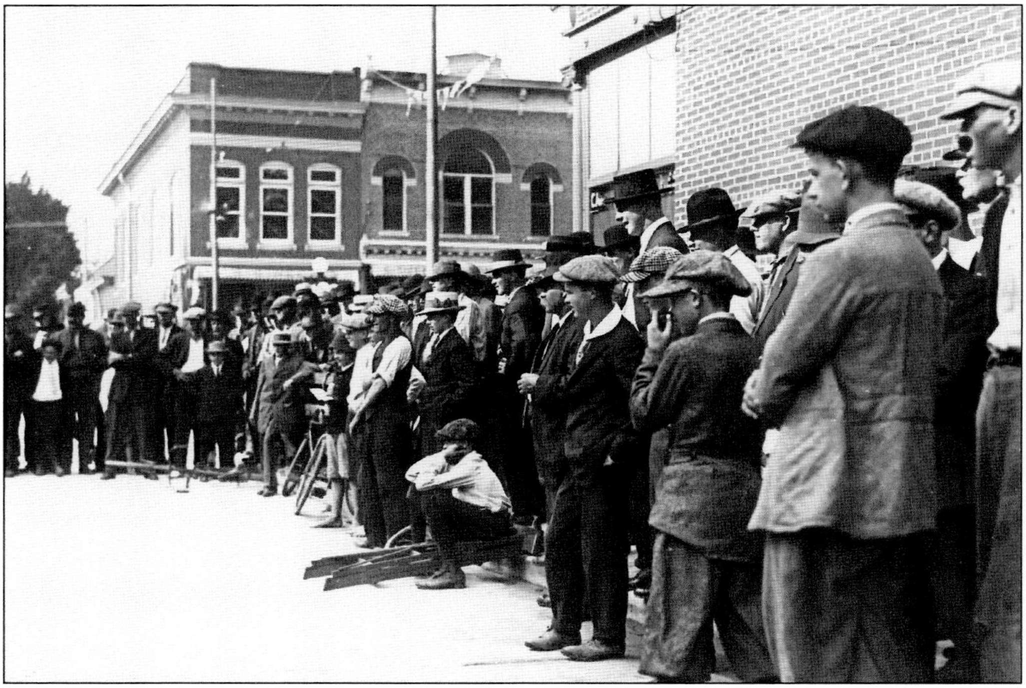

Over the years, events on the Public Square have attracted attention and crowds. In this *c.* 1900 photograph, something has piqued the interest of a sizeable group of gentlemen, some sporting cameras. It was not uncommon to encounter salesmen, political addresses, and even livestock on the Public Square in Knightstown's younger days. The area was, after all, set aside by Waitstill Cary and Jonathan Knight when Knightstown was platted as a place for business and social activities. Note some of the details in this photograph: the group contains old and young alike, but all the observers are men; also notice the boy in the front row of the crowd sitting on a ladder.

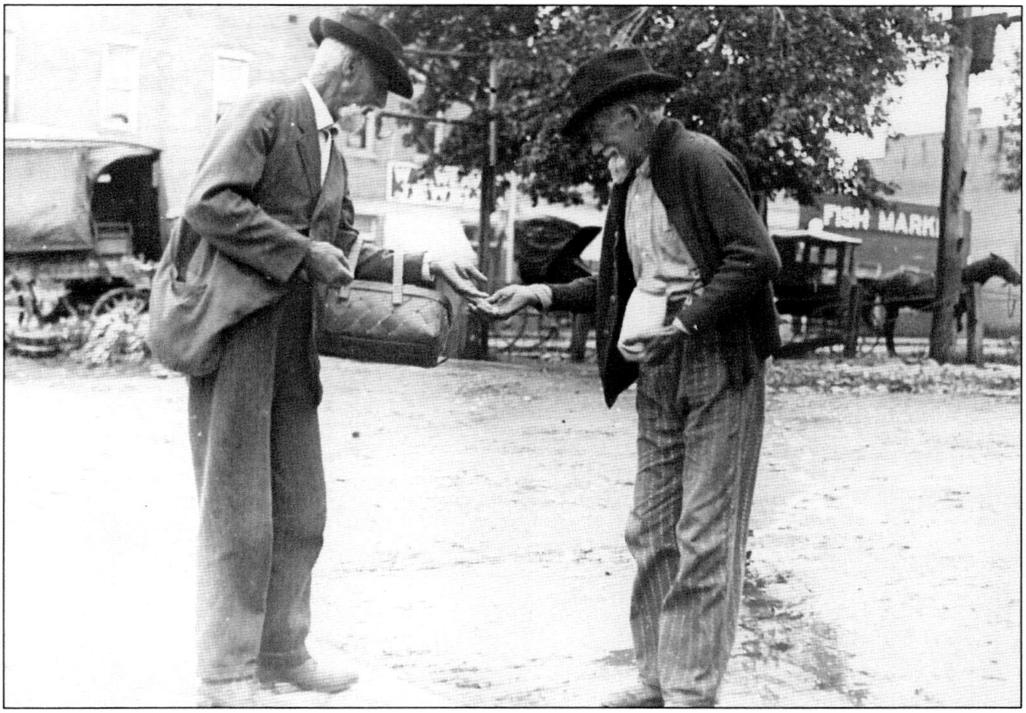

Two older men conduct business and exchange pleasantries on Knightstown's Public Square around 1900. Scenes such as this were common when the square served as an open public market that attracted locals and visitors alike. In fact, the square was so familiar that many early businesses listed their addresses simply as "east side" or "west side" of it.

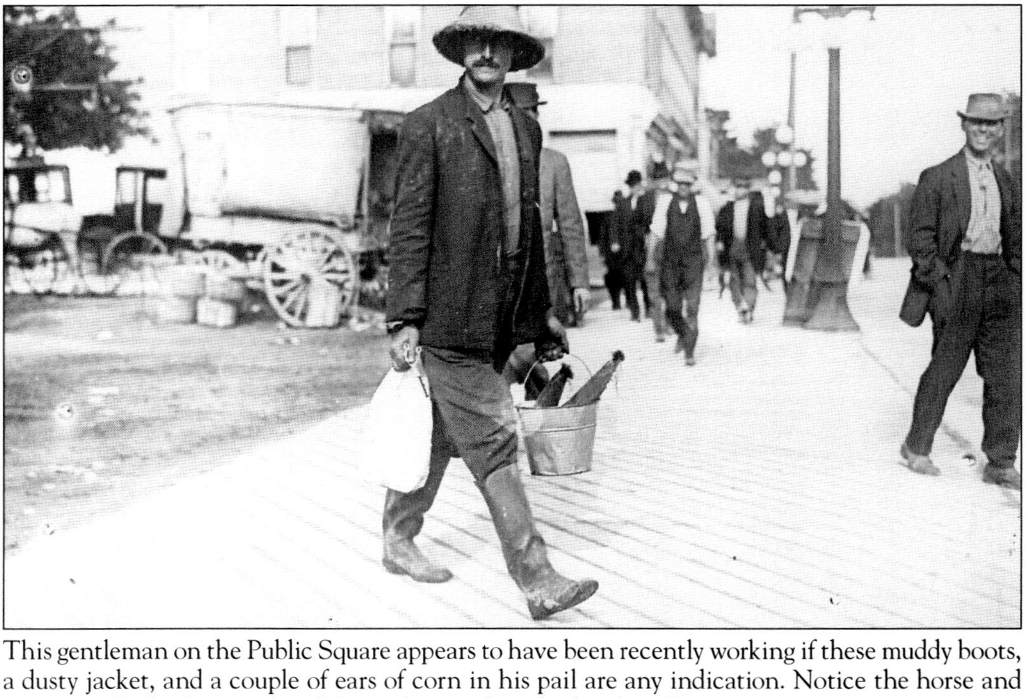

This gentleman on the Public Square appears to have been recently working if these muddy boots, a dusty jacket, and a couple of ears of corn in his pail are any indication. Notice the horse and wagon in the background and the wide, wooden-plank sidewalk.

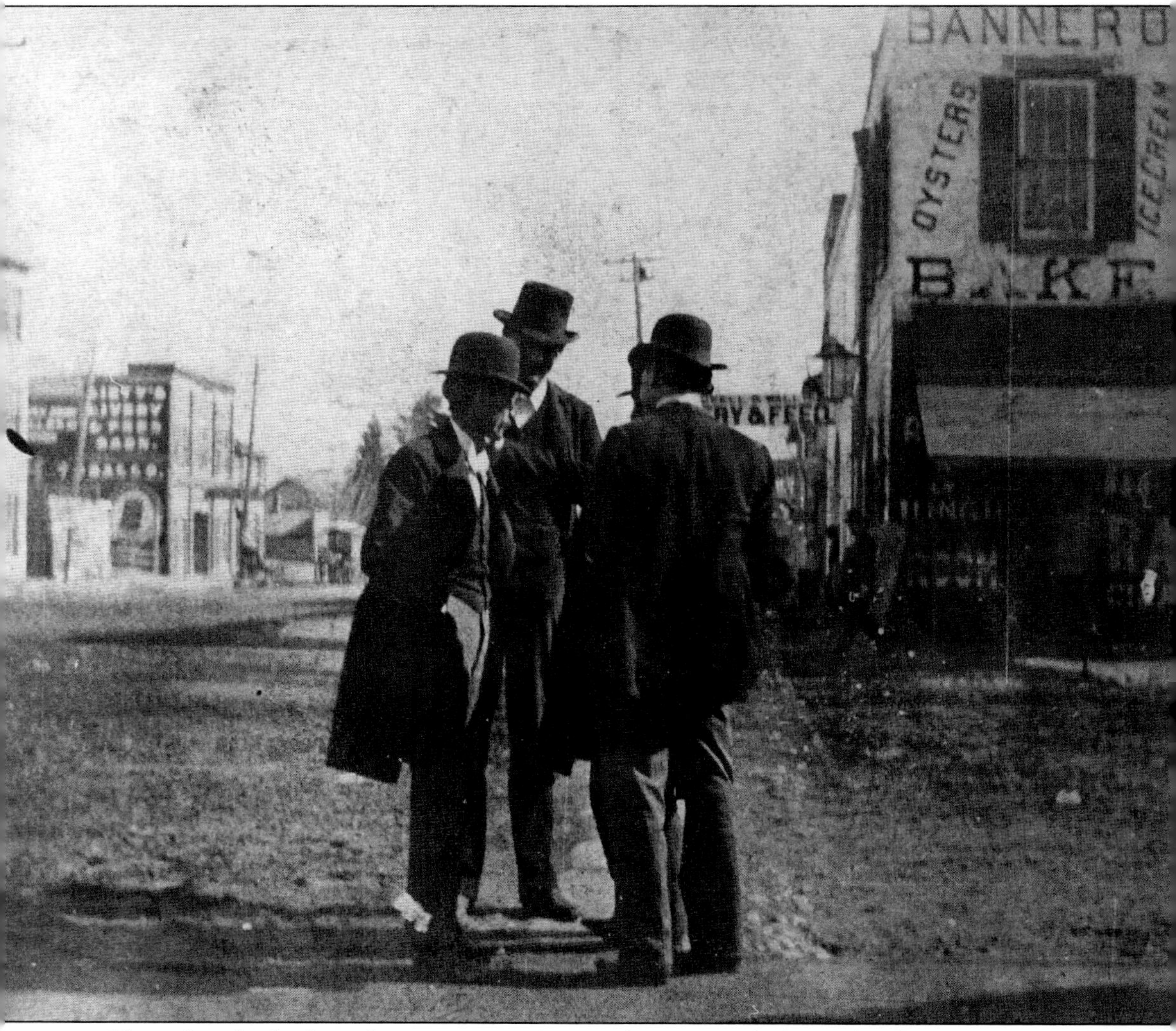

These four finely dressed gents are standing at the corner of Clay and Jefferson Streets in this c. 1900 photograph. They are wearing boots, however, which was a necessity even in finery due to the dirt roads. Sol Hittle's bakery was located on the corner, and the building's painted advertising offers an interesting combination of items—oysters and ice cream. Also in view is the Knightstown Banner office and a livery and feed down the street. Knightstown's position on the National Road, the nation's "Main Street," ensured plenty of business for the little town's commercial establishments.

Two

A Way of Life

> In writing of my boyhood days, old neighbors, old playmates, I confess to feelings of nostalgia at times. How clearly life in my old home at 25 South Adams Street comes back. A typical evening in the living room, for instance. I recall Dad's pride in a new style coal-oil lamp he had bought with a large round wick to make a brighter light. And my aged grandfather Bell in his easy chair before a blazing log fire in the fireplace, poking the log now and then with his cane to make it blaze higher. There was I, on a stool at his side listening to stories of his boyhood in old Virginia.

Reading the words of early Knightstown resident Frank Edwards is like peeking into the windows of a home years ago. Edwards, the great-grandson of Knightstown founder Waitstill M. Cary and grandson of businessman Harvey Bell, was born in Knightstown in 1876. His efforts in preserving Knightstown history through his remembrances and Cary family genealogy have added personality and insight to Knightstown's life story.

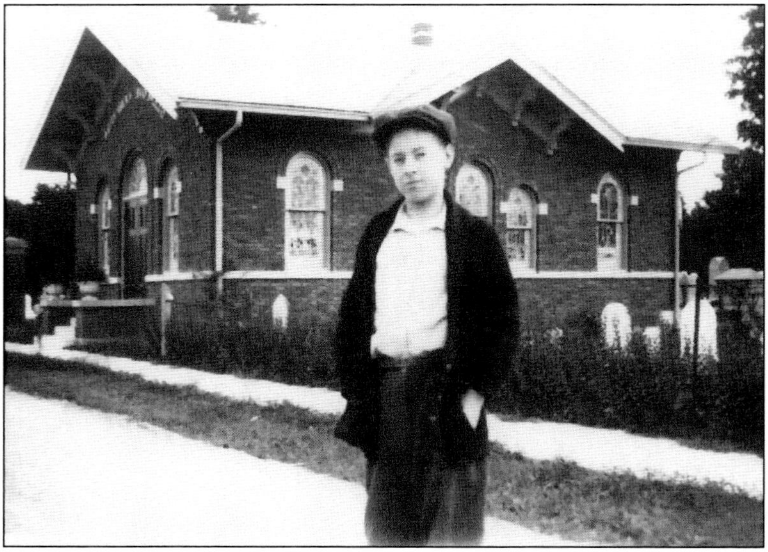

The Old Knightstown portion of the cemetery dates back to the 1830s and includes the graves of some of Knightstown's earliest residents. The newer portion to the north is Glen Cove Cemetery. In this 1918 photograph, a boy stands in front of the chapel, which today serves as the cemetery's office.

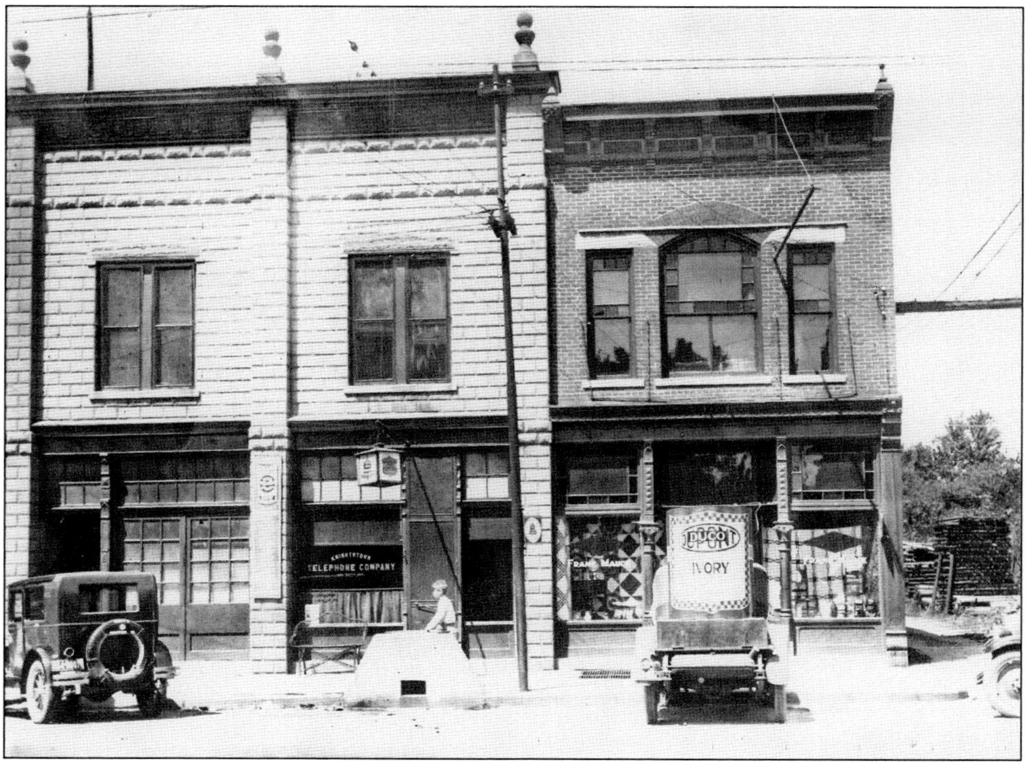

In 1928, a truck parks outside of Frank Mauck's business (notice the quilts and furniture in the windows) and the Knightstown Telephone Company on Clay Street. DUCO was a brand of automotive lacquer developed and sold by the DuPont Company in the 1920s.

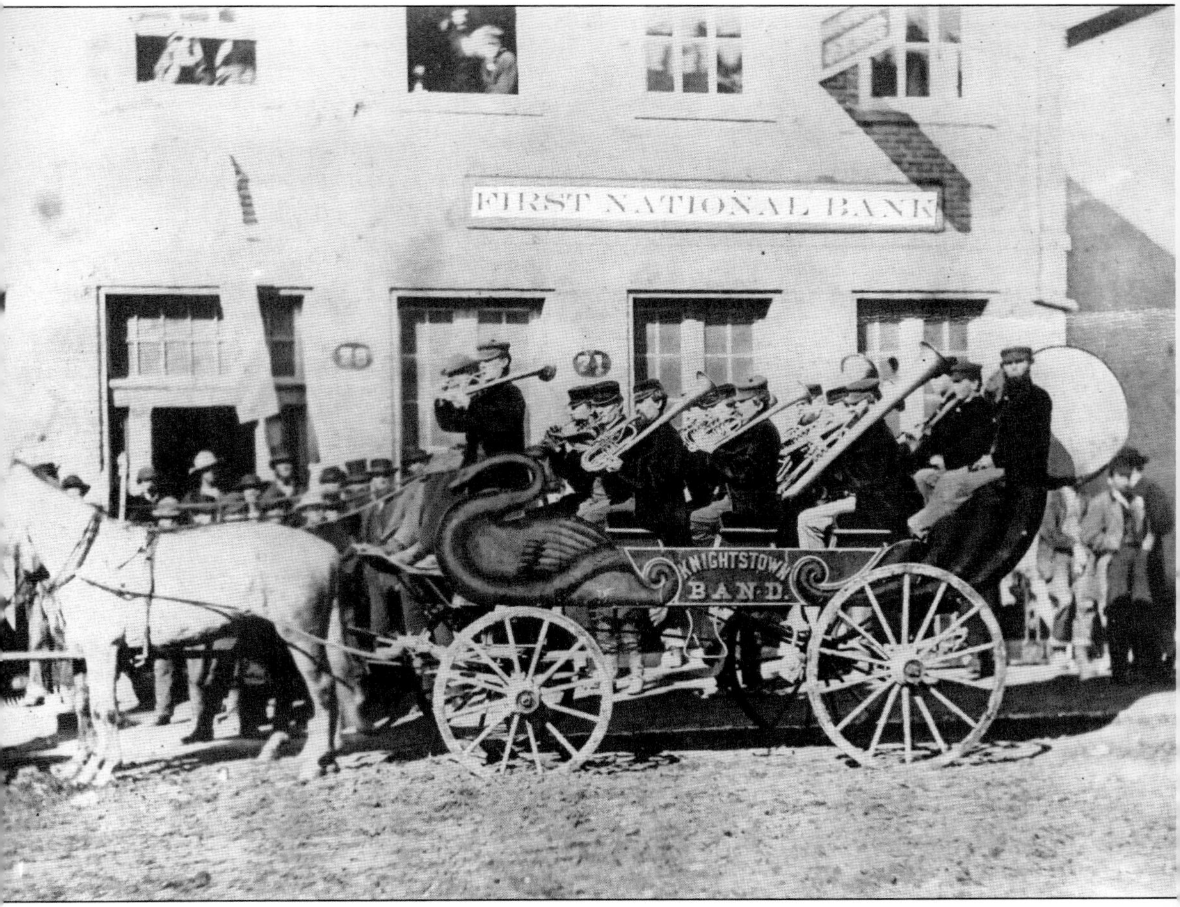

Comprised of Civil War veterans as well as men who remained at home, Knightstown's Silver Cornet Band was organized in 1866. The brass band entertained audiences both locally and in nearby communities, including concerts on Knightstown's Public Square and in Bell's Hall. They evidently took their music seriously. A notice in an 1890 issue of the *Knightstown Banner* reminded Silver Cornet Band members that regular practices were held weekly on Tuesday and Friday nights.

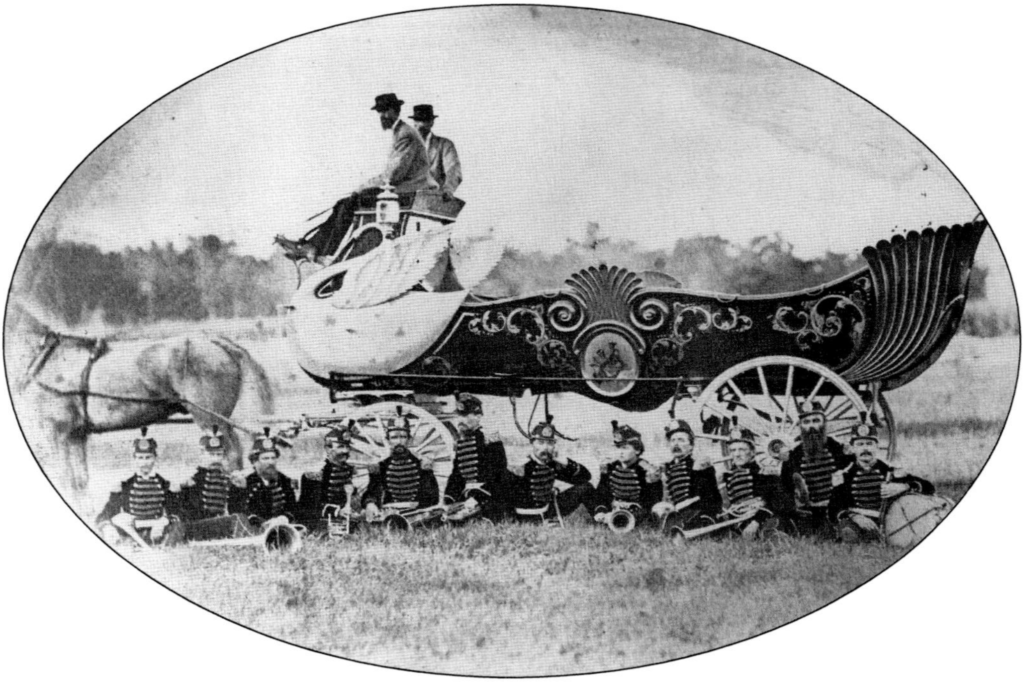

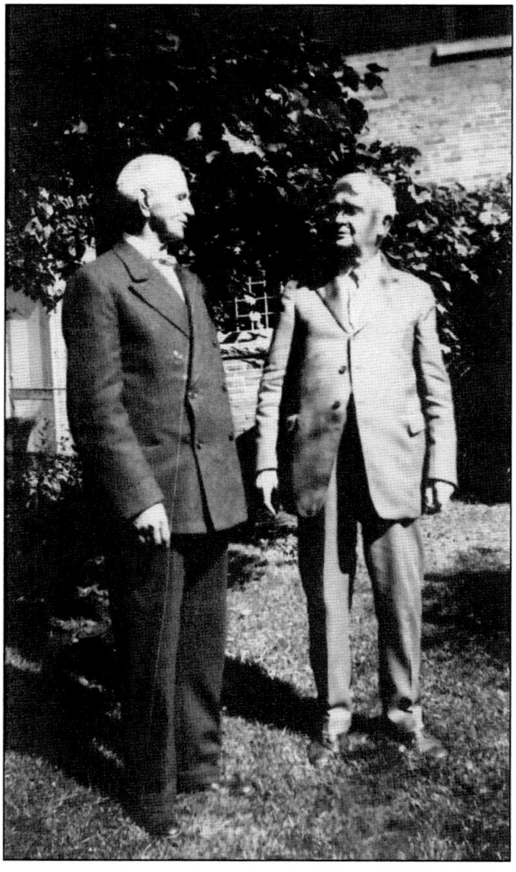

In October 1868, the Knightstown Silver Cornet Band obtained its first bandwagon, but its pride and joy was the new "chariot" it received in 1872 (above). The band members and their chariot were a familiar sight on the Public Square during the band's active years. Pictured in 1927 (at left) are the only two members of the band still living at the time—William Edwards (left) and W. C. Welborn.

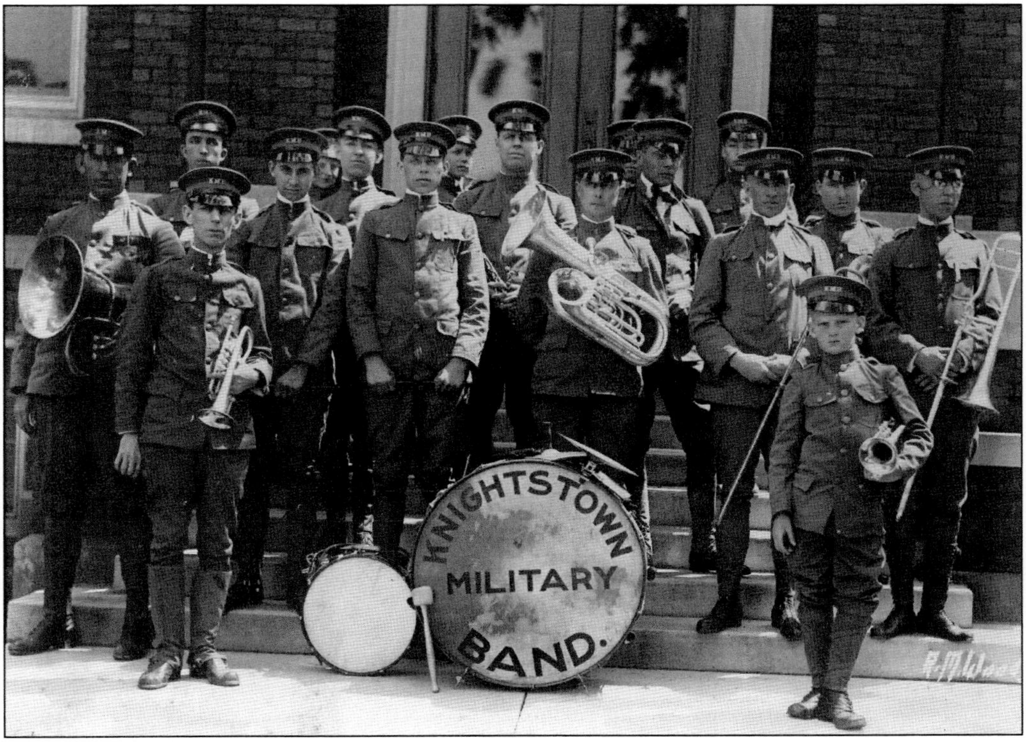

Brass bands were a fashionable form of entertainment in the late 1800s and early 1900s, and many communities, including small ones, were home to local bands. Military bands were especially popular, and not to miss that bandwagon was the Knightstown Military Band (above), pictured after 1912 on the front steps of the Knightstown Public Library. Knightstown's Thomas Band (below) was most likely musically active at around the same time.

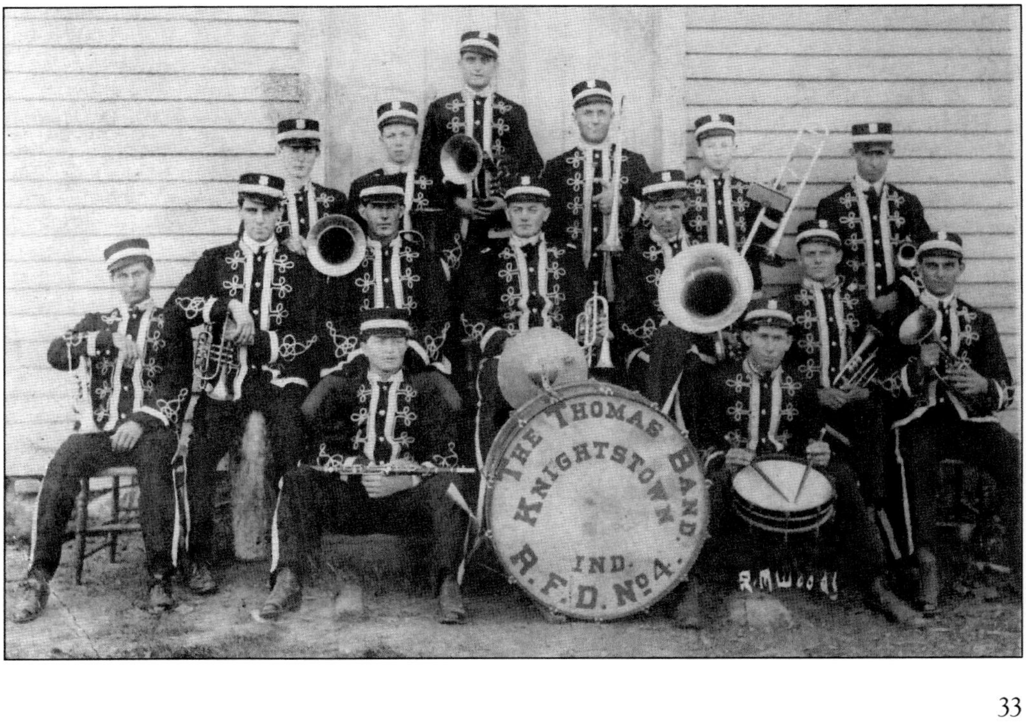

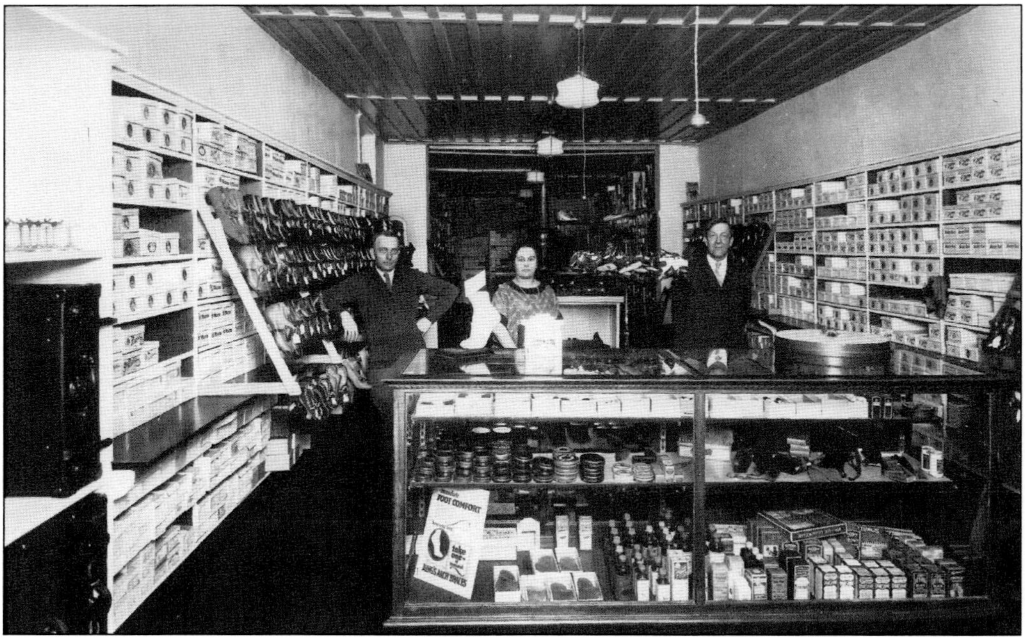

Hill's Shoe Store was located west of Jolly's Drugstore in downtown Knightstown. It is obvious from this 1920s photograph that the Hills kept a very tidy shop. Notice the advertisement in the front case promoting "Jung's Arch Braces for immediate foot comfort." Herbert B. Hill is the man on the right.

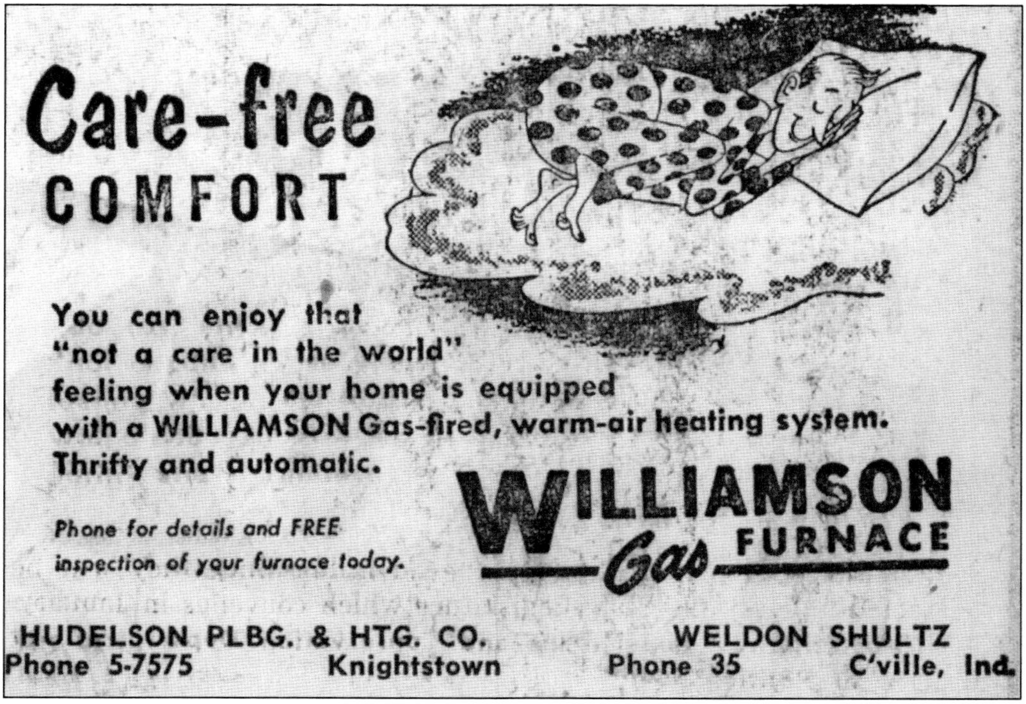

With a cute and comfortable illustration, Hudelson Plumbing and Heating Company promotes Williamson Gas Furnaces in this advertisement in the *Knightstown Banner* on November 27, 1952. (Courtesy of the *Knightstown Banner*.)

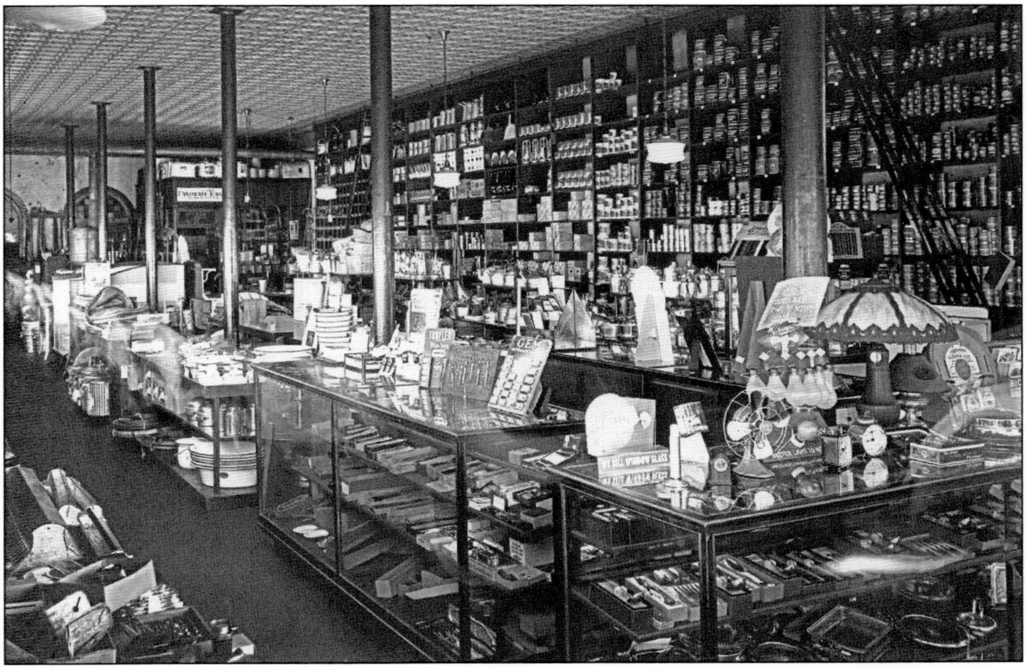

Wagoner Hardware was established in 1886 by T. P. Wagoner and Ralph Wagoner and was a feature of the Knightstown business landscape until the 1950s. This photograph of the interior of the store was taken in the 1930s. A close inspection of the inventory reveals spoons, razor blades, light bulbs, scissors, and window glass among many other housewares and hardware items.

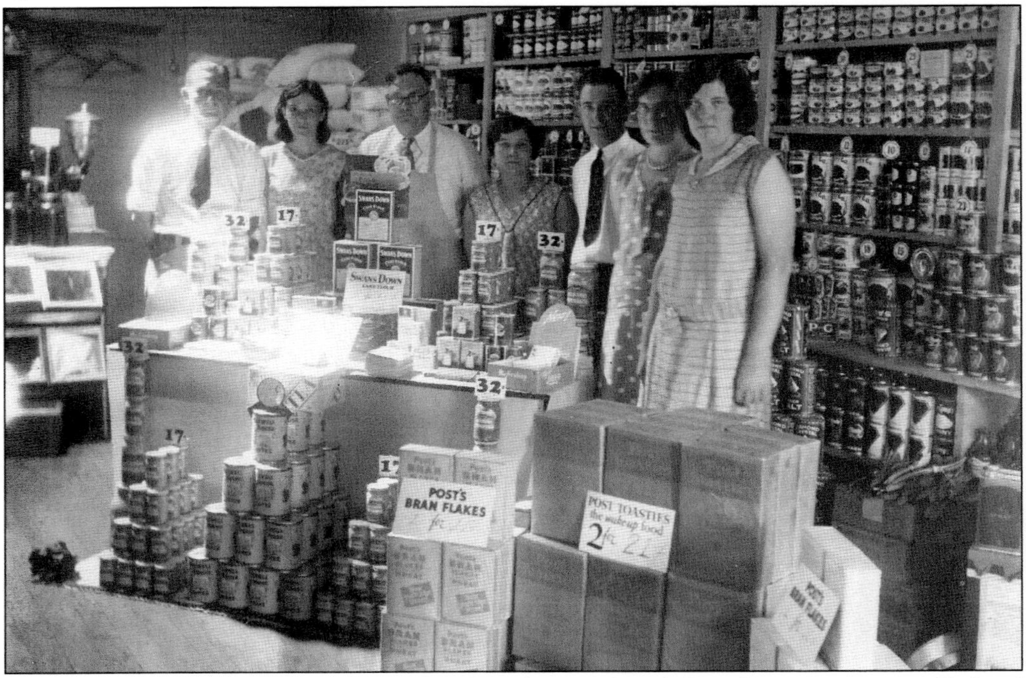

Ralph Lord bought his business in 1928, and employees of Lord's Regal Store are pictured behind the counter a year later. At the time, it was located on the west side of the Public Square. In 1941, the store was moved to a larger spot on the corner of Main and Jefferson Streets.

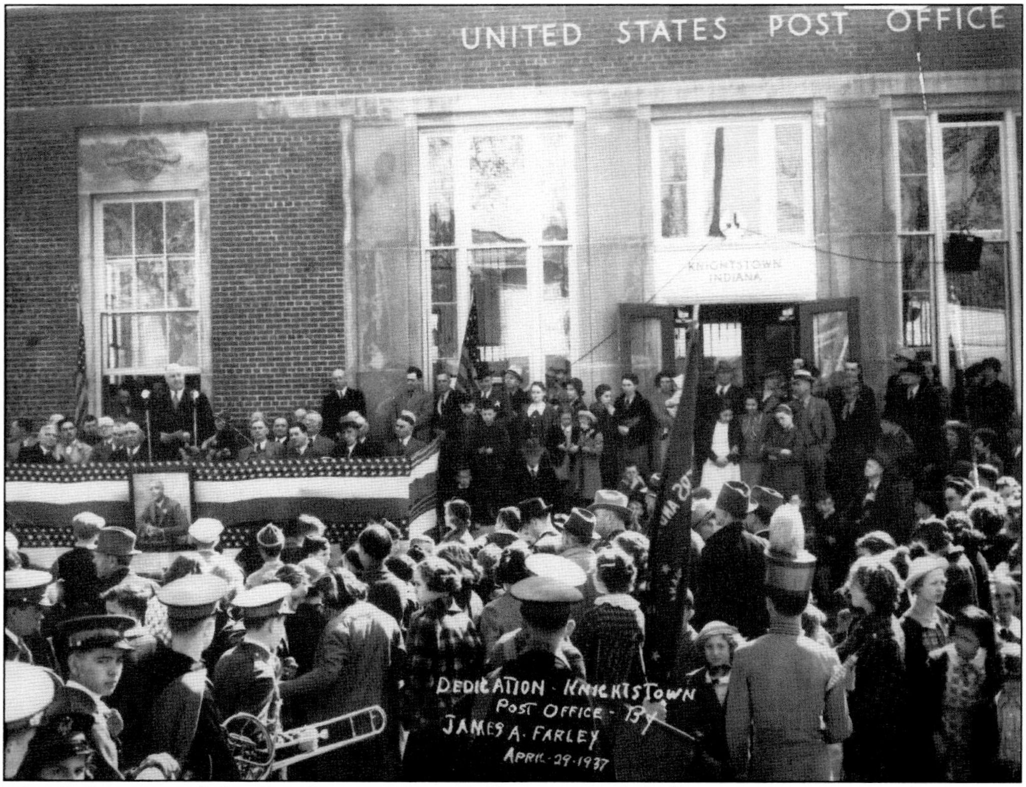

The dedication of the Knightstown Post Office on north Jefferson Street on April 29, 1937, attracted a crowd of 2,000 and featured an address by U.S. Postmaster General James A. Farley. The building features a 12-foot-by-5-foot mural titled, "The Evening Mail," which was painted by Raymond L. Morris through a New Deal program intended to create jobs for artists.

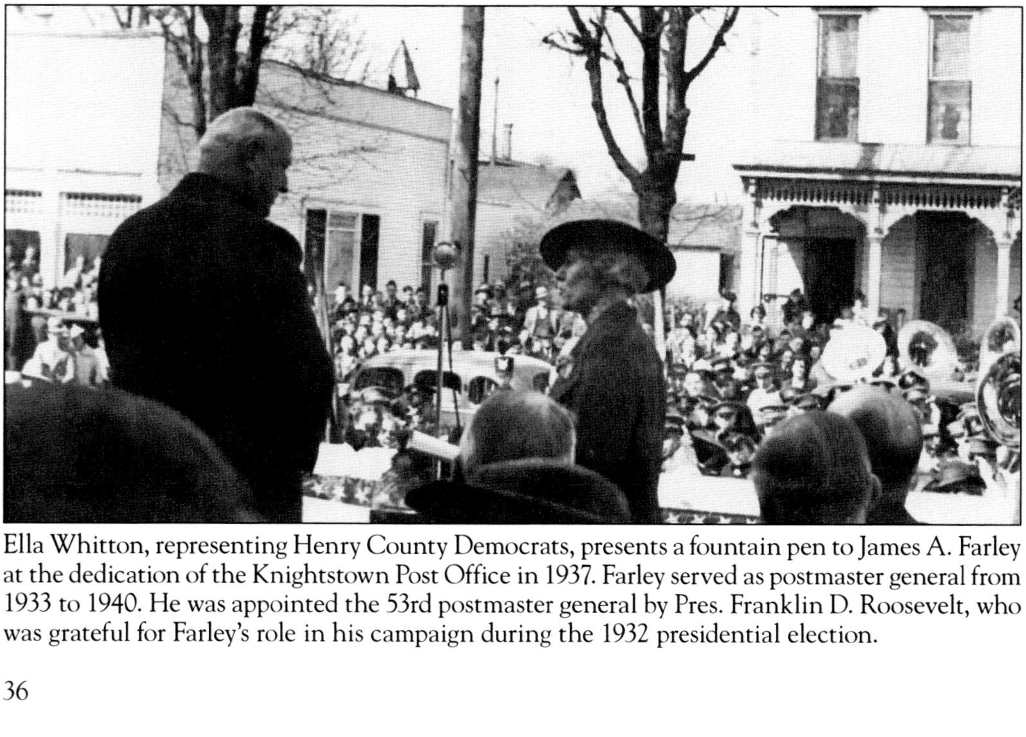

Ella Whitton, representing Henry County Democrats, presents a fountain pen to James A. Farley at the dedication of the Knightstown Post Office in 1937. Farley served as postmaster general from 1933 to 1940. He was appointed the 53rd postmaster general by Pres. Franklin D. Roosevelt, who was grateful for Farley's role in his campaign during the 1932 presidential election.

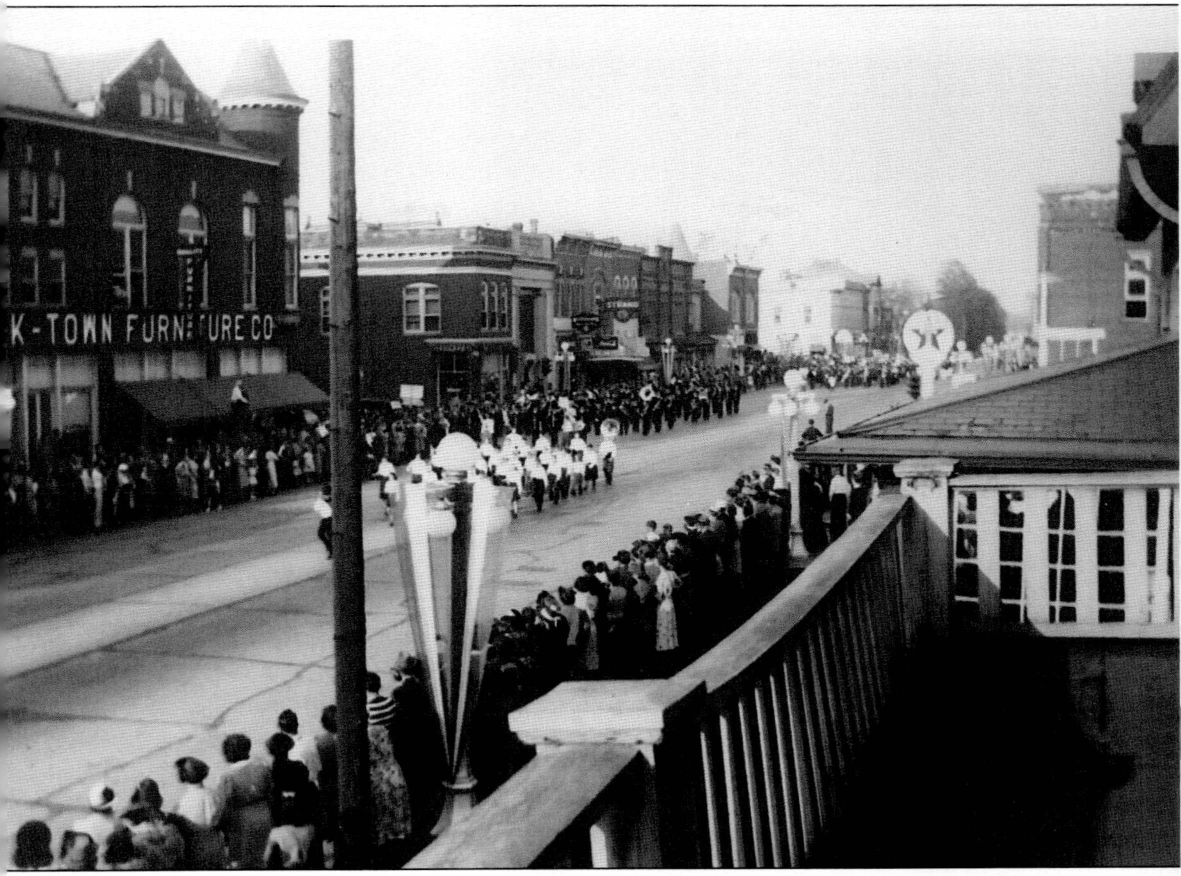

A second-floor porch across from the Masonic Lodge offers a grand view of this parade on Knightstown's main street. The house and its porch are gone; it was located where the Frosty Boy restaurant stands today. The Strand Theater and Public Square are visible down the street.

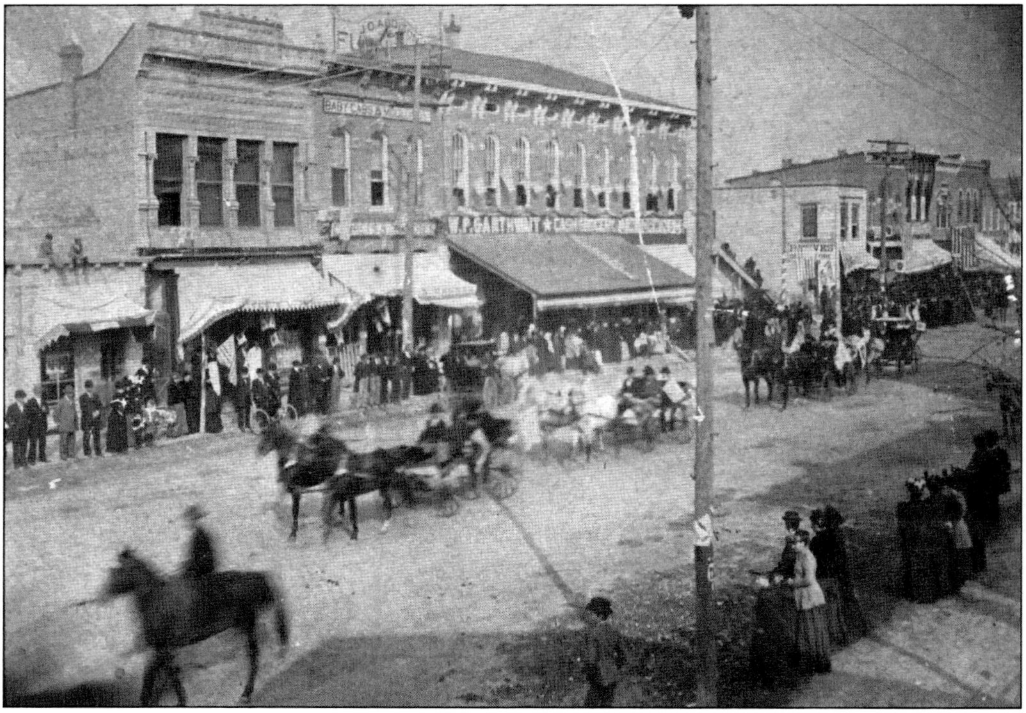

Knightstown's main street has hosted different kinds of traffic as transportation methods have progressed. Horses are leading the way on this occasion, as buggies and wagons are headed east through town.

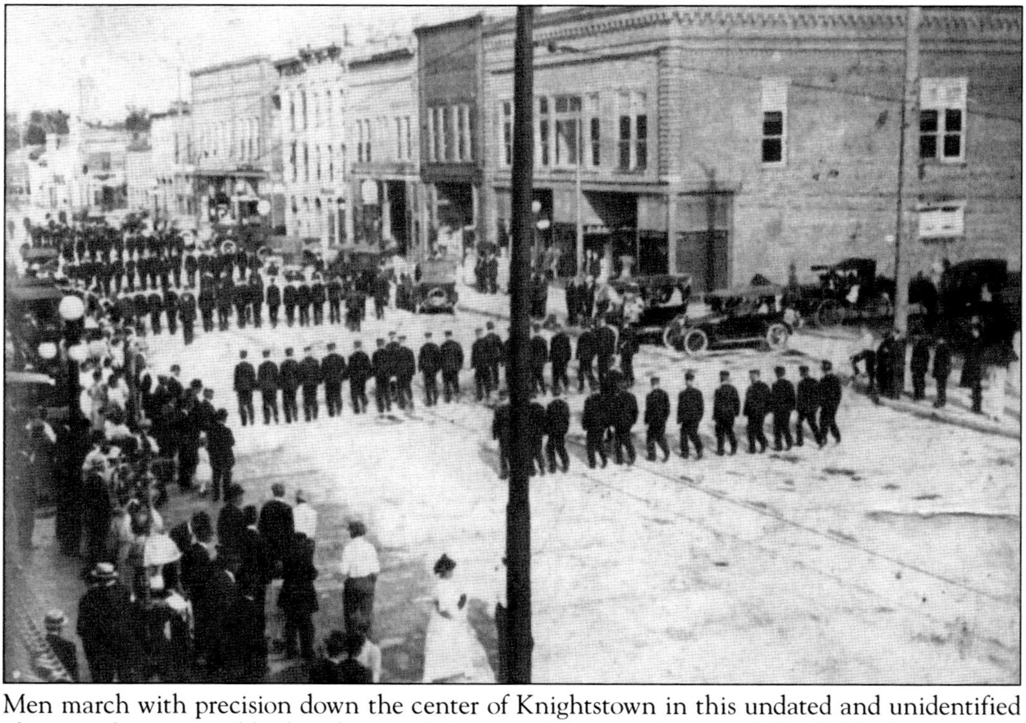

Men march with precision down the center of Knightstown in this undated and unidentified photograph. It is possible that the parade here is celebrating the end of World War I.

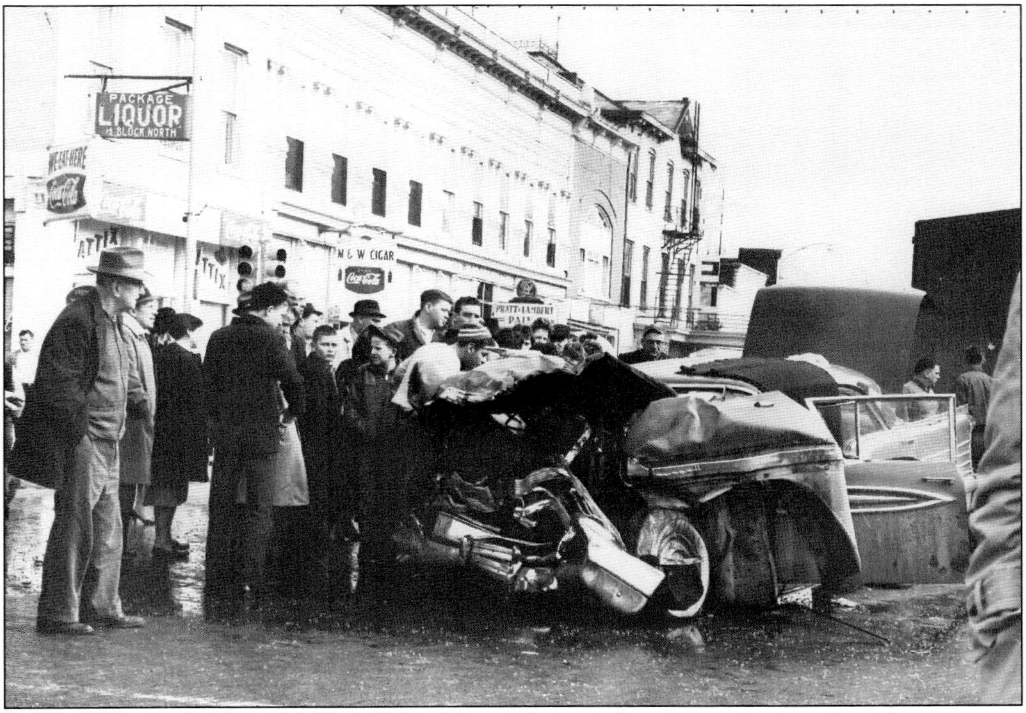

Progress sometimes comes with a price. Automobiles and their drivers back in the day were just as susceptible to accidents as they are today, as is shown by this wreck on Knightstown's main street across from the Mattix Restaurant. They were also just as capable of drawing a crowd.

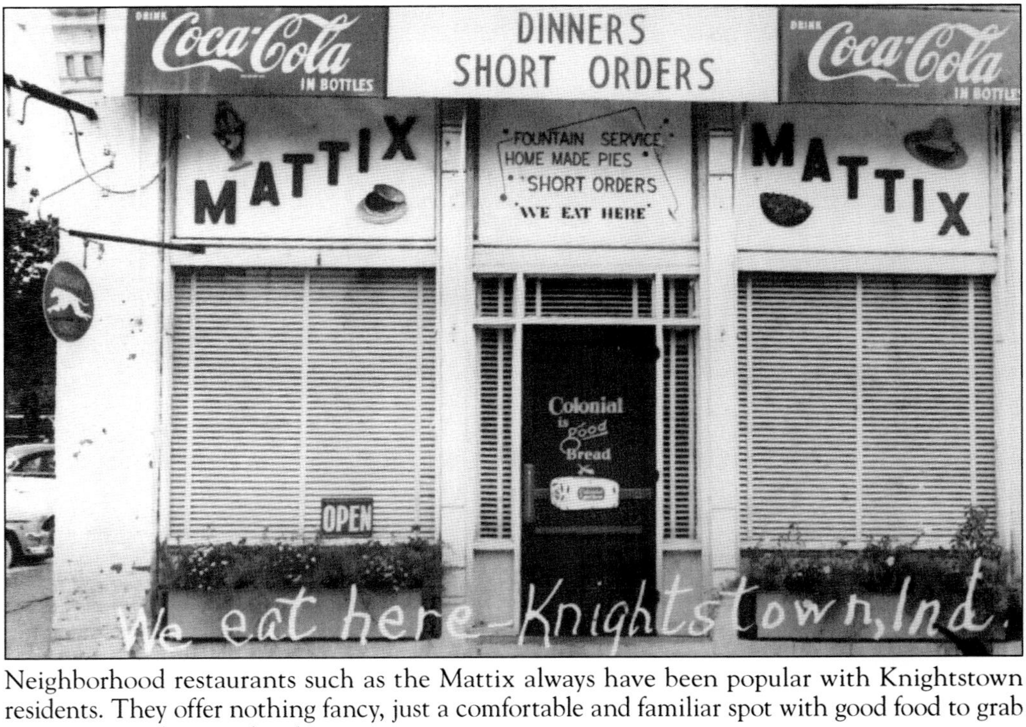

Neighborhood restaurants such as the Mattix always have been popular with Knightstown residents. They offer nothing fancy, just a comfortable and familiar spot with good food to grab a bite and catch up on local news.

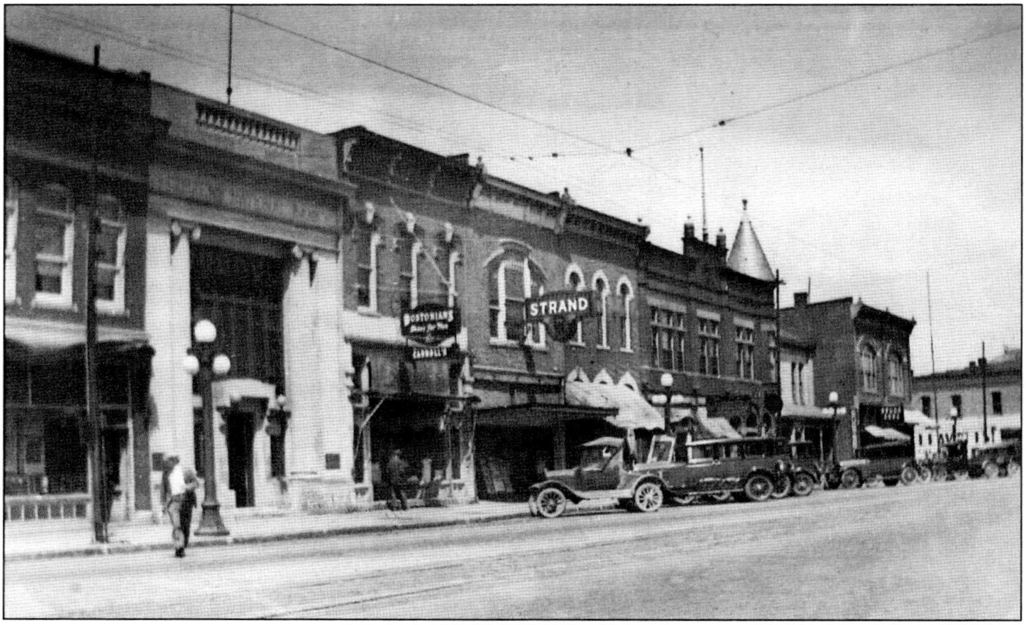

Many of today's teenagers are surprised to learn that Knightstown once boasted two movie theaters, one in the Alhambra and the other the Strand, seen here in a 1920s photograph. Providing even more entertainment opportunities for Knightstown teens was the Duck Pin Bowling Alley, which in the 1940s was situated next door to where the Strand had been located on the north side of Main Street.

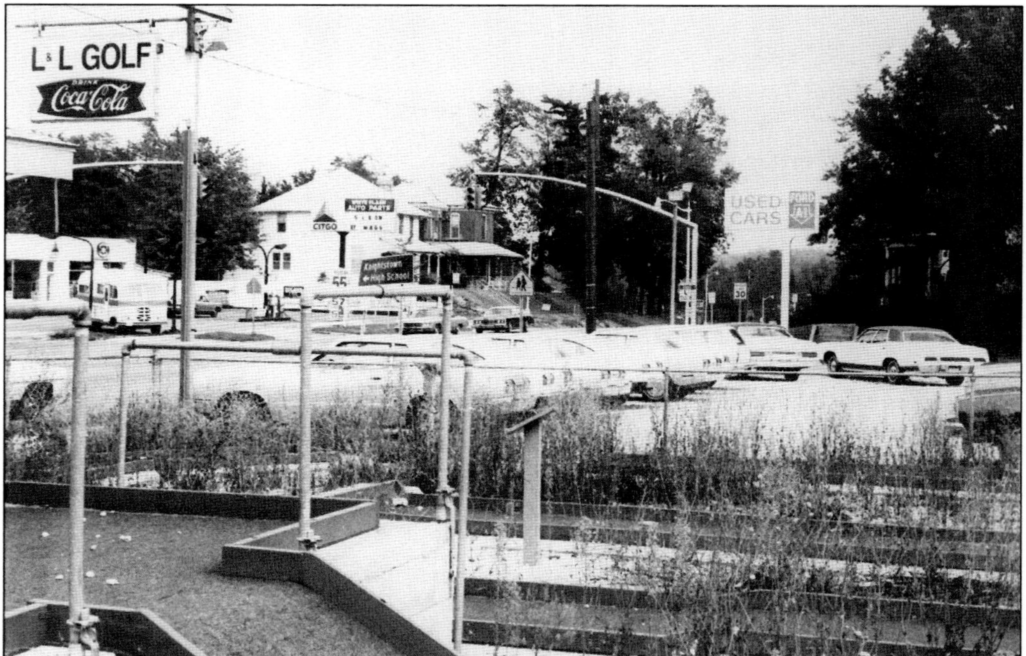

By the time this photograph was taken, weeds and disrepair had taken over the L and L miniature golf course on Main Street just west of the intersection of Main and Adams Streets. The golf course is another example of entertainment sources that no longer exist in downtown Knightstown.

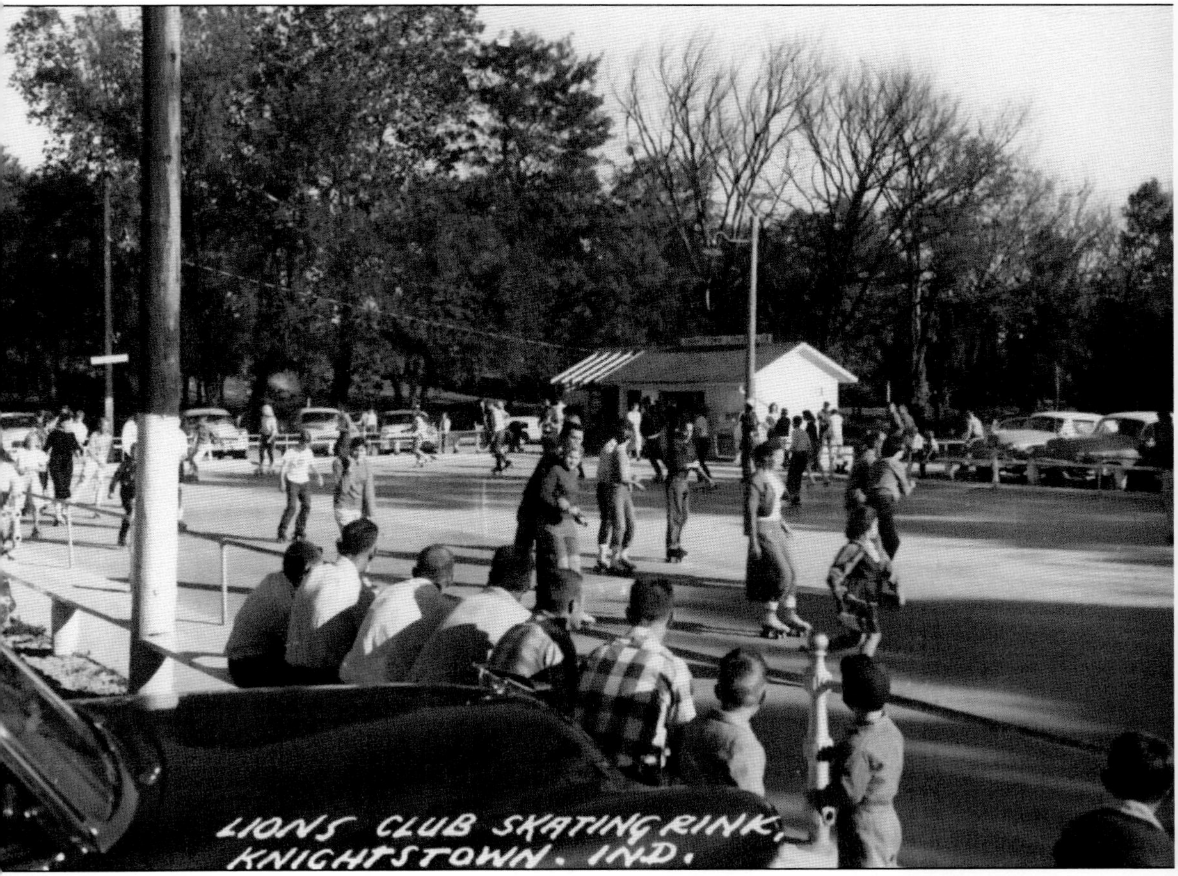

The outdoor Lion's Club skating rink at Knightstown's Sunset Park on the west side of town was an attractive spot for locals, especially teenagers, in the late 1950s and early 1960s. Well supervised and attended by Lion's Club volunteers, the rink offered teenagers at the time a safe and well-maintained place to hang out. At no charge, roller skaters were able to dance and skate to the music of a jukebox (some took stereos before the jukebox was installed) and enjoy soft drinks and popcorn in the evening on the lighted rink. "It was a happening place back then," says longtime Knightstown resident Carol Duncan. When roller-skating slipped out of fashion, so too did the rink. Now long gone, the skating rink was replaced with picnic shelters and an outdoor basketball court.

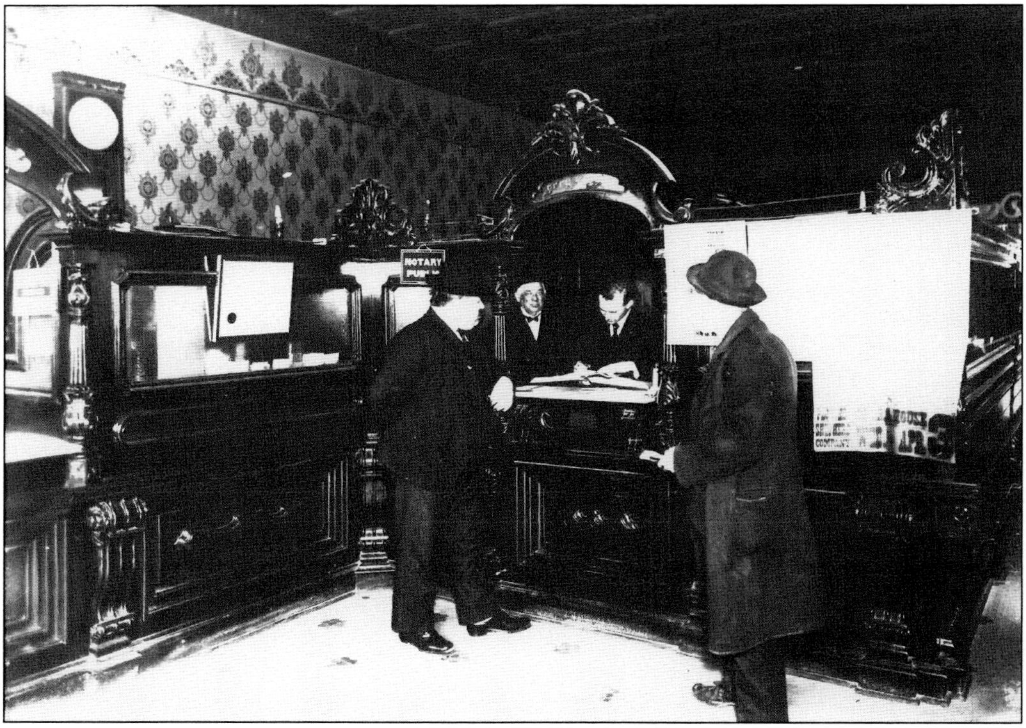

Banking was big business in Knightstown's early days, as is evident by the ornate, and expensive, interior of the First National Bank on Clay Street. Founder Charles D. Morgan (left) and his son Erie are pictured here inside the bank teller's window looking out.

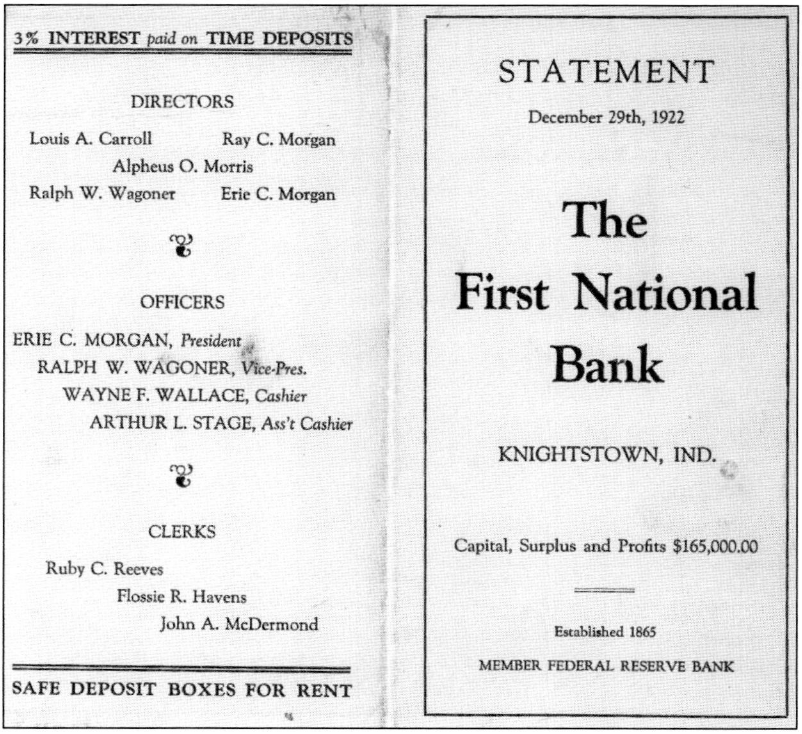

3% INTEREST *paid on* TIME DEPOSITS

DIRECTORS

Louis A. Carroll — Ray C. Morgan
Alpheus O. Morris
Ralph W. Wagoner — Erie C. Morgan

OFFICERS

ERIE C. MORGAN, *President*
RALPH W. WAGONER, *Vice-Pres.*
WAYNE F. WALLACE, *Cashier*
ARTHUR L. STAGE, *Ass't Cashier*

CLERKS

Ruby C. Reeves
Flossie R. Havens
John A. McDermond

SAFE DEPOSIT BOXES FOR RENT

STATEMENT

December 29th, 1922

The First National Bank

KNIGHTSTOWN, IND.

Capital, Surplus and Profits $165,000.00

Established 1865

MEMBER FEDERAL RESERVE BANK

This statement from the First National Bank is dated December 29, 1922. Erie C. Morgan, a former cashier at the bank, is listed as one of the bank's directors. Erie was the son of First National Bank founder Charles Dayton Morgan, who died in 1911.

Founded by local businessmen, the Citizens National Bank was one of the early banks in Knightstown. The neoclassical Citizens Bank building on Main Street was constructed in 1910. Obviously by its style, the bank's right side was remodeled much later when the drive-through was added.

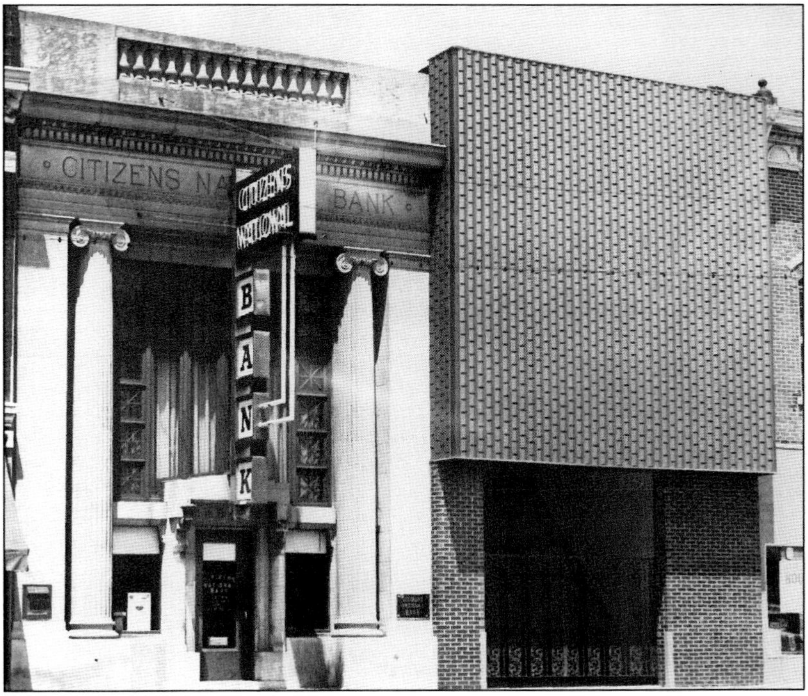

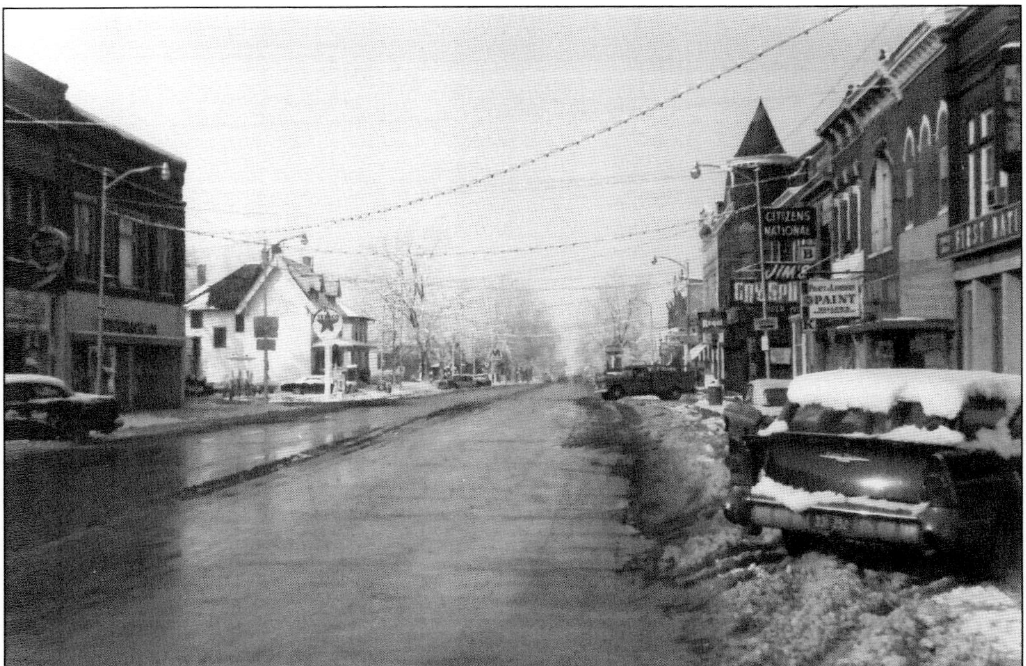

Snow-covered cars are a familiar sight during the winter months in Knightstown. Fortunately, with the arrival of automobiles, snow removal on a large scale became possible. In the 1800s, the horses had to fend for themselves.

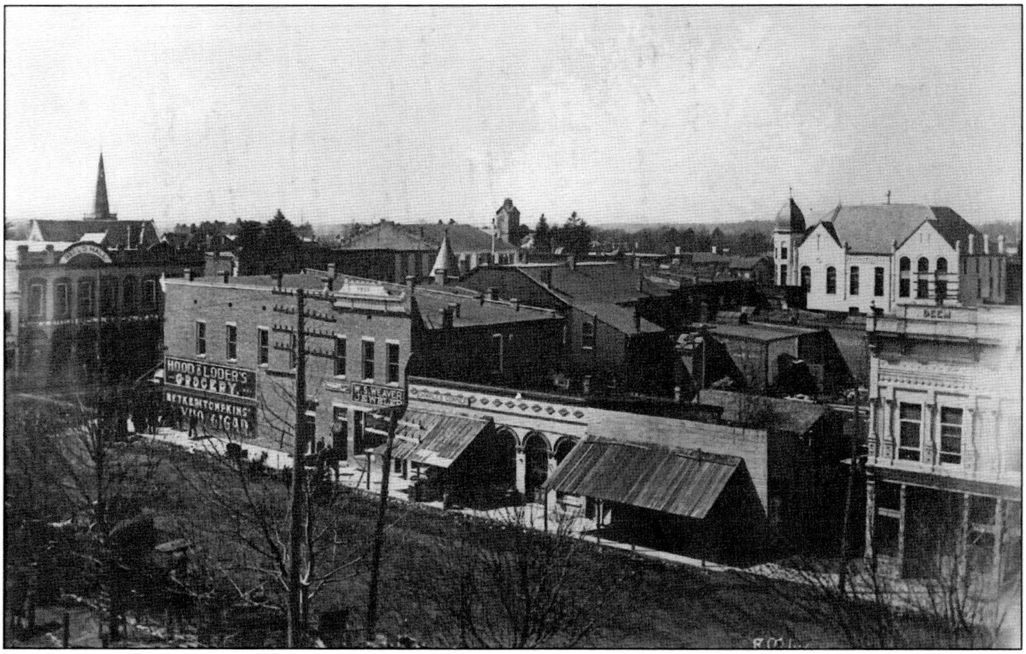

Taken before 1899, this aerial shot of downtown Knightstown (above) shows the first Masonic Temple, which is the large, white building to the right. Tragedy struck on a Wednesday morning in October 1899, when the Masonic Temple and the Kennard Building on Clay Street were destroyed by fire. Even more heartbreaking were the deaths of three men, firemen Charles Scudder and Truman Rhodes and citizen Fone F. Davy, when the front walls of the buildings caved in. The tribute (below) includes a photograph of the building before the fire, one of the ruins afterward, and those of the three men who died.

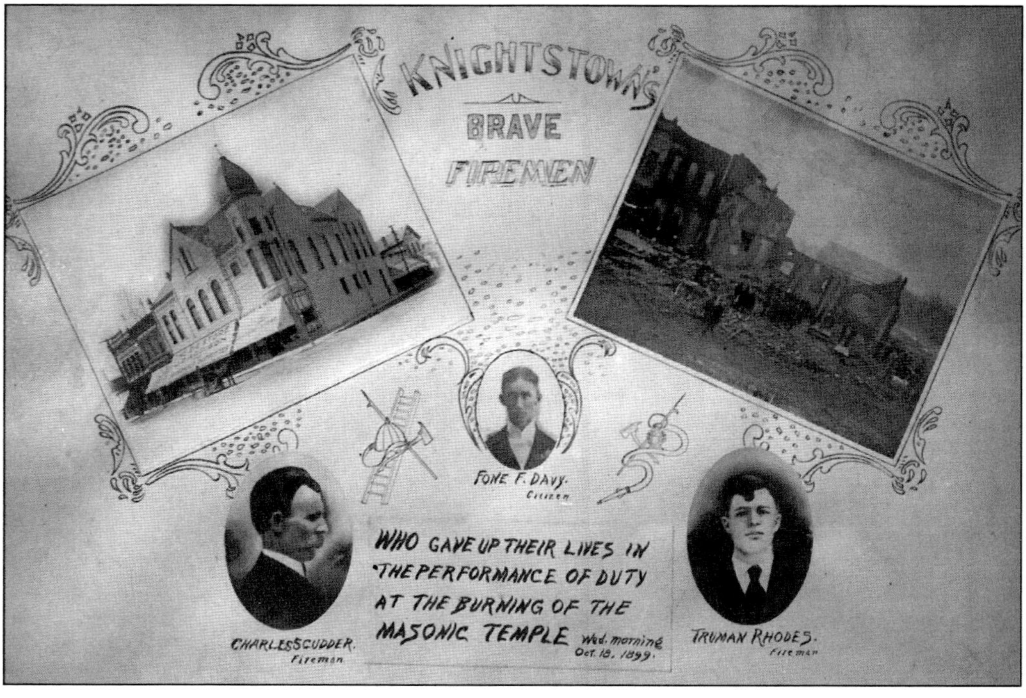

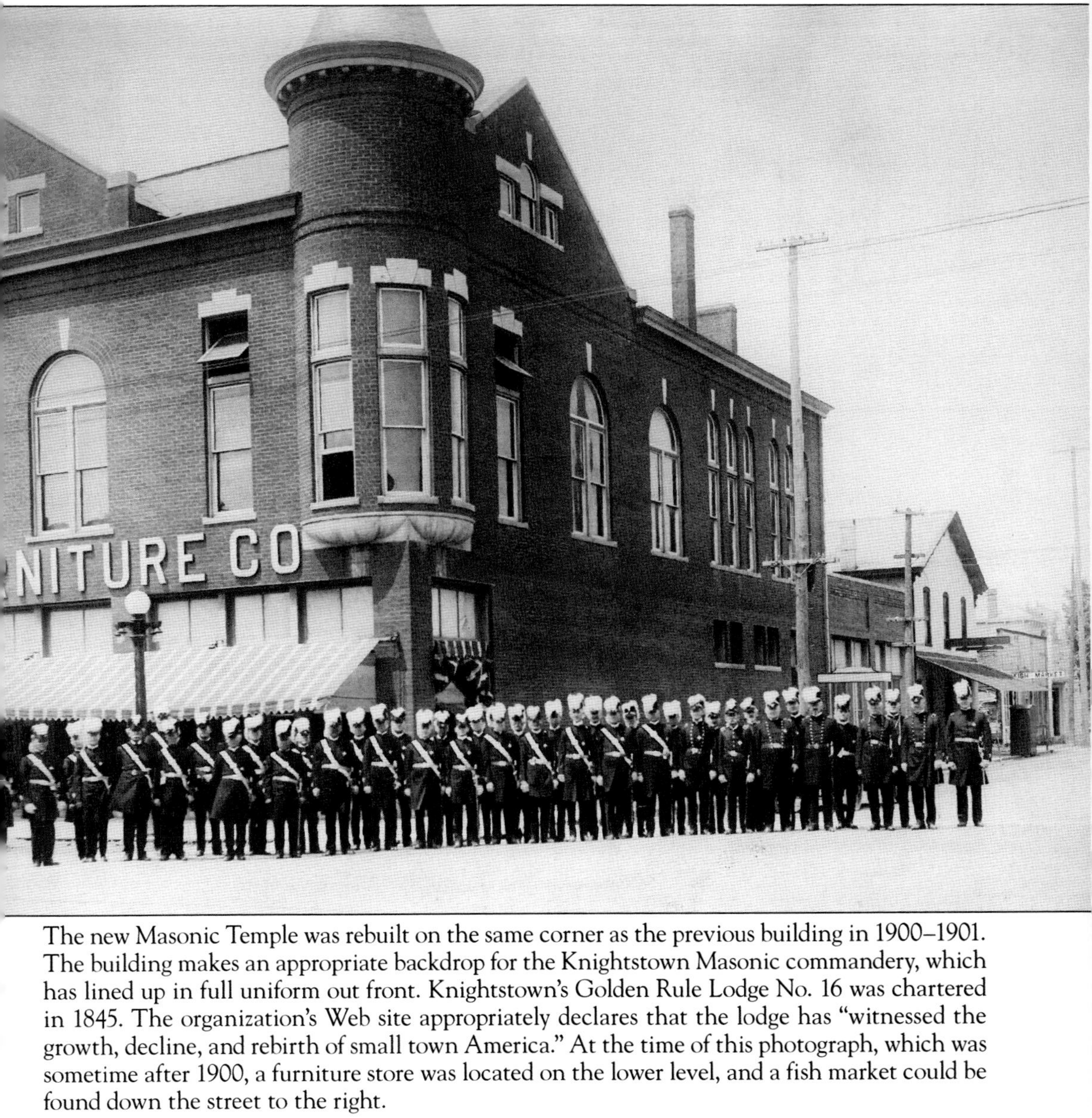

The new Masonic Temple was rebuilt on the same corner as the previous building in 1900–1901. The building makes an appropriate backdrop for the Knightstown Masonic commandery, which has lined up in full uniform out front. Knightstown's Golden Rule Lodge No. 16 was chartered in 1845. The organization's Web site appropriately declares that the lodge has "witnessed the growth, decline, and rebirth of small town America." At the time of this photograph, which was sometime after 1900, a furniture store was located on the lower level, and a fish market could be found down the street to the right.

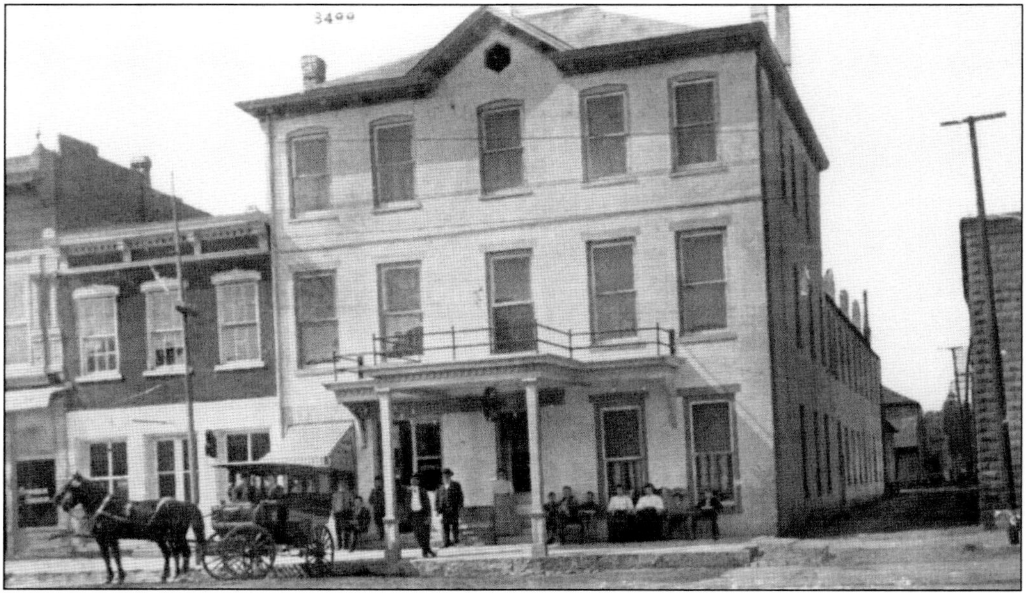

This hotel was built in 1856, and over the years it has gone by several different names. In this *c.* 1910 photograph (above), it went by the Hotel Jack. Later the building was called the Lindsay Manor Hotel (below) and the Shipman Hotel. More than the name had changed between these two views, however, as is seen by the larger lower right window and the addition of the fire escape in the later example. Also, notice the updated facade on the building to the left, as well as the differences in modes of transportation apparent in each photograph. The hotel was demolished in 1993.

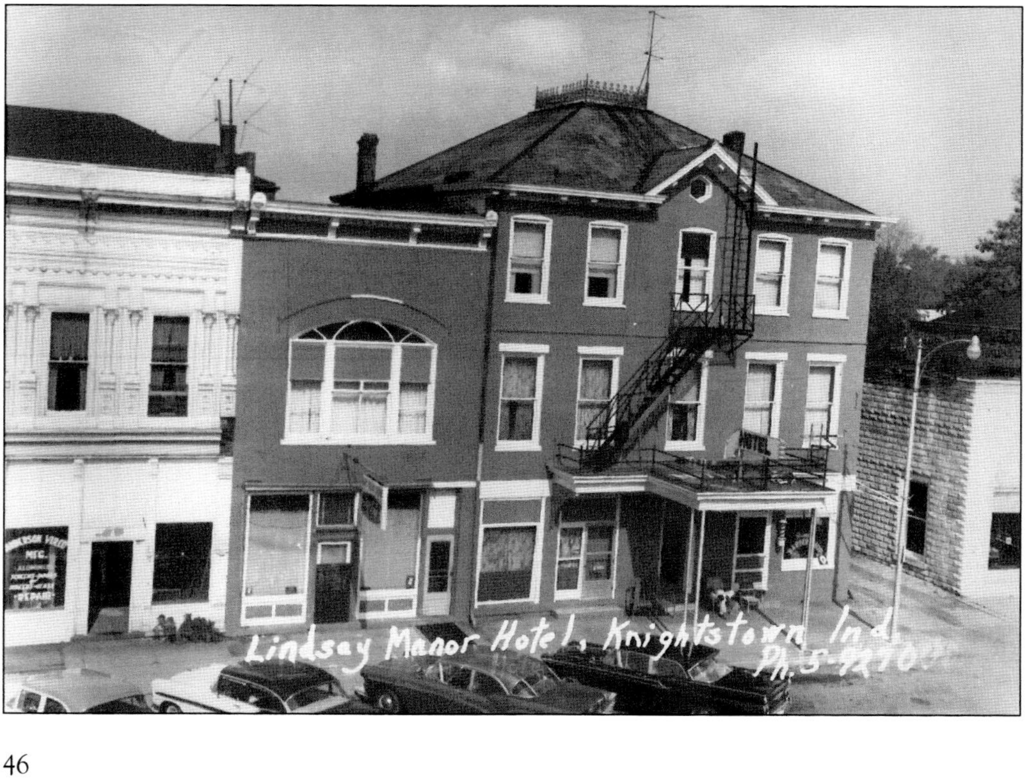

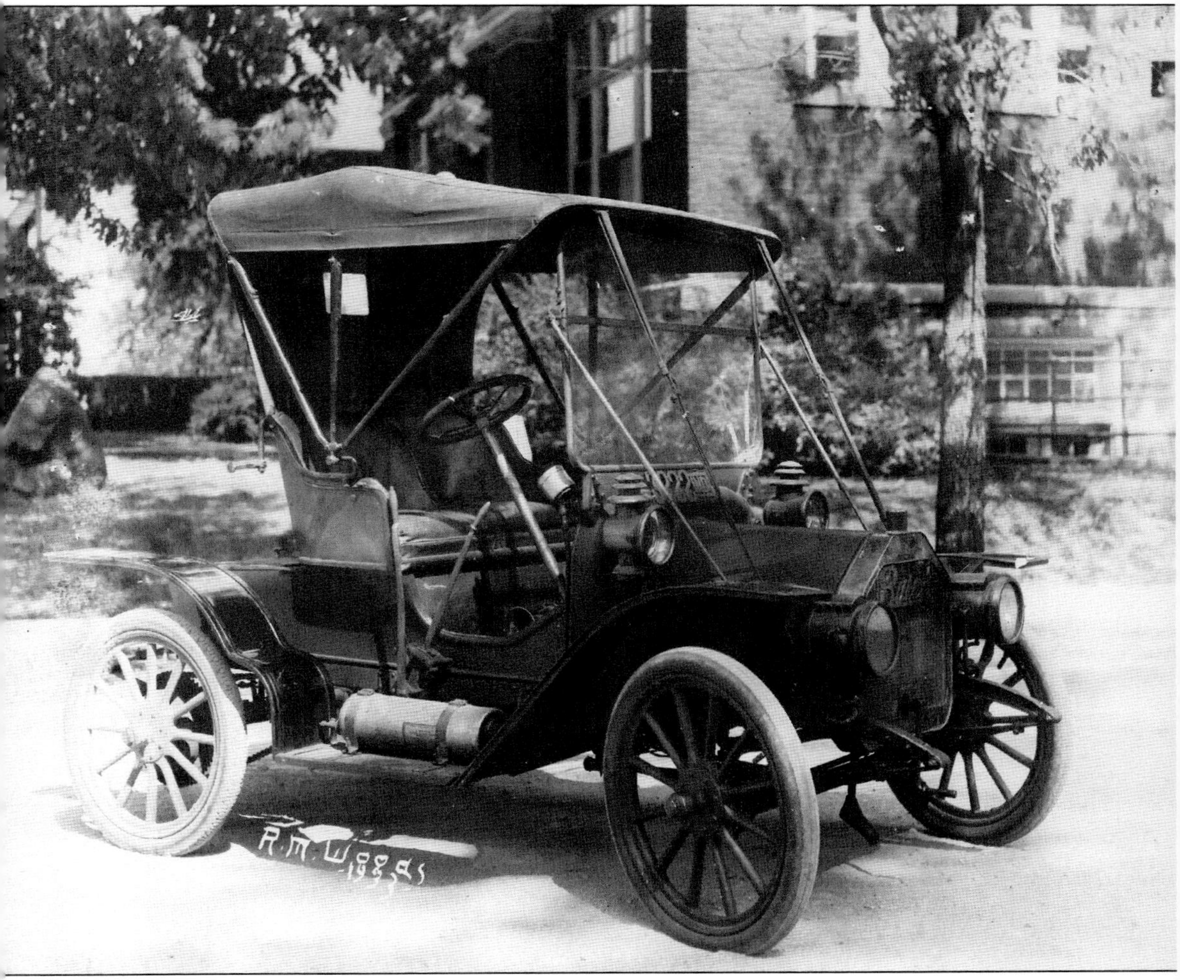

Someone proudly displays a Buick in this 1933 snapshot outside of the Knightstown Public Library. It seems Knightstown citizens have demonstrated a connection to the automobile from early on. An early issue of the local newspaper, for example, included an article that listed prominent local citizens and the vehicles they were driving—52 of them in all.

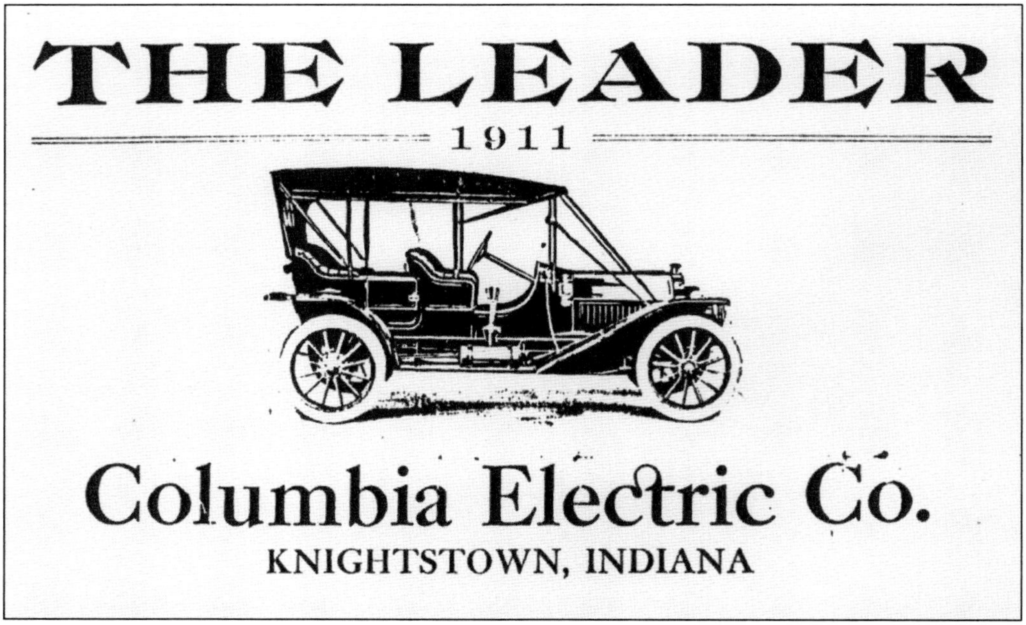

The Leader automobile was manufactured in Knightstown from 1907 until 1912. The business moved from nearby McCordsville to Knightstown after negotiations with the Merchants and Manufacturers' Association of Knightstown resulted in a free, new facility for the company.

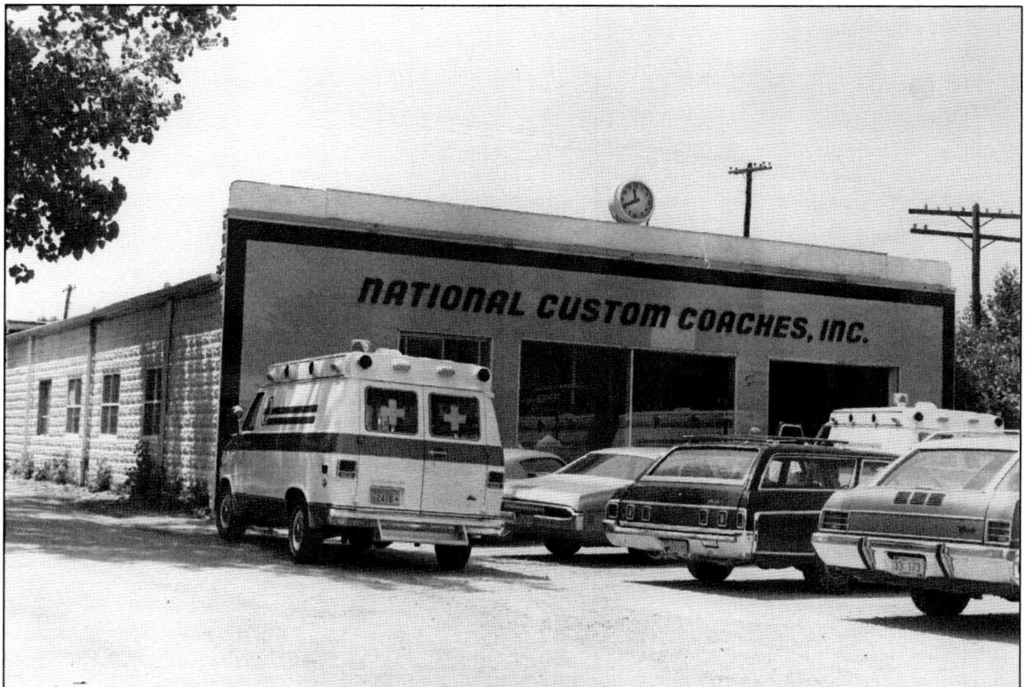

Knightstown has seen more than its share of ambulances over the years, but it has not been for emergencies. Several manufacturers of hearses, funeral wagons, and ambulances have done business in this small town. National Custom Coaches, for example, was alive and well in Knightstown in the 1960s and 1970s.

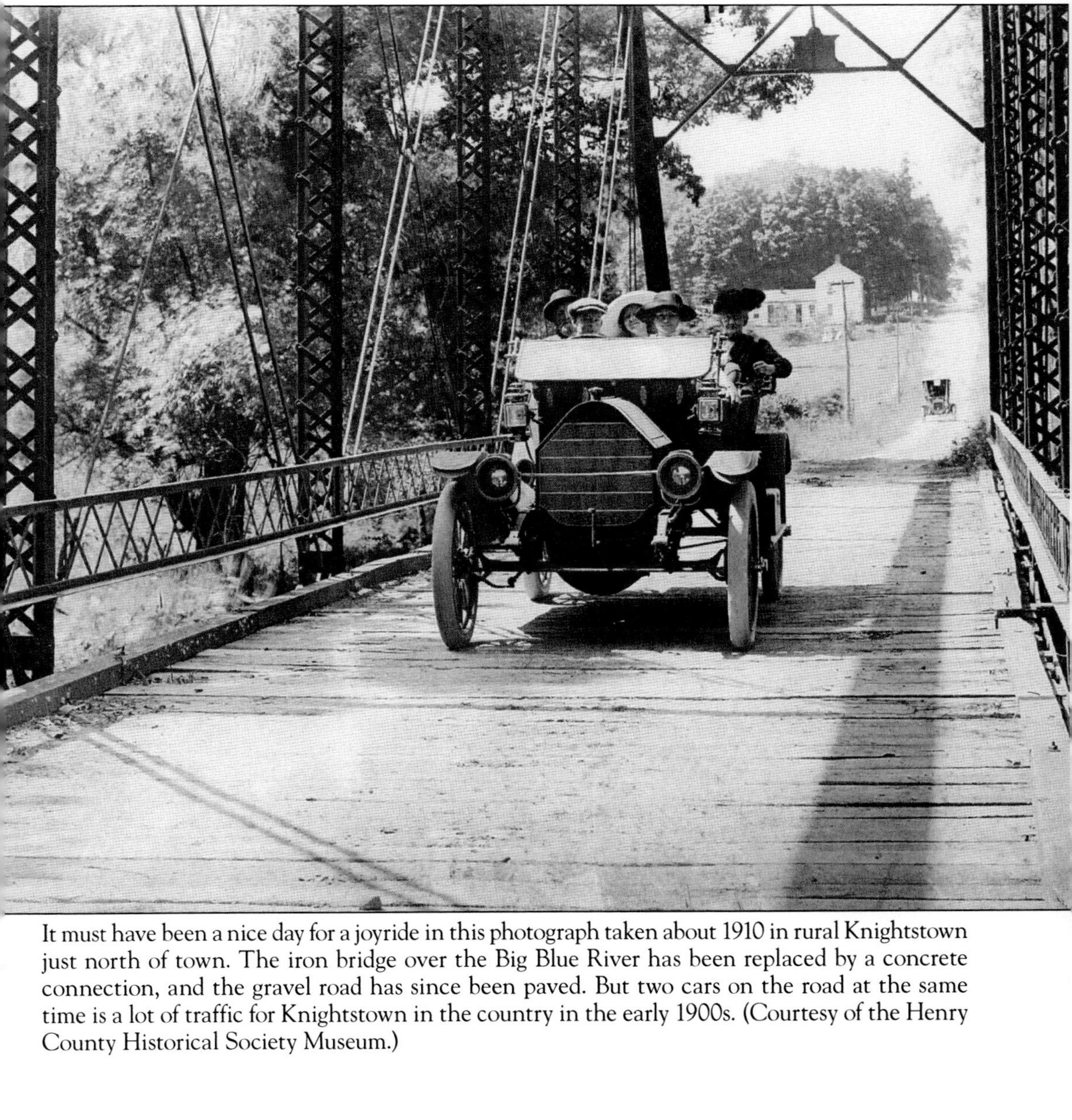

It must have been a nice day for a joyride in this photograph taken about 1910 in rural Knightstown just north of town. The iron bridge over the Big Blue River has been replaced by a concrete connection, and the gravel road has since been paved. But two cars on the road at the same time is a lot of traffic for Knightstown in the country in the early 1900s. (Courtesy of the Henry County Historical Society Museum.)

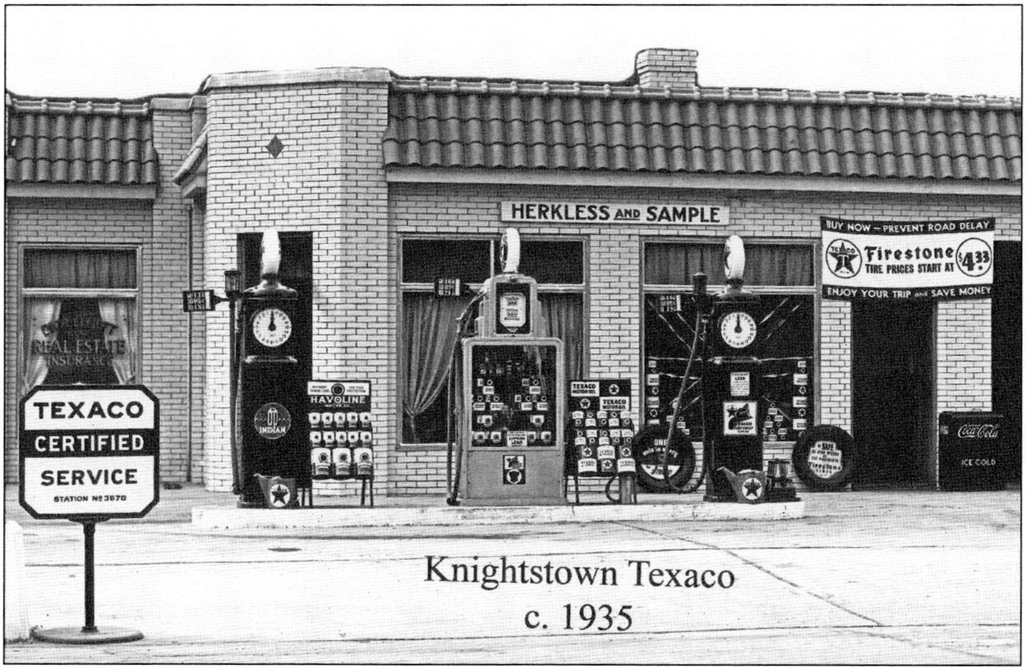

The arrival of the automobile sparked the construction of gas stations along the National Road, such as this 1934 Spanish Eclectic Texaco station at the corner of Main and Jefferson Streets in downtown Knightstown. Older gas stations often provide appealing examples of the architecture of the time. This one still stands and is the home of a telecommunications company.

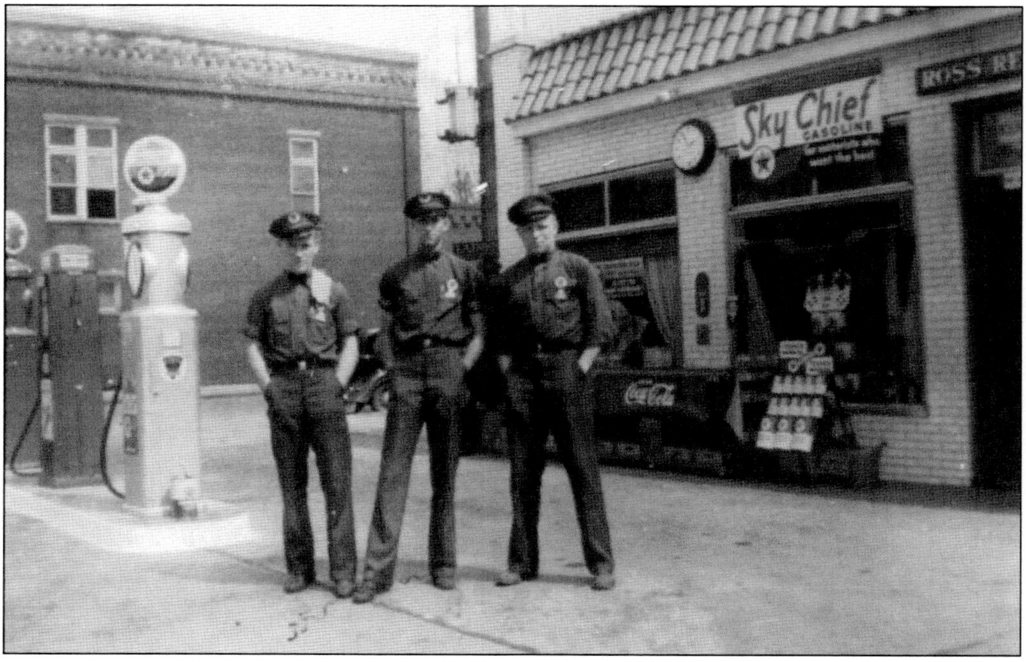

In 1939, gas station attendants wore crisp uniforms with shirts tucked in and matching hats, and stations were "full service." These three employees of the Texaco station on the corner of Jefferson and Main Streets are ready for work—definitely no self-serve gasoline available here.

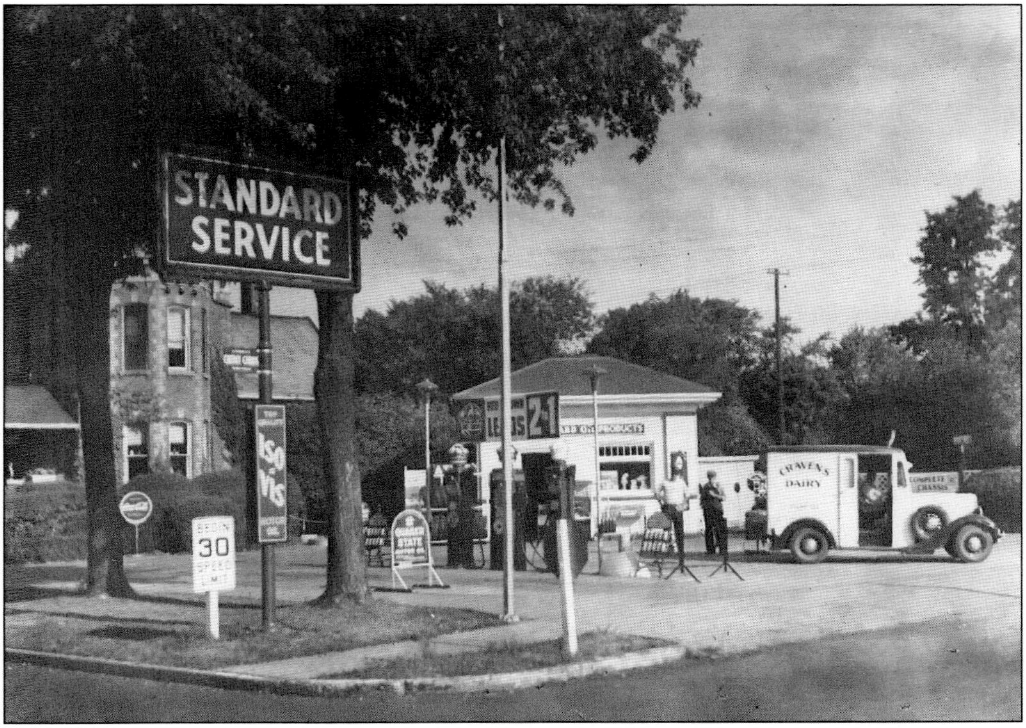

This little service station wore several identities over the years. The Standard Service Station (above) sits next to the Elias Hinshaw house on Main Street, where the local Craven's Dairy truck has made a quick stop. As Phil's Service (below), the station offers many of the same products and services, and the building is the same. The offerings seem simpler, however, with fewer products displayed outside. The Hinshaw house again is visible on the left. Today a modern gas station has replaced the small building, and the Hinshaw house still can be found next door.

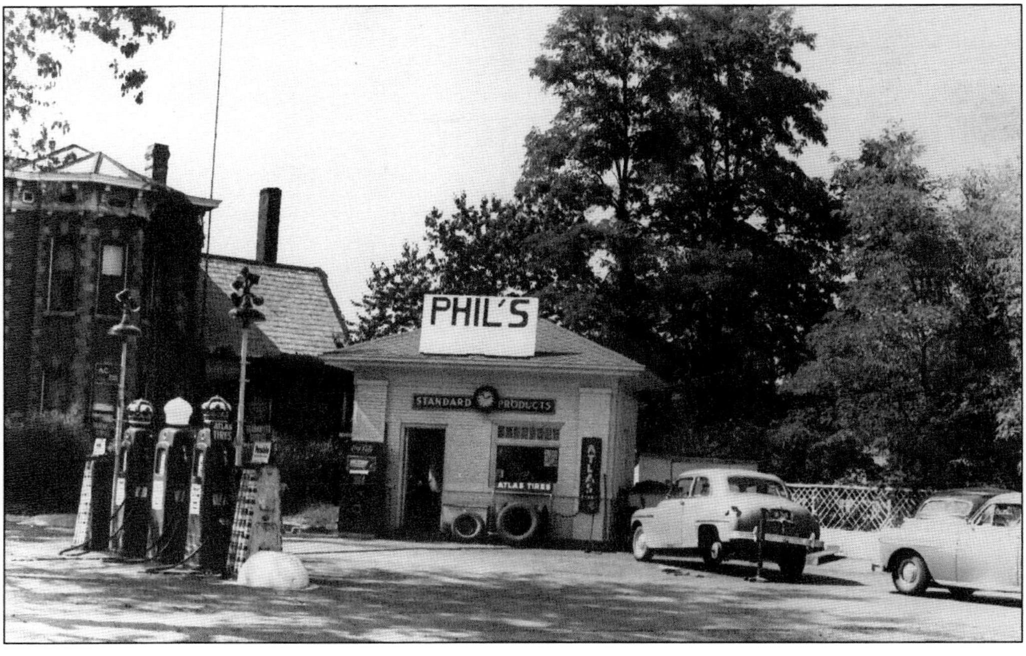

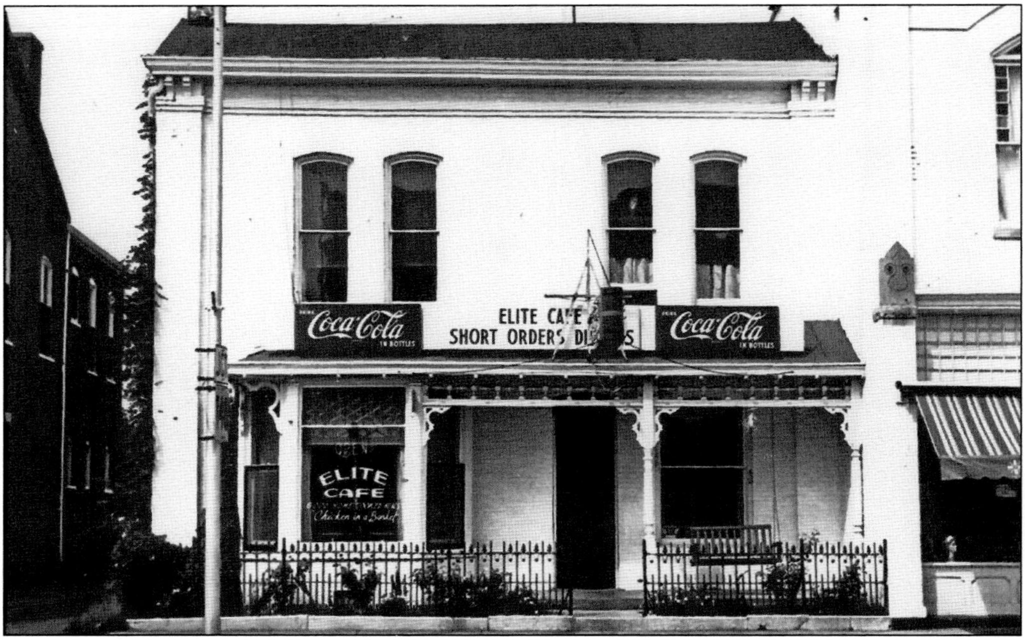

Many locals and visitors stopped for a bite to eat at the Elite Café on Main Street, which advertised "chicken in a basket" and featured on its menu "really good pie," says longtime resident Peg Mayhill. Many residents have fond memories of the porch swing and the homey atmosphere. Over the years, the two-story building housed another restaurant, Vestal's, and Grace Tyner's Millinery Parlor among others. Though the building no longer stands (the space is now a parking lot), the wrought-iron fence still does and offers a reminder of good meals and good company.

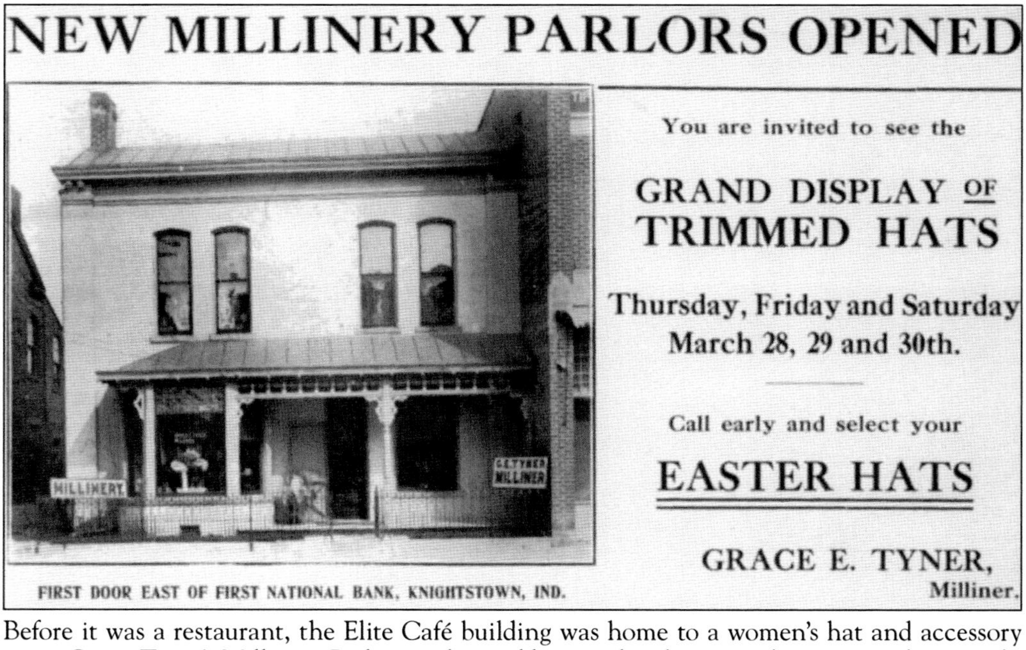

Before it was a restaurant, the Elite Café building was home to a women's hat and accessory store. Grace Tyner's Millinery Parlor was located here and is shown in this c. 1907 photograph. Recognizable are the front porch and the wrought-iron fence out front. No chicken was advertised in the window, however, just hats.

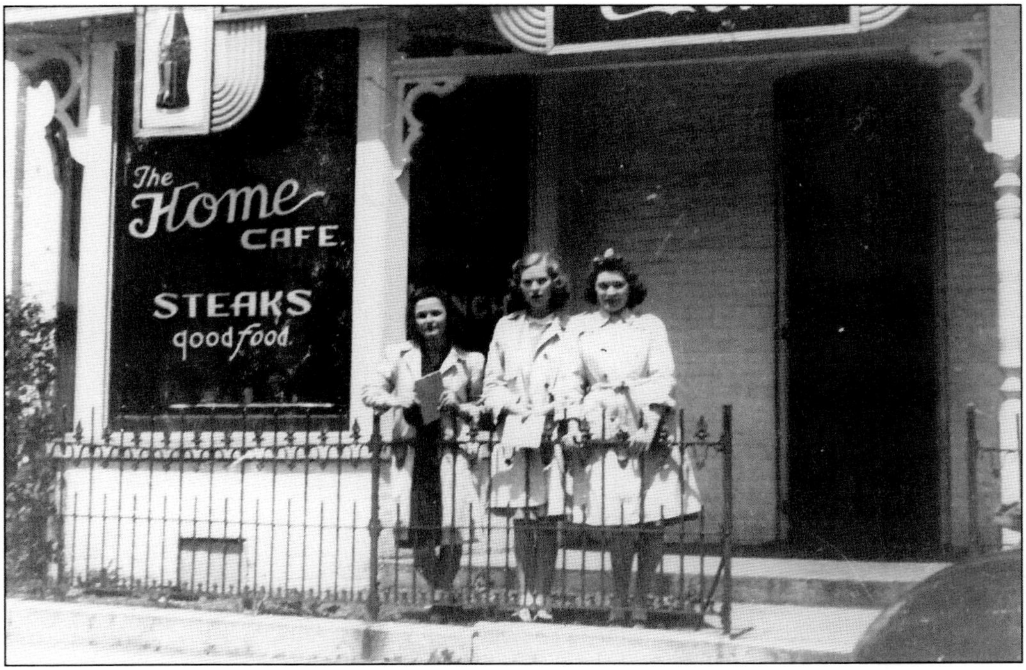

It is in the same location as the Elite Café, but in 1945 the restaurant was known as the Home Café. These three young ladies have paused for the camera, but maybe they were on their way inside for the "steaks and good food" that were promised by the writing in the front window.

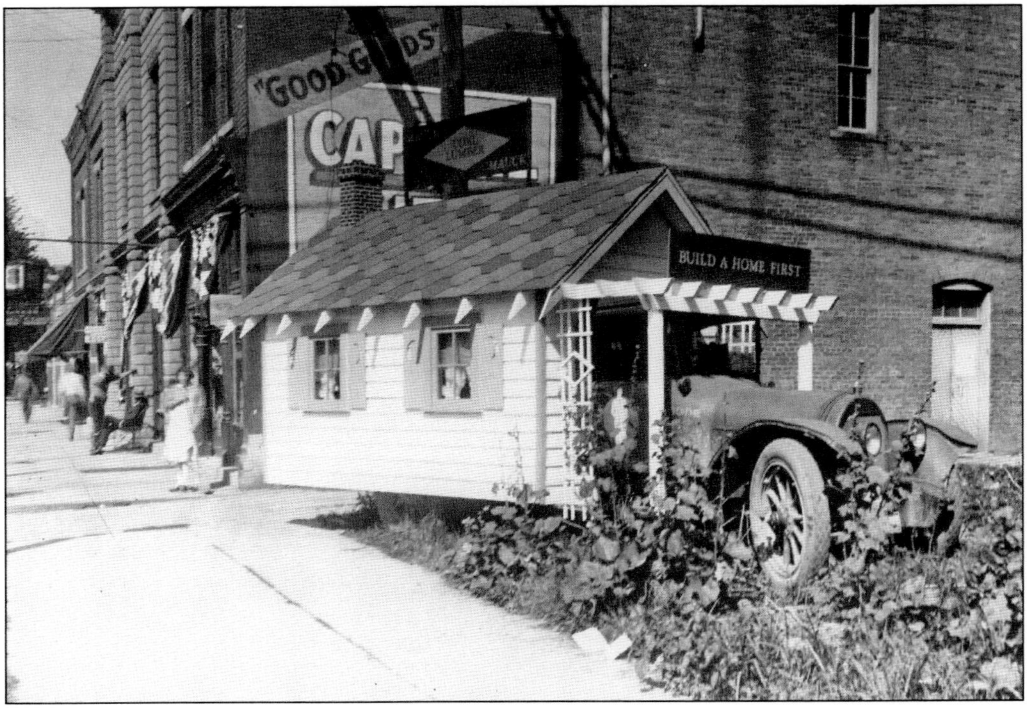

A house on the back of a truck is an unusual sight, even in Knightstown. The sign in this 1928 photograph reads, "Build a Home First." The *what* in the message seems clear, but the *why* is a bit blurred.

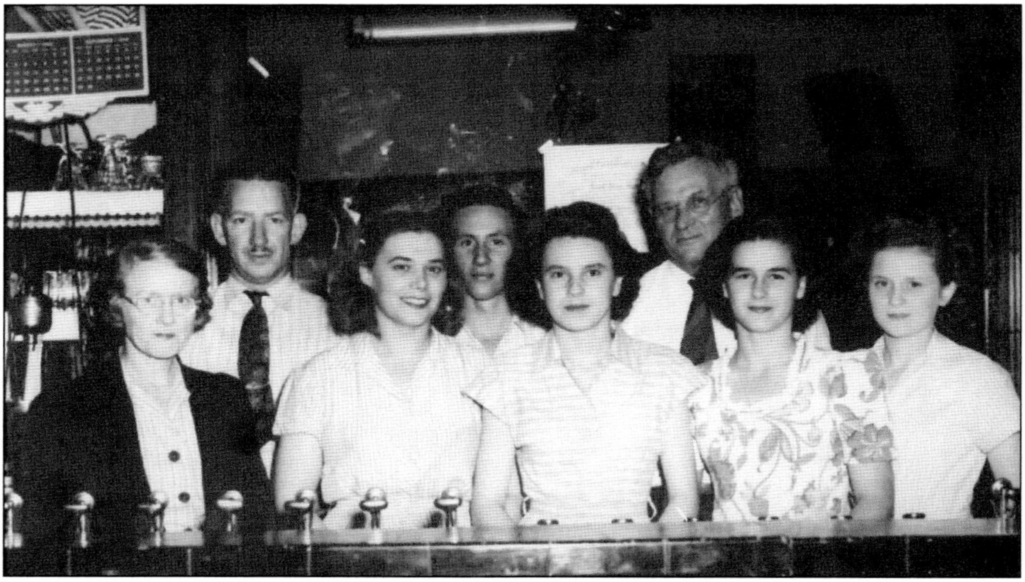

Jolly's Drugstore (above) was one of longest running and most popular businesses in Knightstown. It was founded by Walter Jolly in 1906 and was originally located on the Public Square before moving into the building on Main Street that once had housed Bell's Hall upstairs. In this c. 1940 photograph, local teens enjoy treats at Jolly's, which featured a soda fountain, much to the enjoyment of Jolly's regulars. The business closed its doors on June 30, 1992, when it was bought out by Hooks Drugs. Following a ball game, Knightstown teenagers (below) gather at another local hangout, the Mattix Restaurant.

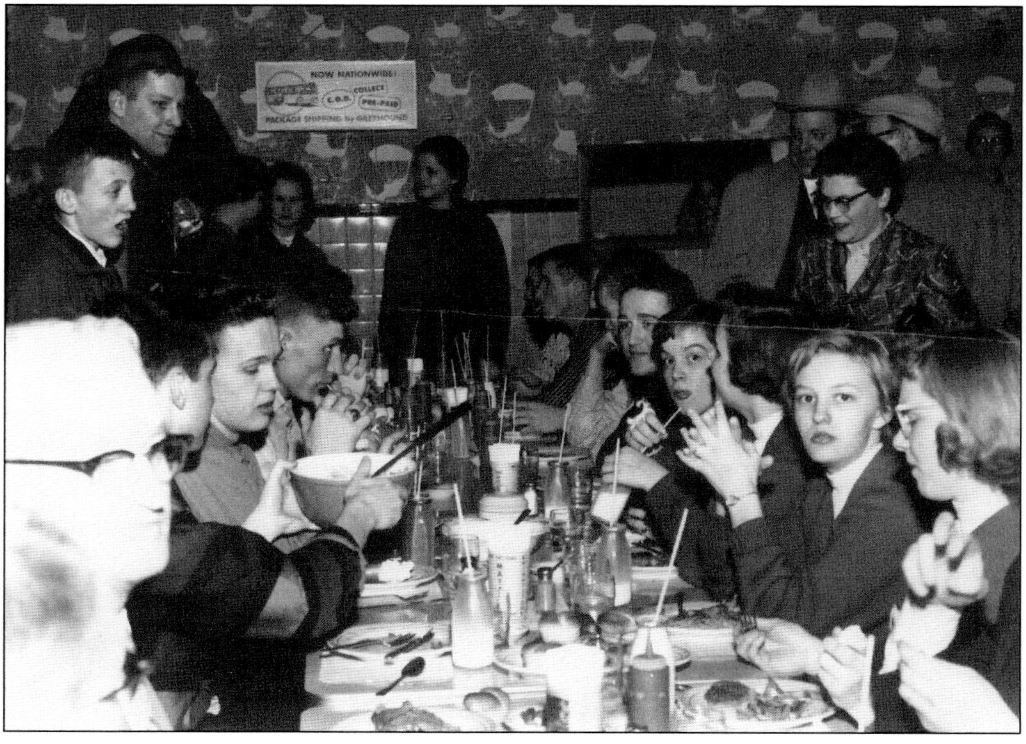

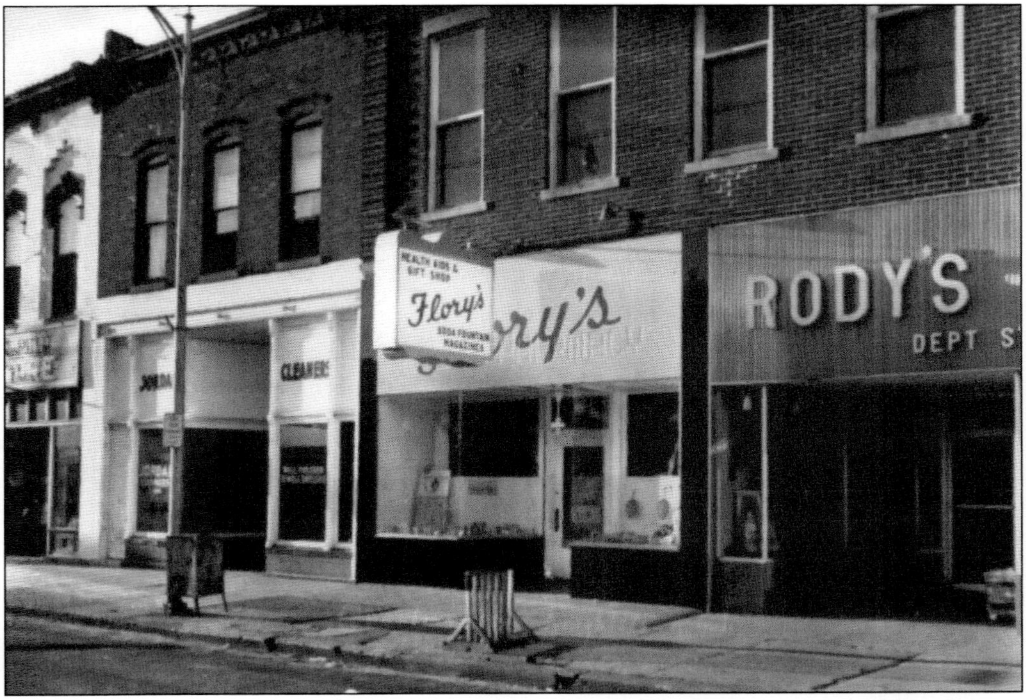

Flory's was another popular gathering spot for folks in Knightstown. Originally located on the first floor of the Alhambra Theater building, the shop moved to Main Street and lived out the remainder of its days there. It closed on December 24, 1978. Flory's might best be remembered for its Coney dogs; the sauce was made from Mrs. Flory's secret recipe.

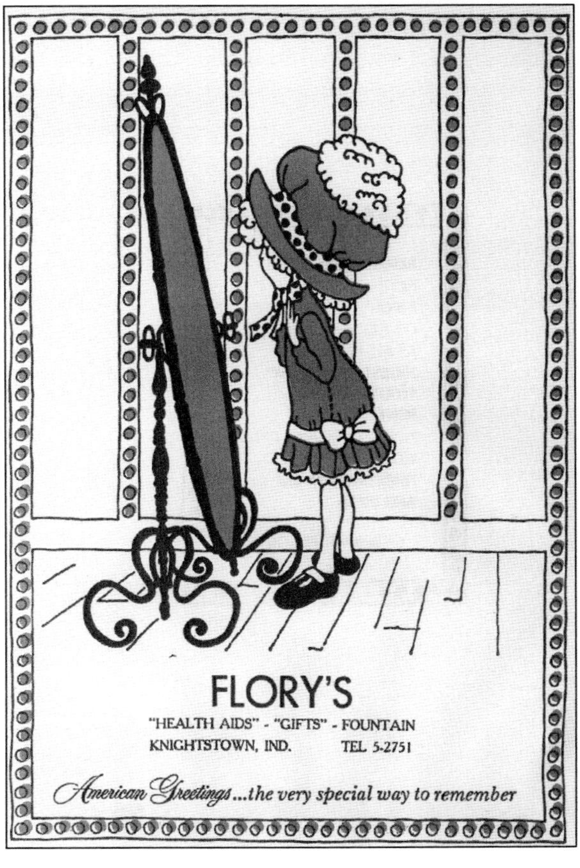

In this Flory's drugstore paper sack, customers could take home items that they had purchased, such as greeting cards, health aids, and gifts. Originally printed in blue-and-white ink, the sack also advertised Flory's well-loved soda fountain.

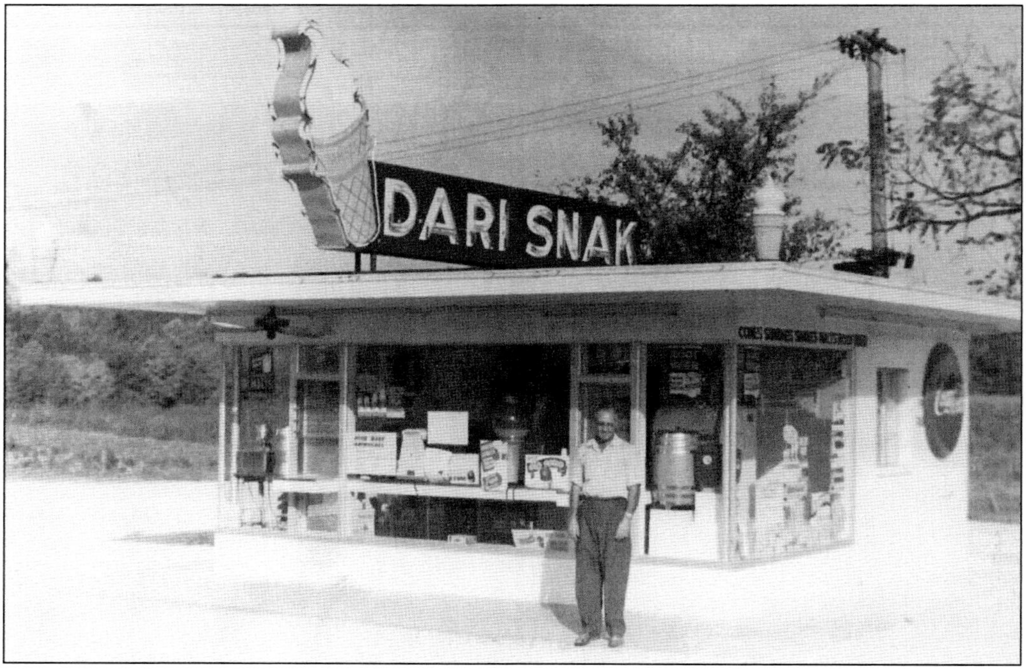

In the 1950s and 1960s, the Ramsey's Dari Snak (above) was one of the hangouts before and after Knightstown High School ball games. The Ramsey family (below) served up ice cream and grilled burgers to the hungry crowds. Customers could eat inside at the booths or pull up outside for carhop service to their cars. Headlights turned on signaled that they were ready to order.

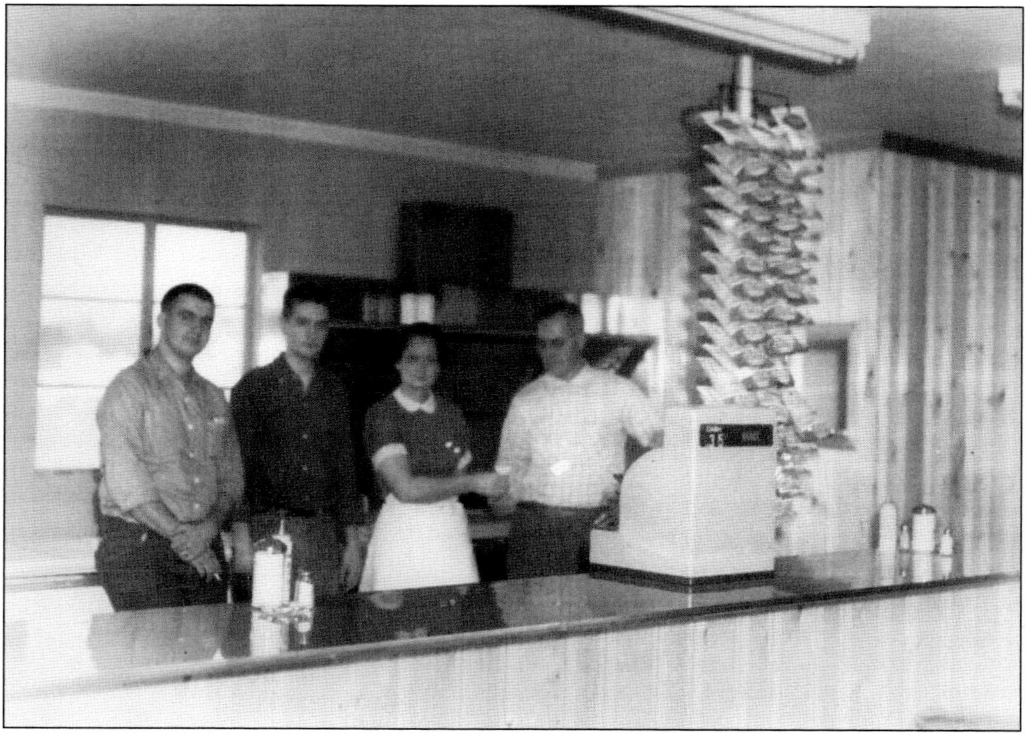

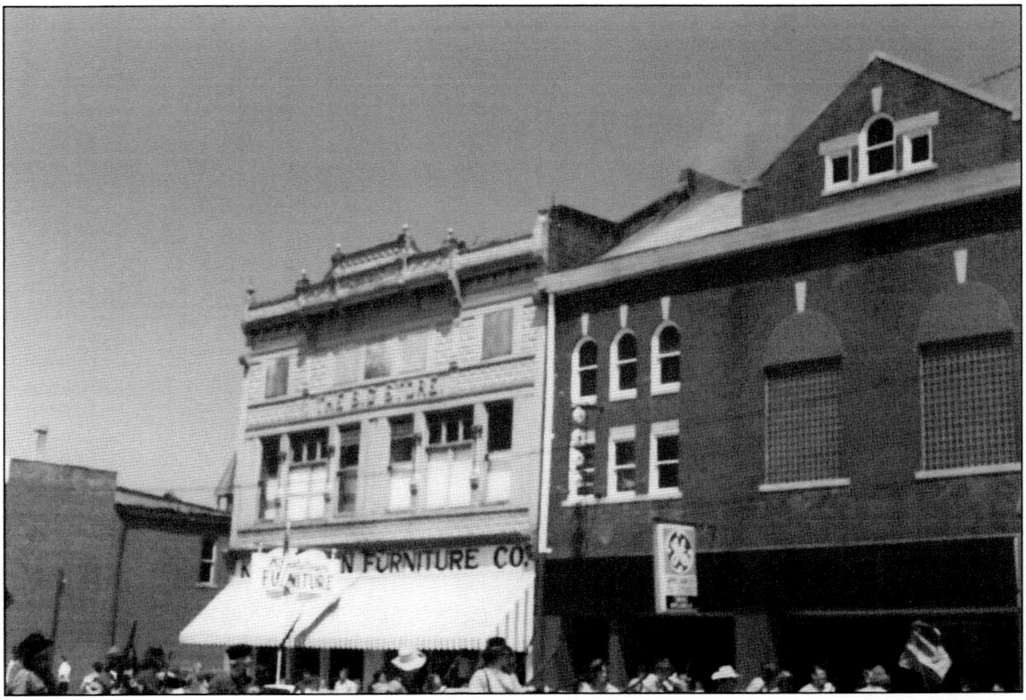

The ornate facade of this early commercial structure (to the left) on Main Street is today hidden beneath a smooth, flat front that was added much later. The building has been home to a furniture store, an antique mall, and an archery range.

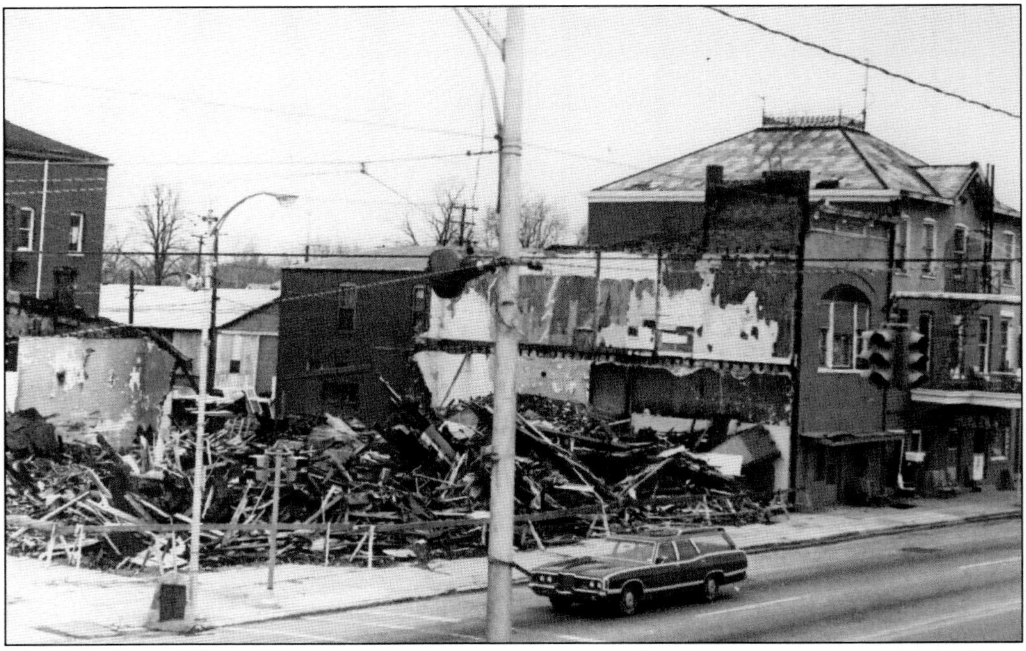

The demolition of historic buildings has been no stranger to Knightstown residents. This building on the southeast corner of the Public Square at Main and Washington Streets was torn down in 1973. It was one of the oldest commercial buildings still standing in town at the time. The Hotel Jack is on the right.

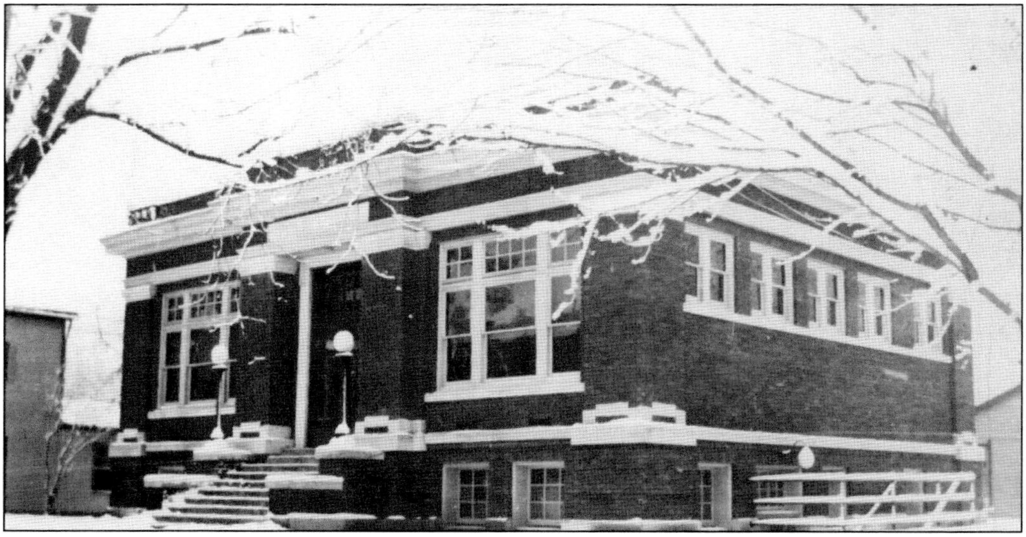

The Knightstown Public Library on Main Street was constructed in 1912 with funds provided by steel magnate and philanthropist Andrew Carnegie. Carnegie, who believed in the importance of local libraries, funded many public libraries across the country. The Knightstown Library has changed little in its nearly 100 years, and it still offers books and services to Knightstown readers.

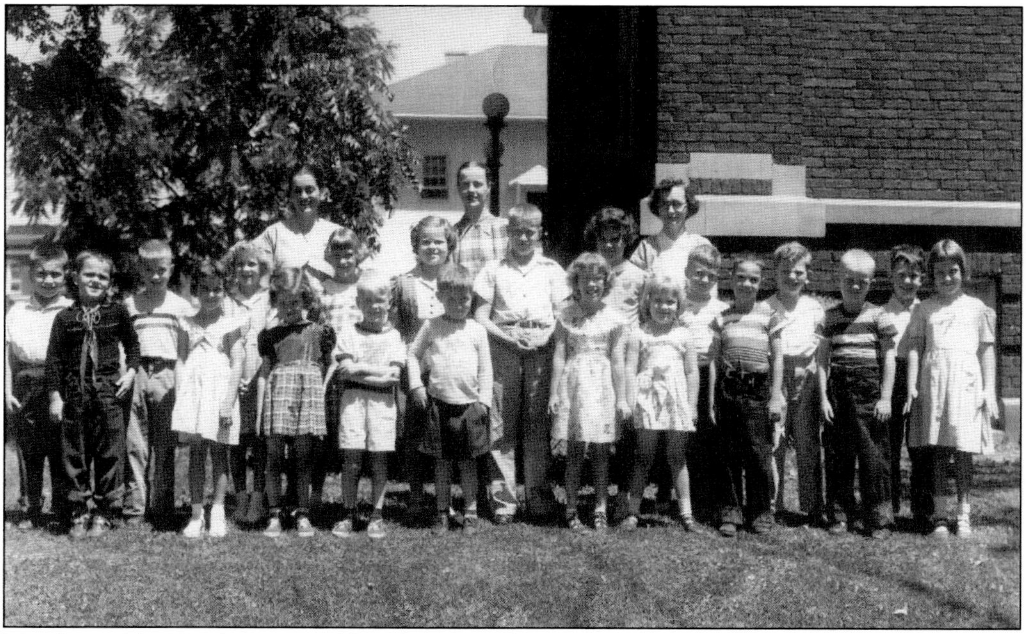

Members of the Knightstown Public Library's reading program around 1950 are pictured outside the library building, and the young ladies are wearing their summer dresses. Summer reading programs for children are a staple of public libraries everywhere; this one met every Saturday afternoon.

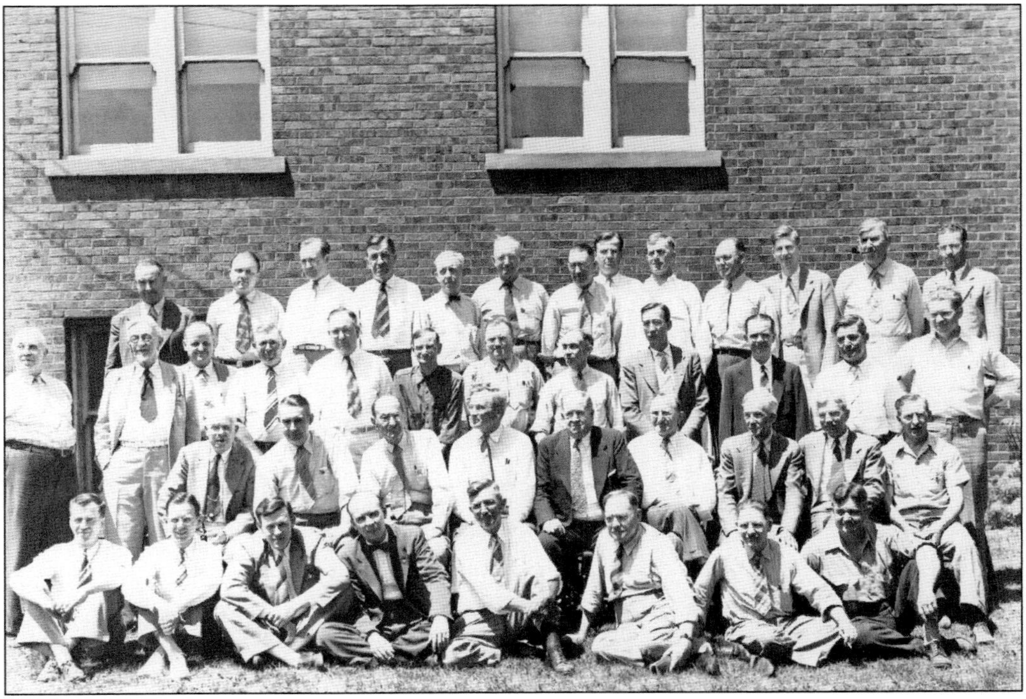

Kiwanis Club of Knightstown members are pictured here in 1941. Kiwanis is an international service organization with clubs in local communities. Chartered in 1922, the Knightstown Kiwanis Club supported the community in many ways for many years, until it was disbanded in 1997.

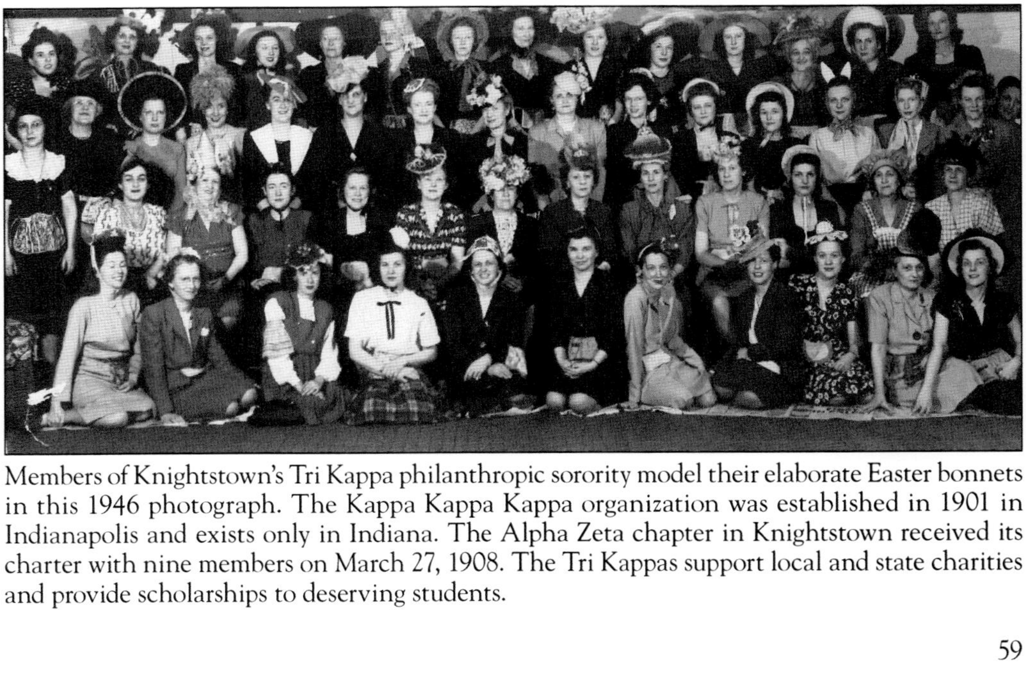

Members of Knightstown's Tri Kappa philanthropic sorority model their elaborate Easter bonnets in this 1946 photograph. The Kappa Kappa Kappa organization was established in 1901 in Indianapolis and exists only in Indiana. The Alpha Zeta chapter in Knightstown received its charter with nine members on March 27, 1908. The Tri Kappas support local and state charities and provide scholarships to deserving students.

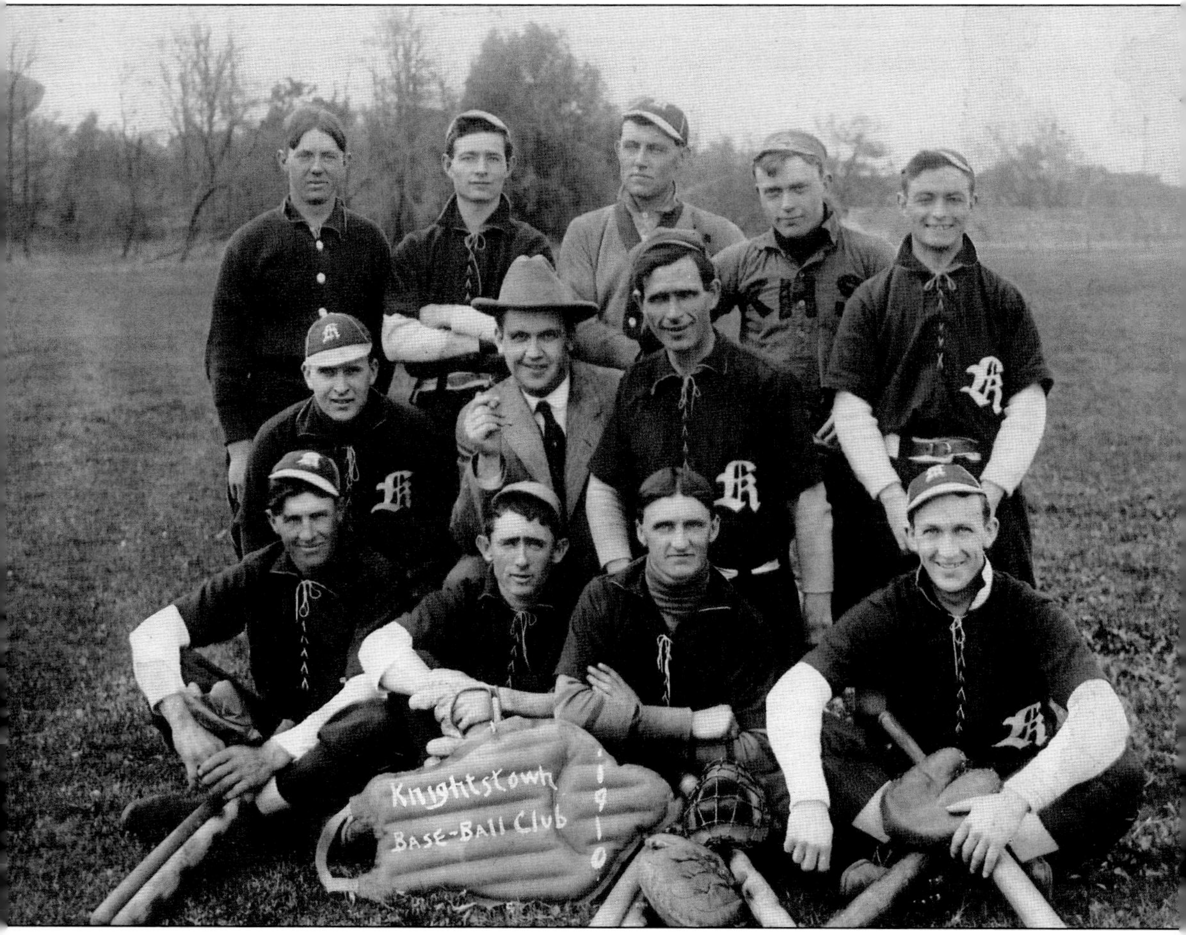

Sports clubs provided opportunities for men in rural communities to participate in their favorite games. Clubs were hot in the early 1900s, when sports such as baseball and football were catching on. The baseball club in Knightstown is pictured here in 1910. Note the old-style mitts and catcher's mask.

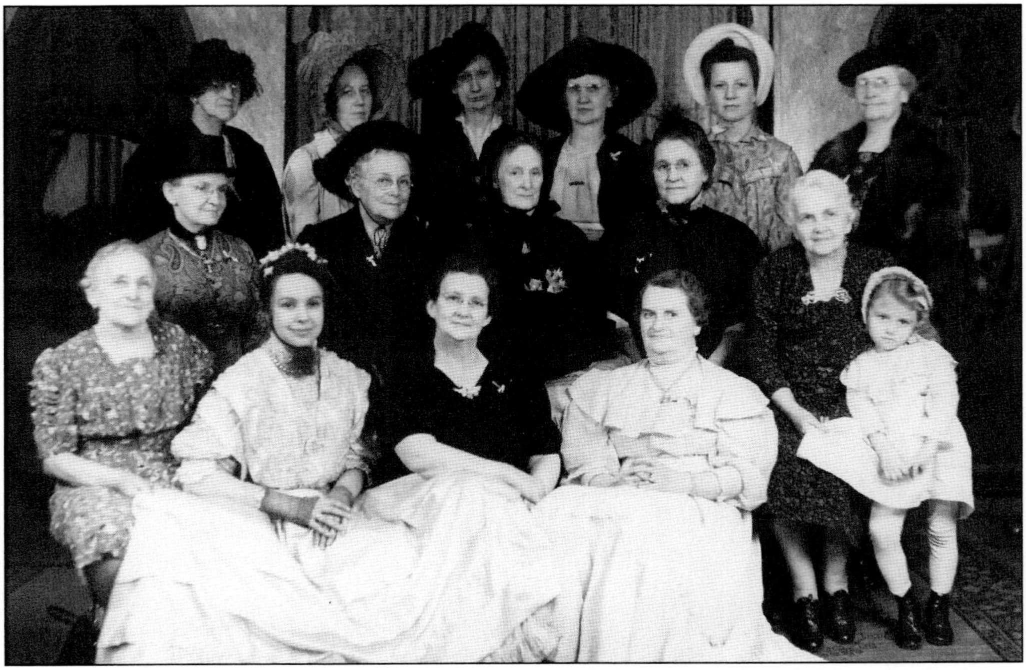

This is an early photograph of Knightstown's Fortnightly Historical Club (above), which was organized in 1907 with the colors black and yellow and the motto "Count Your Blessings." In January 1957 (below), members celebrated the club's 50th anniversary. The attire might have changed, but not the ladies' dedication to and enjoyment of their club.

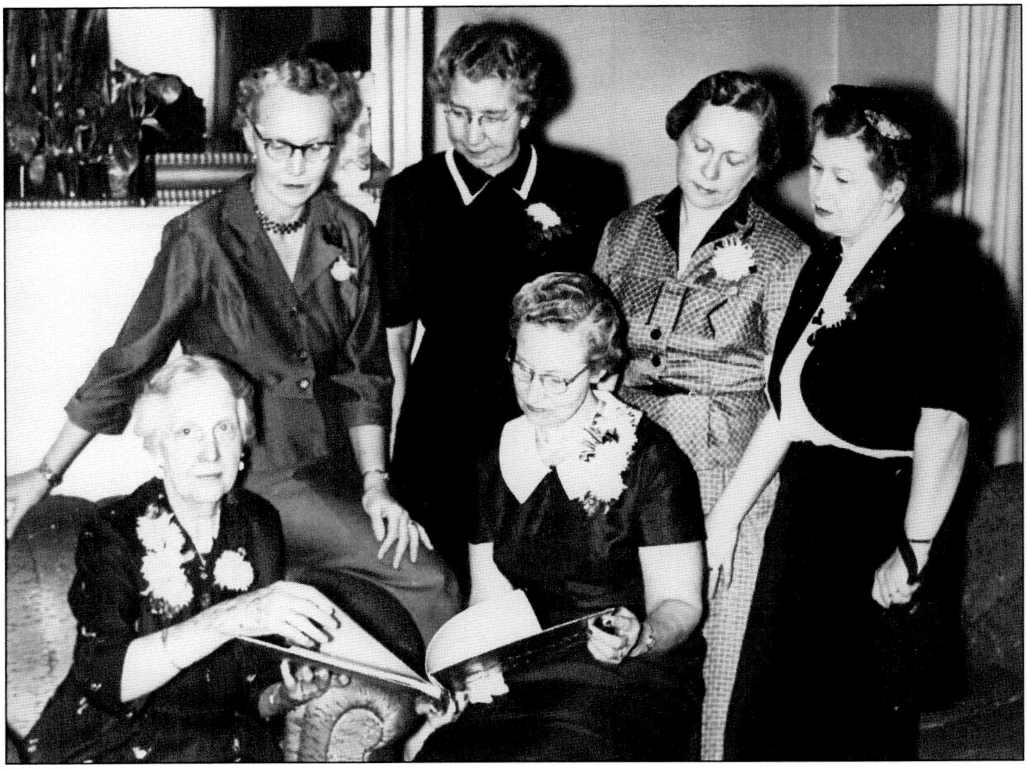

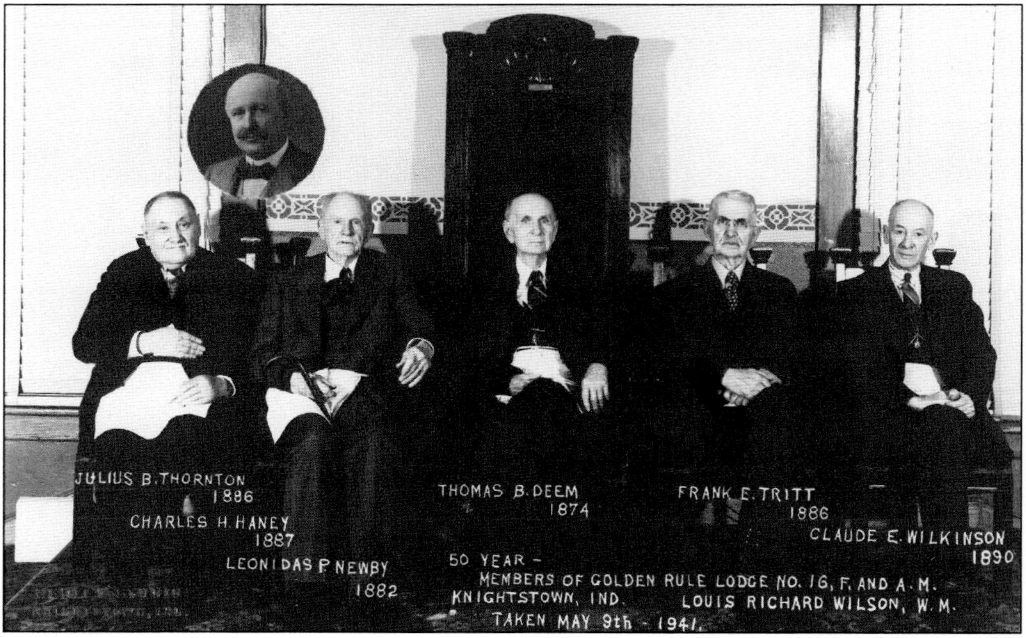

Fifty-year members of Knightstown's Masonic Golden Rule Lodge No. 16 are pictured here in honor of their dedication to the Freemasons. Some of the names are very familiar in Knightstown history, such as publisher T. B. Deem, bank president and state senator Leonidas P. Newby, and businessman Frank Tritt.

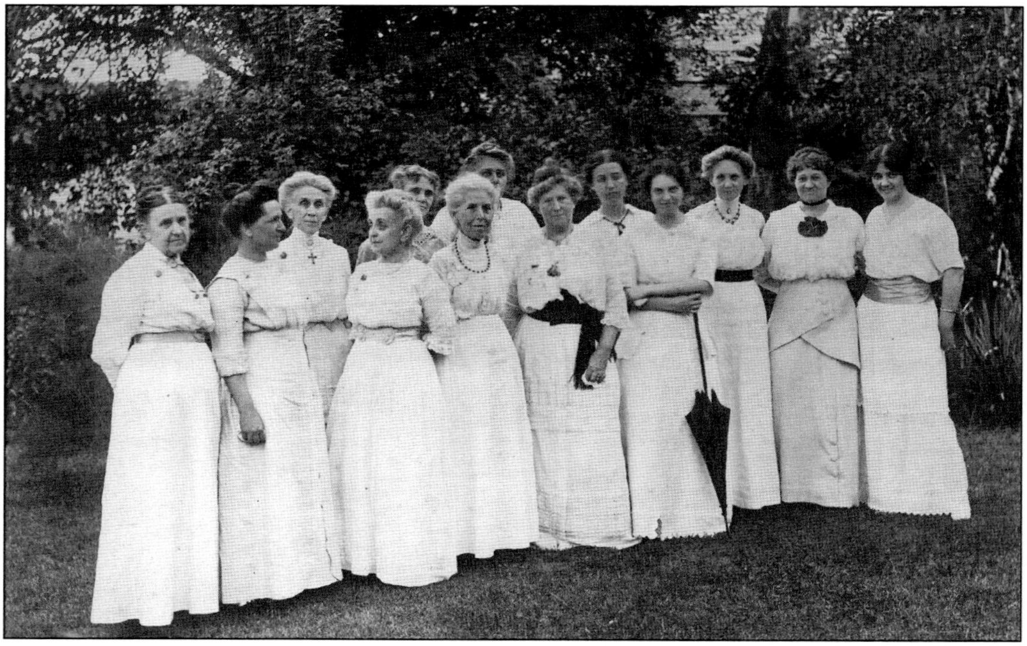

Literary clubs were fashionable in the late 1800s and early 1900s, possibly as an outgrowth of ladies' social and reading circles. Knightstown had several, including the American Literary Club, Avon Club, and Shakespeare Club. Here members of Knightstown's Shakespeare Club are pictured in 1914. The Shakespeare Club was chartered in 1889, and it still exists today; so does the Avon Club, which began in November 1894.

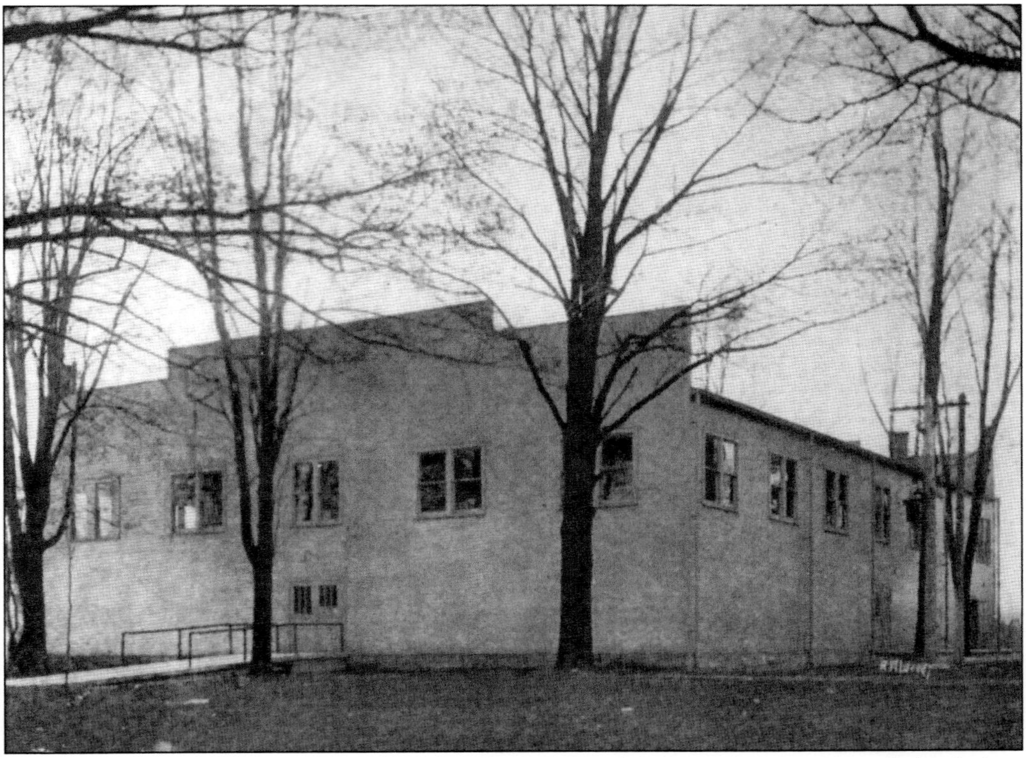

Knightstown's Hoosier Gym was constructed in 1922 and improvements were made (including a front lobby) using Works Progress Administration funds in 1936. Many Knightstown residents remember playing and watching basketball games here or dancing on the slick gym floor at sock hops following games. In 1966, Knightstown High School played its last official regular season basketball game at the Hoosier Gym. Interest in the old building was revived when it was chosen as the sight of a major film. Still full of charm, the gym now is used as a community center.

Actor Gene Hackman (right) pauses during a scene in the 1986 movie *Hoosiers*, which was filmed in Knightstown's Hoosier Gym. Barbara Hershey and Dennis Hopper also starred in the Oscar-nominated film, which tells the tale of a tiny Indiana high school that makes it to the state championship tournament in the mid-1950s.

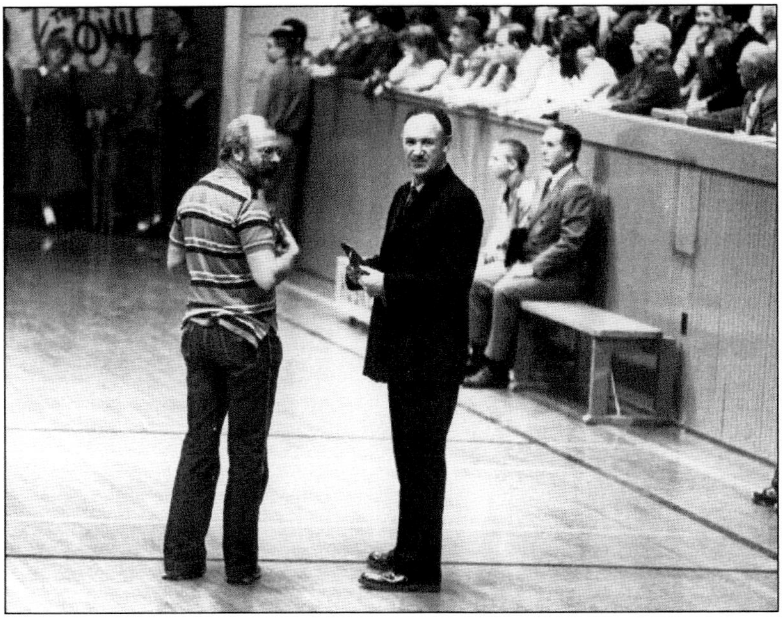

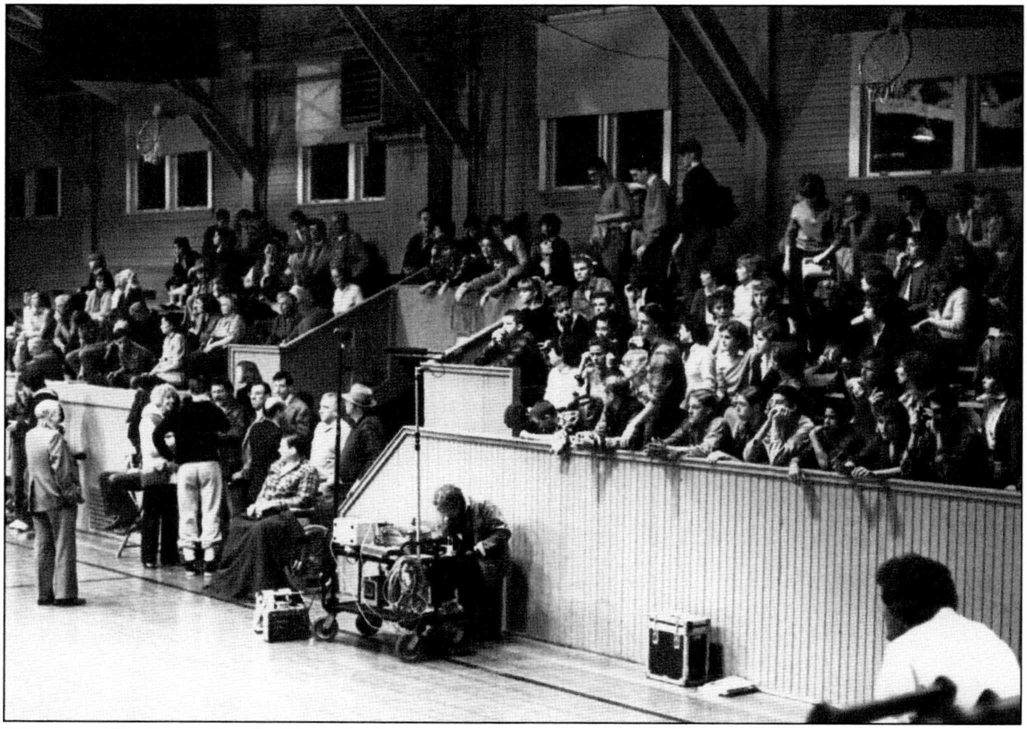

The crowd takes a break (above), the actors relax, and equipment is adjusted during filming of *Hoosiers* inside Knightstown's Hoosier Gym. Many of the extras for the film were Knightstown residents. Outside the gym and the Knightstown Academy (below), film crew trailers line the street almost as far as the eye can see.

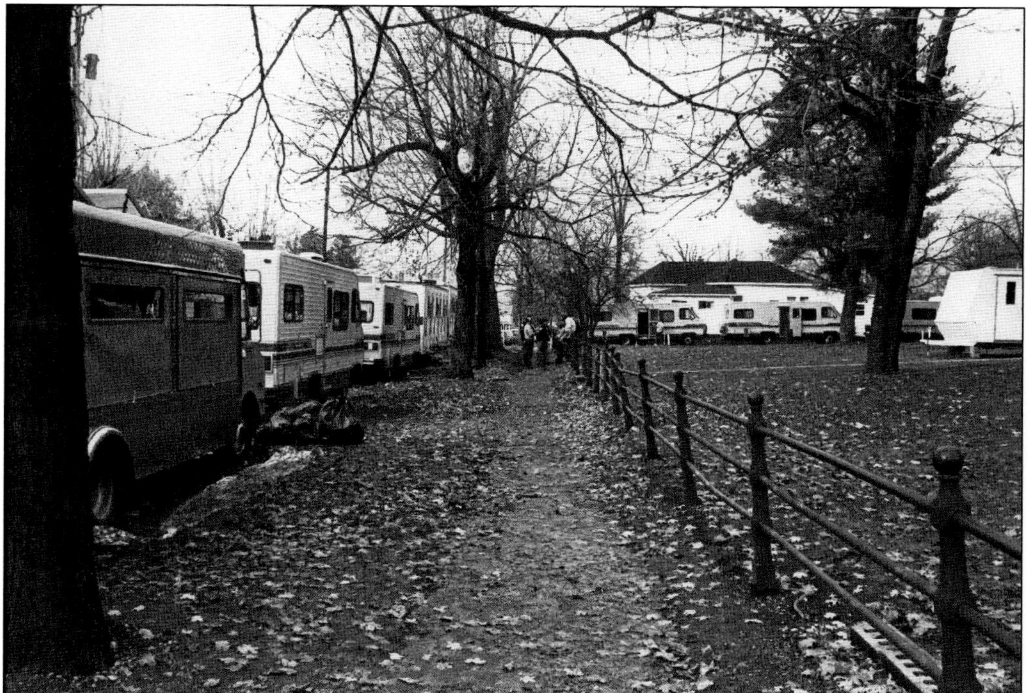

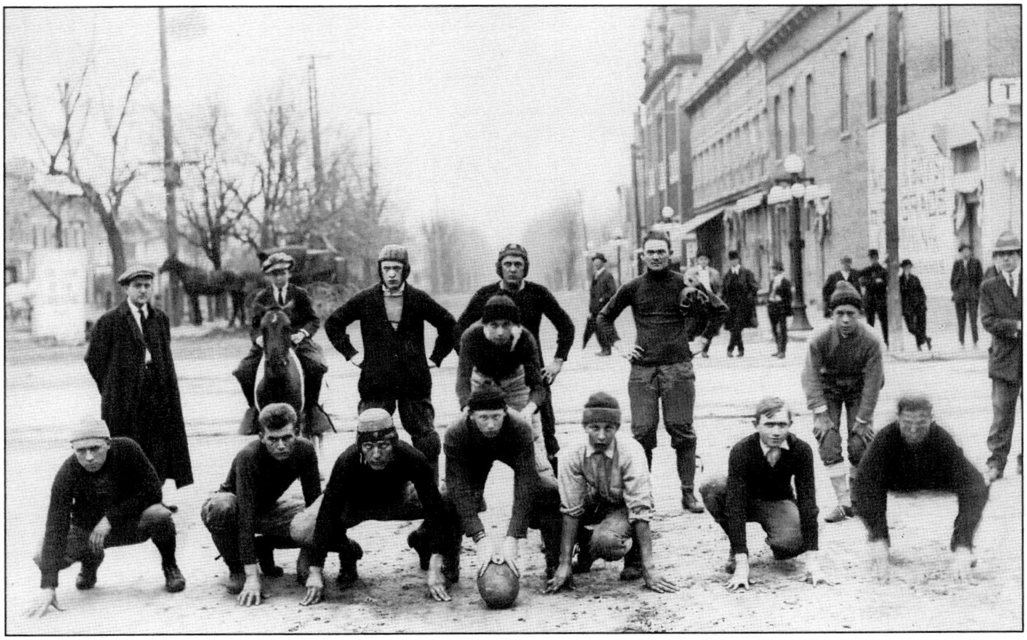

The south end of the Public Square, with horses and buggies and the Alhambra Theater in view, makes an interesting backdrop for football players in 1912—the same year rules were changed and touchdowns were awarded six points and field goals three points.

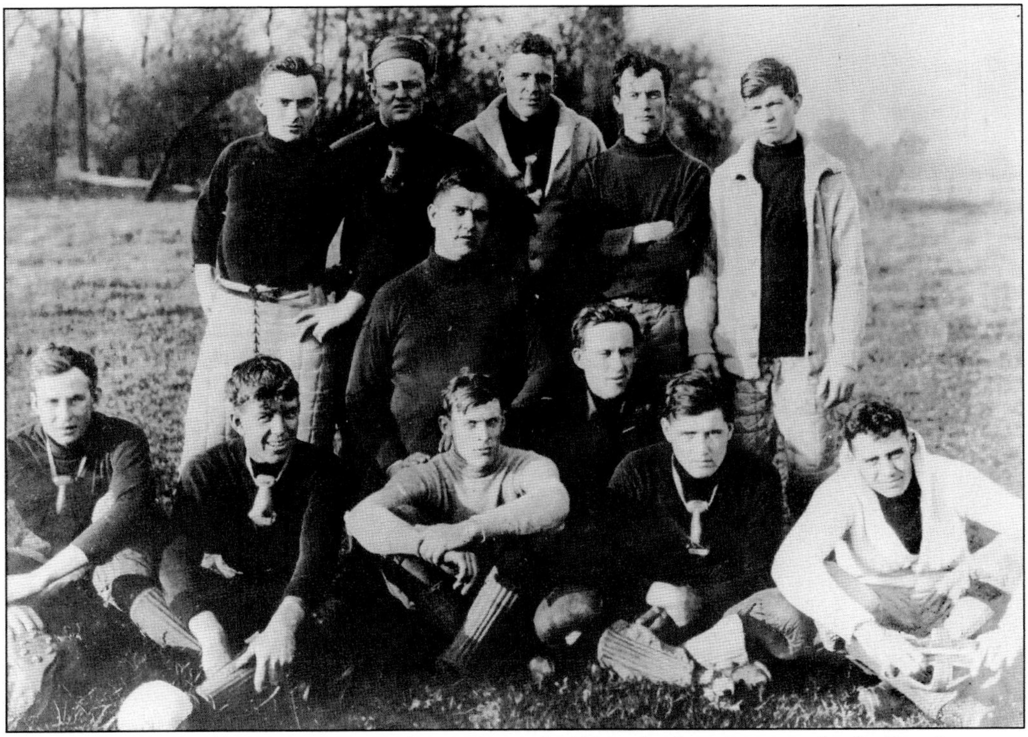

Independent football teams were popular in the early 1900s. In this photograph, the Knightstown Little Giants take time off the field to pose for the camera in 1912. American football started in 1879 and was big with colleges and universities in the early 1900s.

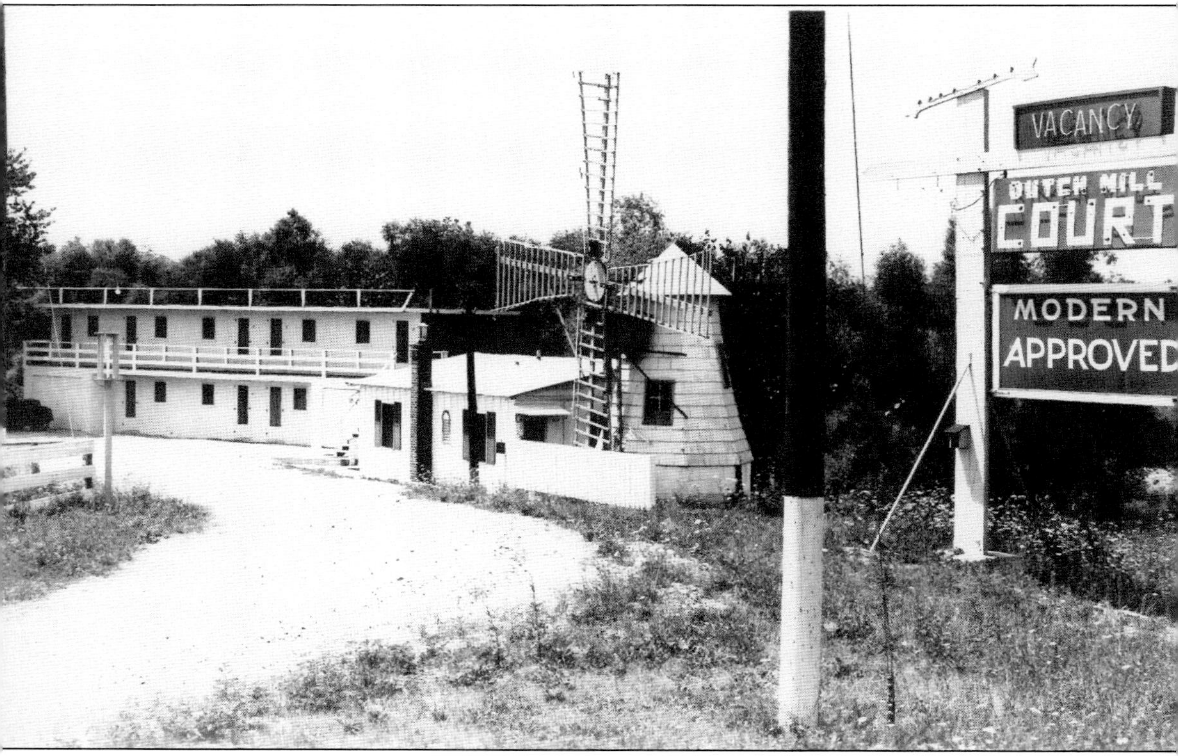

The easy-to-spot Dutch Mill Court was located about two miles west of Knightstown on U.S. 40 and welcomed many visitors over the years. Early highway workers, for example, sometimes stayed there and occasionally headed in to visit Knightstown's taverns after work. Small roadside motels such as the Dutch Mill Court were commonplace along the National Road during the 1940s and 1950s. They lost most of their business when Interstate 70 was built and pulled traffic from U.S. 40.

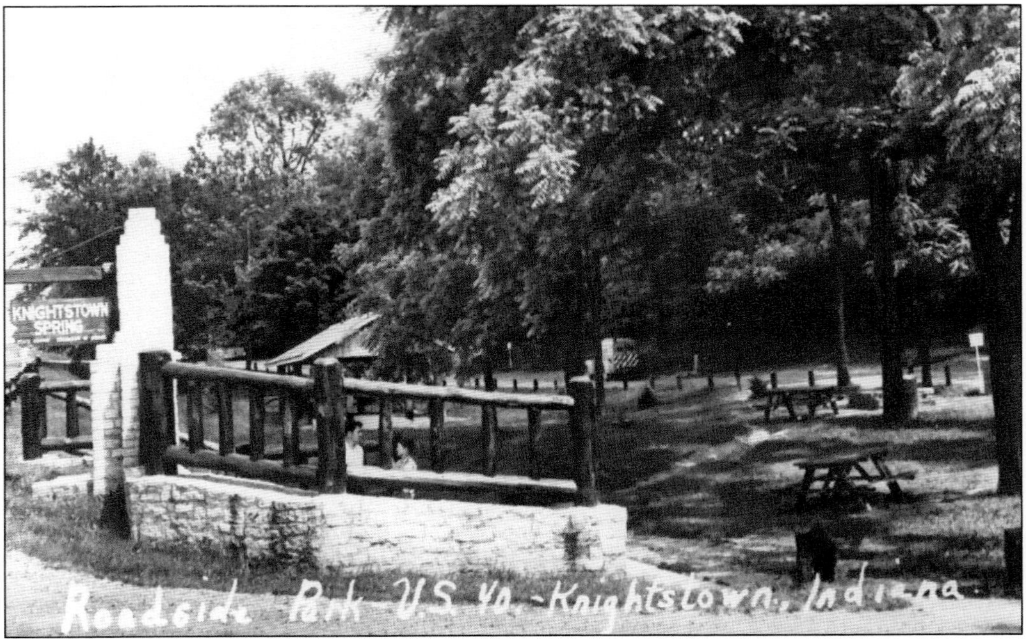

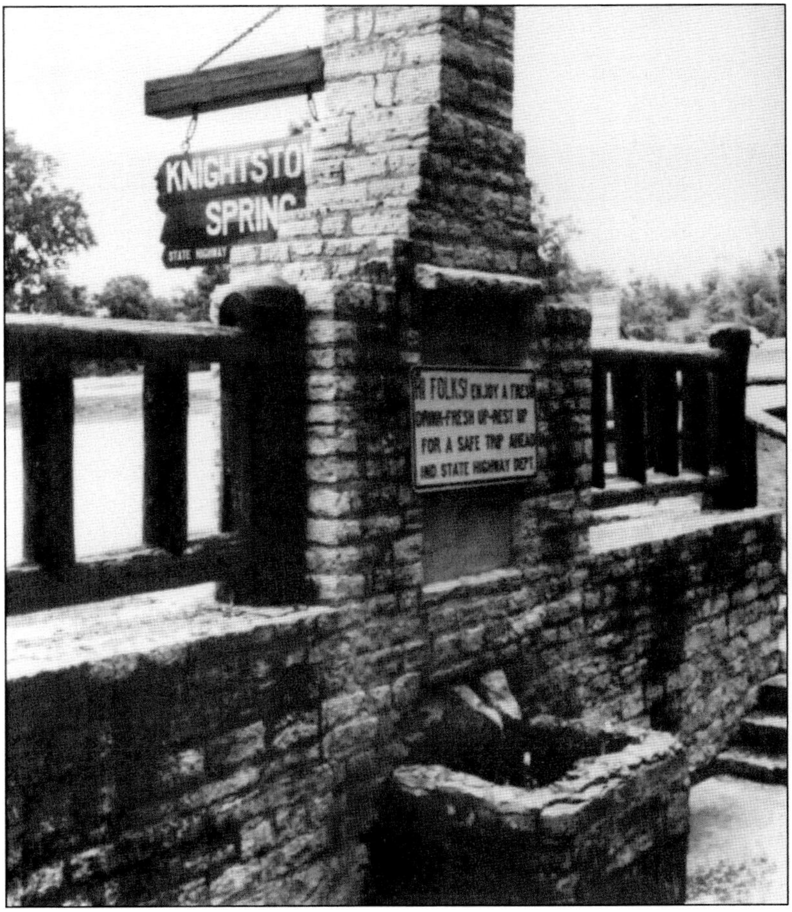

Nestled alongside the National Road just east of town, the Knightstown Spring (above and at right) provided a spot to rest and enjoy a picnic and the fresh spring water. Eventually visitation slowed as the water ceased to pass health department standards. Closed in the 1970s, the site is abandoned and overgrown, and all that remains of the spring is the ruins of the stone wall and spigot and a shadow of the circular drive.

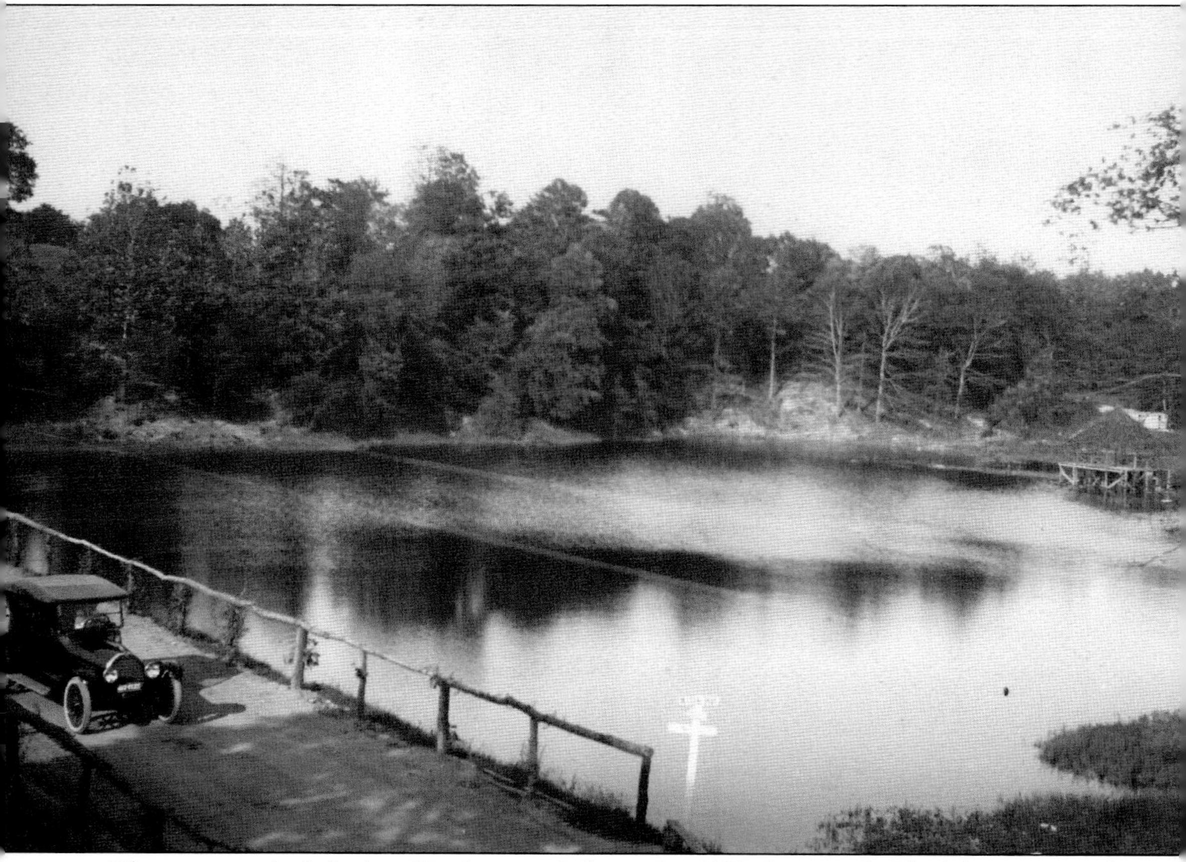

The water is a little high at Knightstown Lake in this 1923 photograph. The lake was part of a promotional plan to increase subscribers to the *Indianapolis Star* newspaper. Readers who subscribed to the paper for six months could purchase a lot at Knightstown Lake for \$58.50 (\$8.50 down plus \$2.50 per month until paid). A 1923 issue of the *Indianapolis Star* advertised the lake as a "new and beautiful summer resort created for the benefit of readers of the *Indianapolis Star*."

Three

A Giant on the Public Square

The Alhambra Theater building reigned over the Public Square's east side during a good portion of the 1900s. It was full of so much life, entertainment, and memories that it is deserving of some attention of its own. It also is a prime example of what neglect can do to both the physical and emotional aspects of a community. Meet the Alhambra—it is missed.

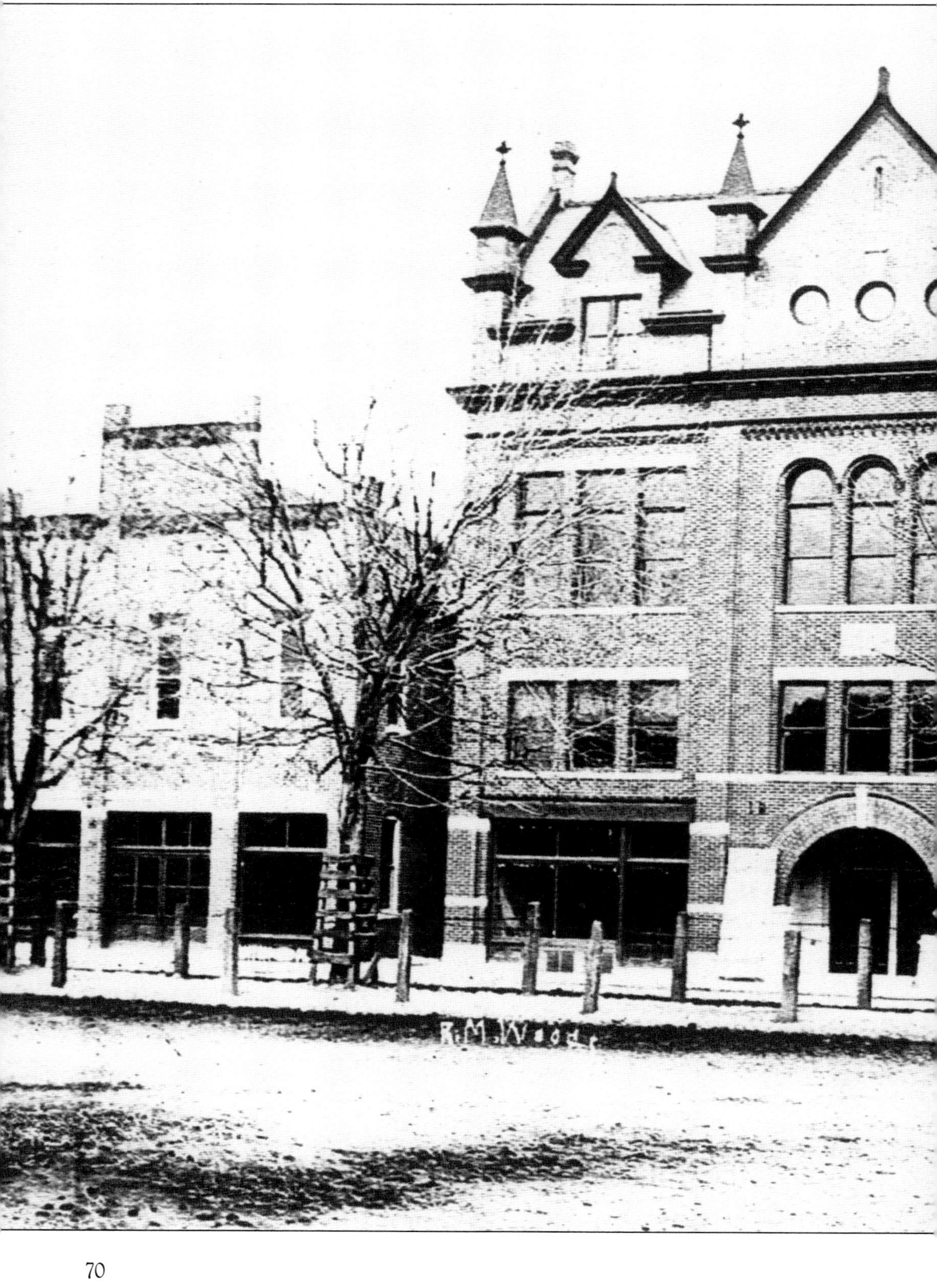
R.M.Wood

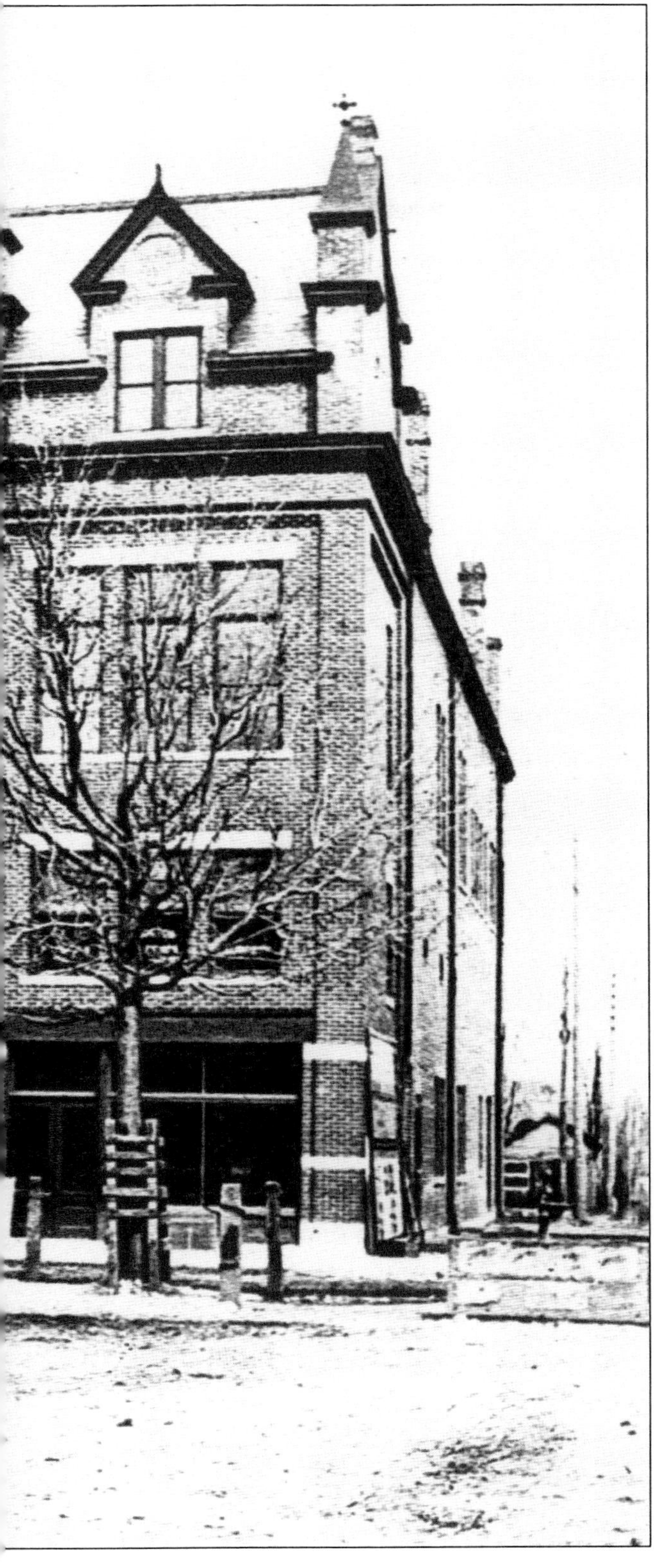

The Alhambra Theater building was a center of Knightstown's civic life since its construction in 1897. A movie theater, apartments, and third-floor Odd Fellows Lodge were once housed in the stately Alhambra. The building also featured a millinery shop and for a while the popular Flory's soda shop, among other businesses over the course of its lifetime. Longtime locals remember attending movies at the Alhambra for 10¢ and buying penny candy at Flory's shop on the first floor. Unfortunately this giant on Knightstown's Public Square fell into disrepair and was demolished in July 1992.

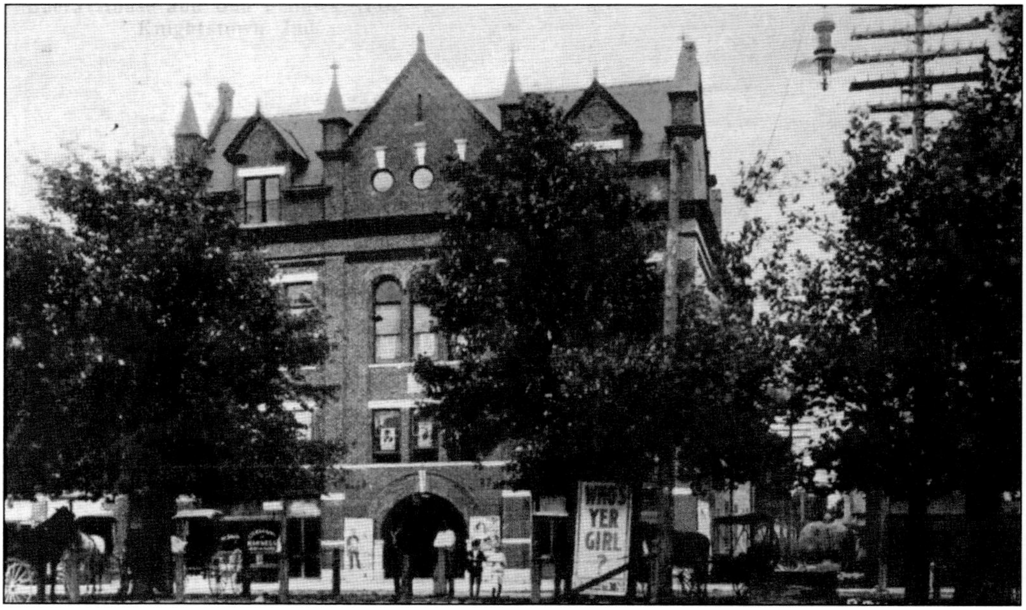

The Alhambra once dominated the east side of Knightstown's bustling Public Square. In its early days, the Public Square exhibited a farmers' market atmosphere and was the heart of town activity. Today only the two buildings to the north of the Alhambra remain on the Public Square's east side: a 1940 gas station and an 1890 commercial building.

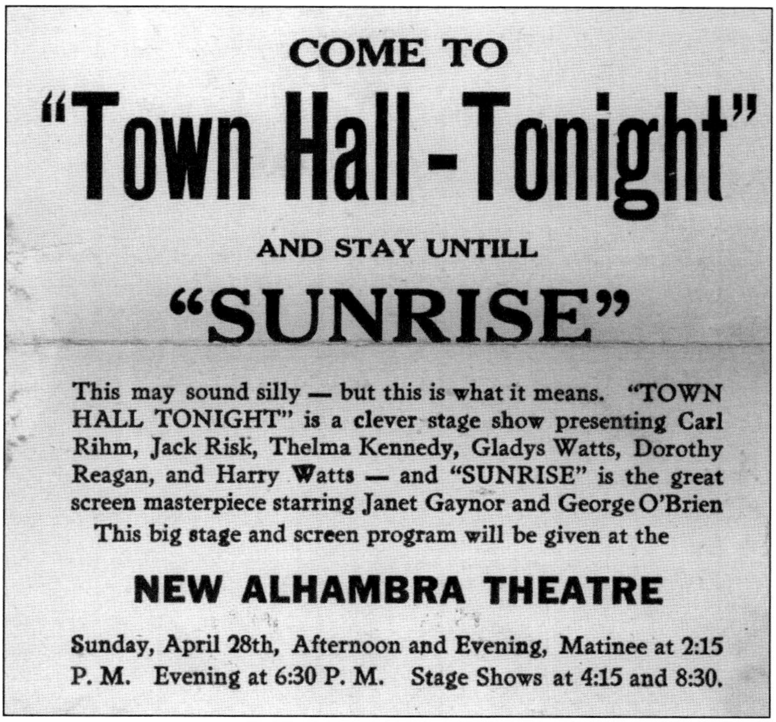

COME TO

"Town Hall-Tonight"

AND STAY UNTILL

"SUNRISE"

This may sound silly — but this is what it means. "TOWN HALL TONIGHT" is a clever stage show presenting Carl Rihm, Jack Risk, Thelma Kennedy, Gladys Watts, Dorothy Reagan, and Harry Watts — and "SUNRISE" is the great screen masterpiece starring Janet Gaynor and George O'Brien This big stage and screen program will be given at the

NEW ALHAMBRA THEATRE

Sunday, April 28th, Afternoon and Evening, Matinee at 2:15 P. M. Evening at 6:30 P. M. Stage Shows at 4:15 and 8:30.

Many Knightstown residents remember afternoons and evenings spent at the Alhambra. Plays were featured early on but were replaced by motion pictures as that industry grew. The production advertised in this notice combines both stage and screen: local talent in the play and Janet Gaynor and George O'Brien on the silver screen.

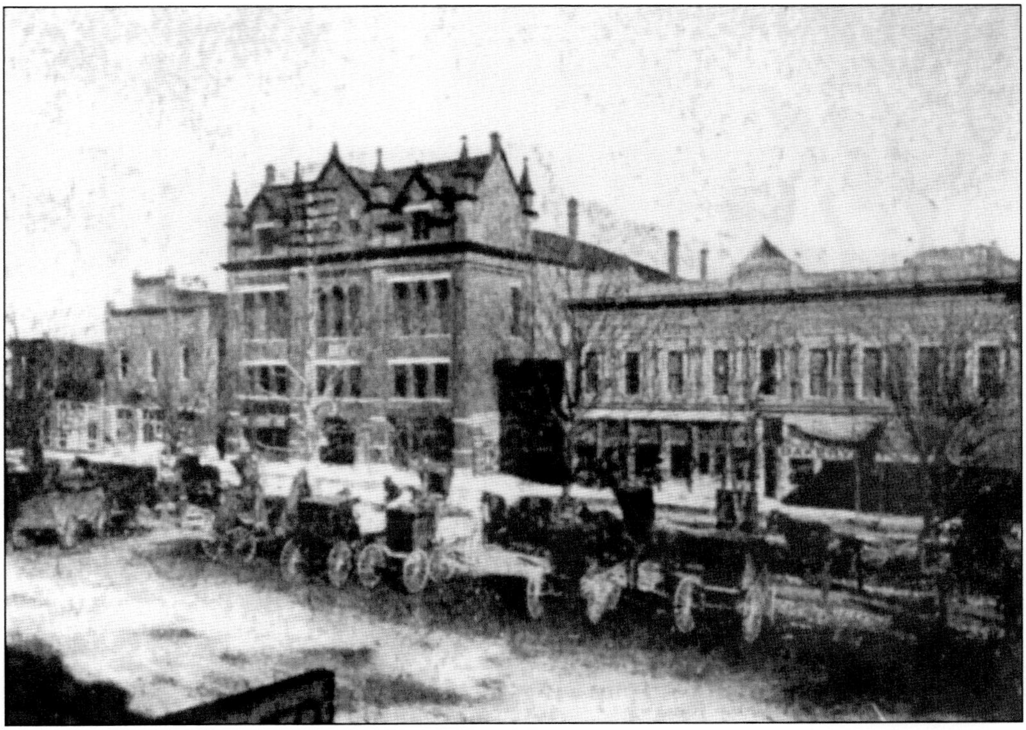

It wouldn't have been the Public Square without the Alhambra Theater and a group of horses and buggies tethered out front. The building to the left in this undated photograph is still around.

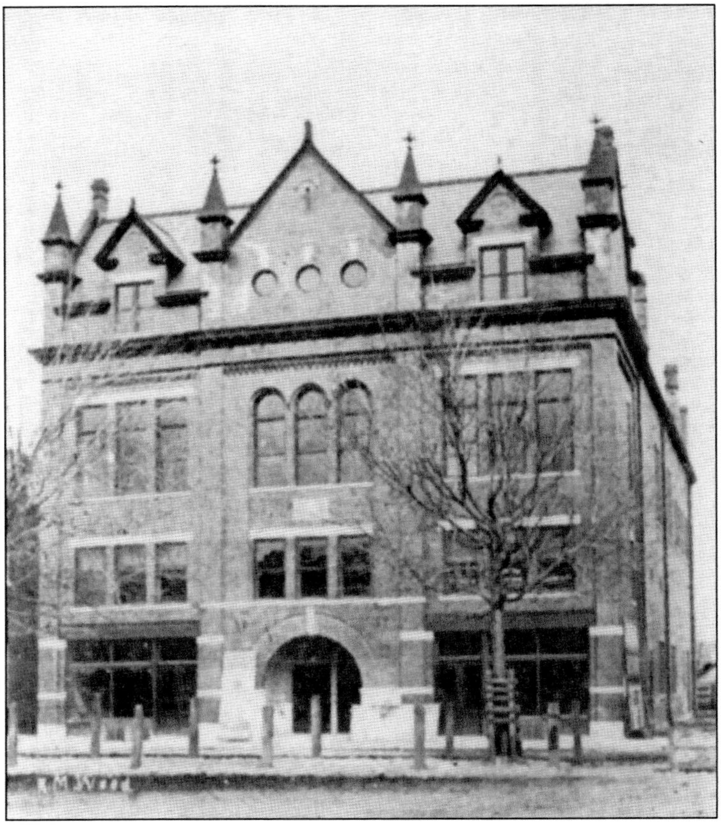

This old photograph was featured on a postcard that advertised the structure as the IOOF (Independent Order of Odd Fellows) Building instead of the Alhambra. But that was all right because the Odd Fellows lodge was located in the building as well.

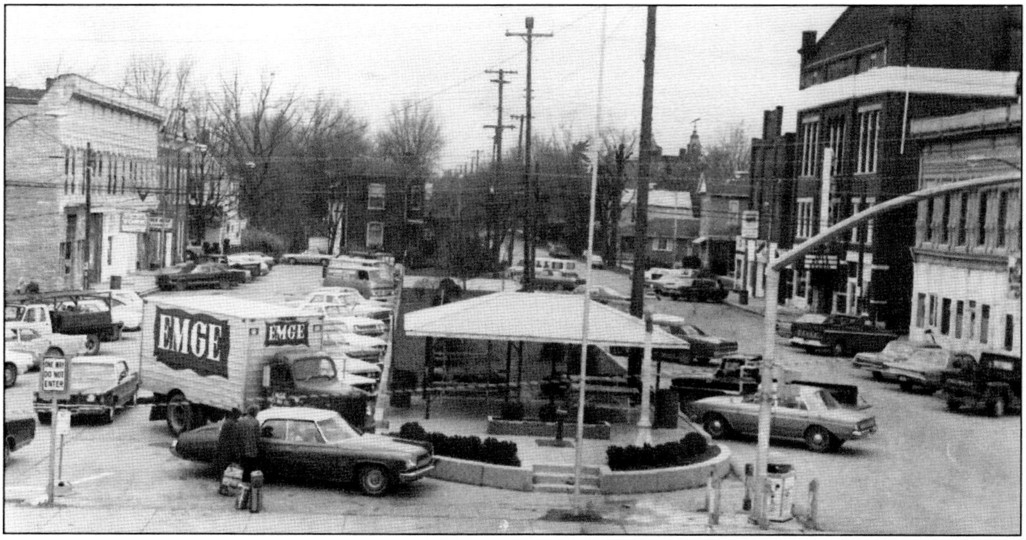

The 1950s saw the Public Square as busy as ever, with the Alhambra still an impressive part of the character of the neighborhood. Notice that the telescope tower from the 1876 Knightstown Academy several blocks north is visible in the background.

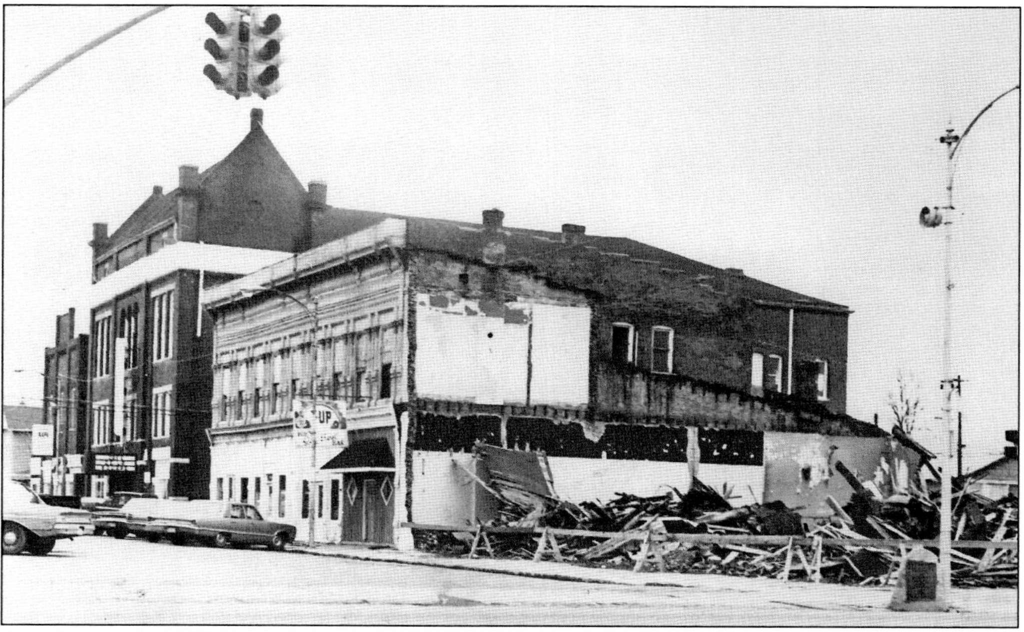

Big changes began to occur on the Public Square. In this photograph, the corner building has been demolished, but the lonely Alhambra still stands. It was the start of a period of fire and neglect that left the east side of the Public Square without several of its original buildings, including the Alhambra.

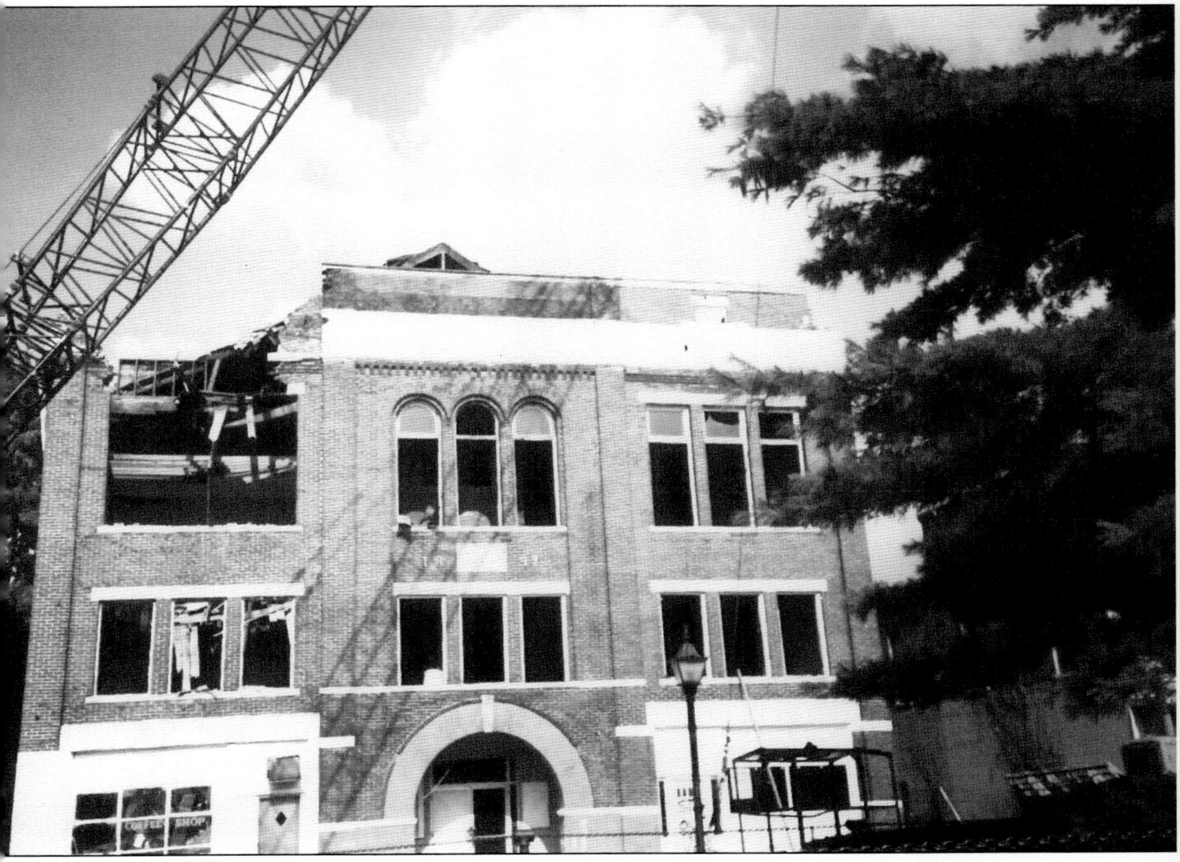

Sadly, Knightstown lost a significant piece of its history when the Alhambra building was demolished in July 1992. Efforts to save the popular structure were unsuccessful, as neglect had taken its toll, and it became a safety hazard to pedestrians walking nearby as well as to the surrounding buildings.

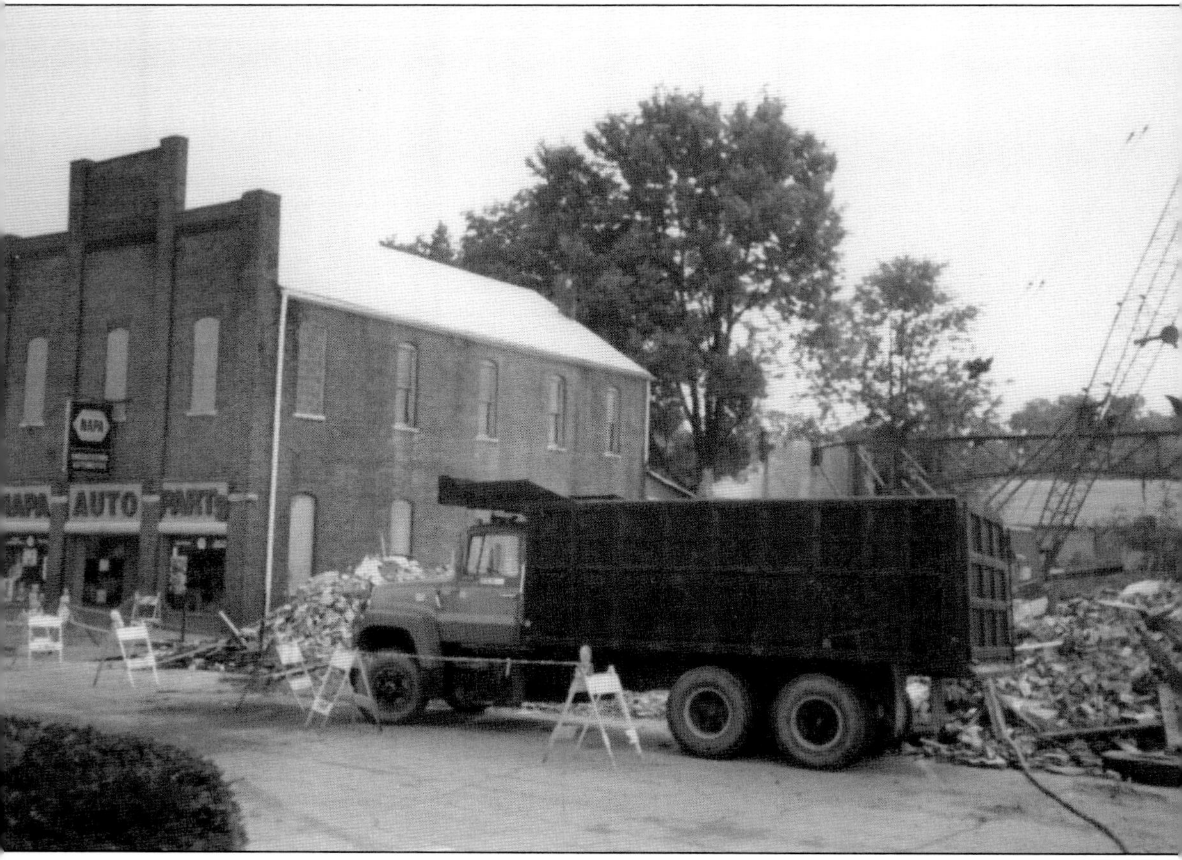

The Alhambra stood strong on the Public Square for more than 95 years. But it did not take long to reduce the three-story building to a pile of bricks. In this 1992 photograph, a truck sits in front of the gaping hole in the Public Square's landscape that was once the Alhambra.

Four

Taking Up Residence

Around 1830, founder Waitstill M. Cary and his family set up housekeeping in a small, wooden house on the southeast corner of Knightstown's Public Square. (The home no longer exists but is recognized by a commemorative marker.) Cary's daughter Mary offered this recollection of the family's first home in Knightstown, "October 1, 1827, we moved to the village of Knightstown. Father put up a frame building about whear [*sic*] Gid Bass Barber Shop was or afterward was or just west of the Shipman Hotel is now. After the roof and siding and flooring was down we moved in our new house and opened our hotel in 1836."

Other roughly built houses soon followed the Carys', as more and more travelers took to the National Road and chose to settle in the community on the west bank of the Big Blue River. But what Knightstown gained in numbers in its early days, it lacked in quality and style. In 1839, for example, an editorial in the *Indiana Sun* described Knightstown's houses as "unsightly, being low, ill-shaped, and some of them not painted at all."

As the little town of Knightstown progressed, so too did the design of its citizens' homes. Crude wooden dwellings slowly made way for more substantial buildings, such as larger houses constructed of stone or brick. Economic success and improvements to the town's streets and roadways, including the National Road, contributed to the community's ability to improve its business establishments as well as its family homes.

During the mid- to late 1800s, Knightstown's accomplishments were reflected in the fashionable houses that began to grace Knightstown's developing neighborhoods. Though the people that first lived and raised their families in the grand homes of Knightstown are gone, the tradition continues as modern families maintain and appreciate the fine old homes that remain.

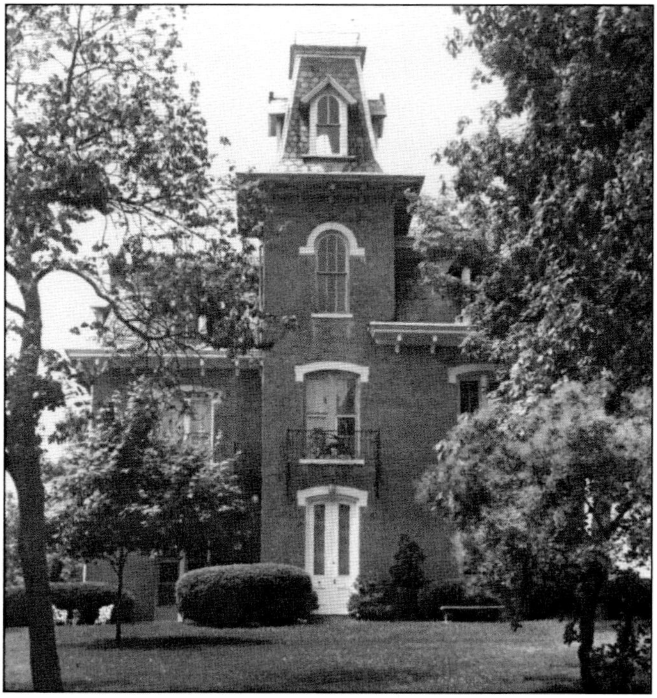

Richard Probasco, a local dry goods store owner, built the Probasco-Morrison house around 1870 (at left). In 1873, he sold it to John I. Morrison, an early leader in Indiana's educational system. Morrison is credited with creating Indiana's Office of State Superintendent of Public Instruction. He also was a school board member when the Knightstown Academy was constructed in 1876, and his daughter Sarah was the first woman to graduate from Indiana University. This elegant home is one of three Knightstown residences featured in Wilbur D. Peat's *Indiana Houses of the Nineteenth Century* and was captured in this early illustration (below).

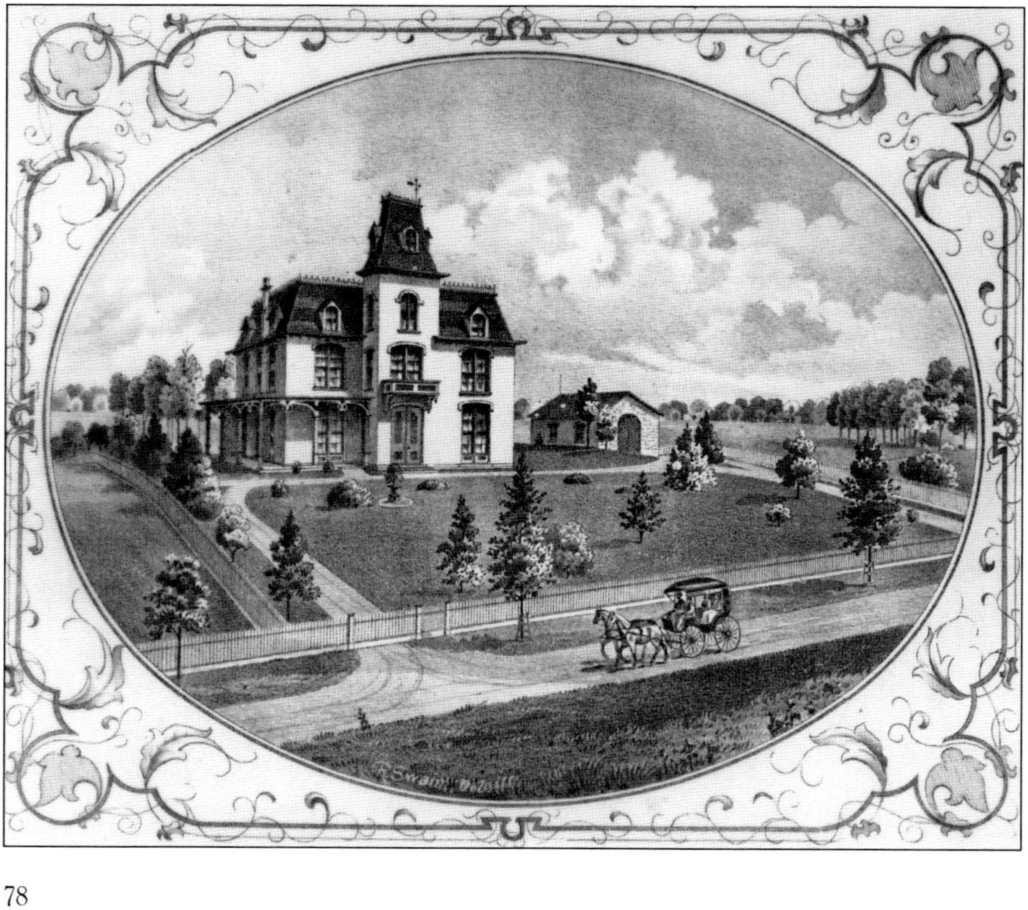

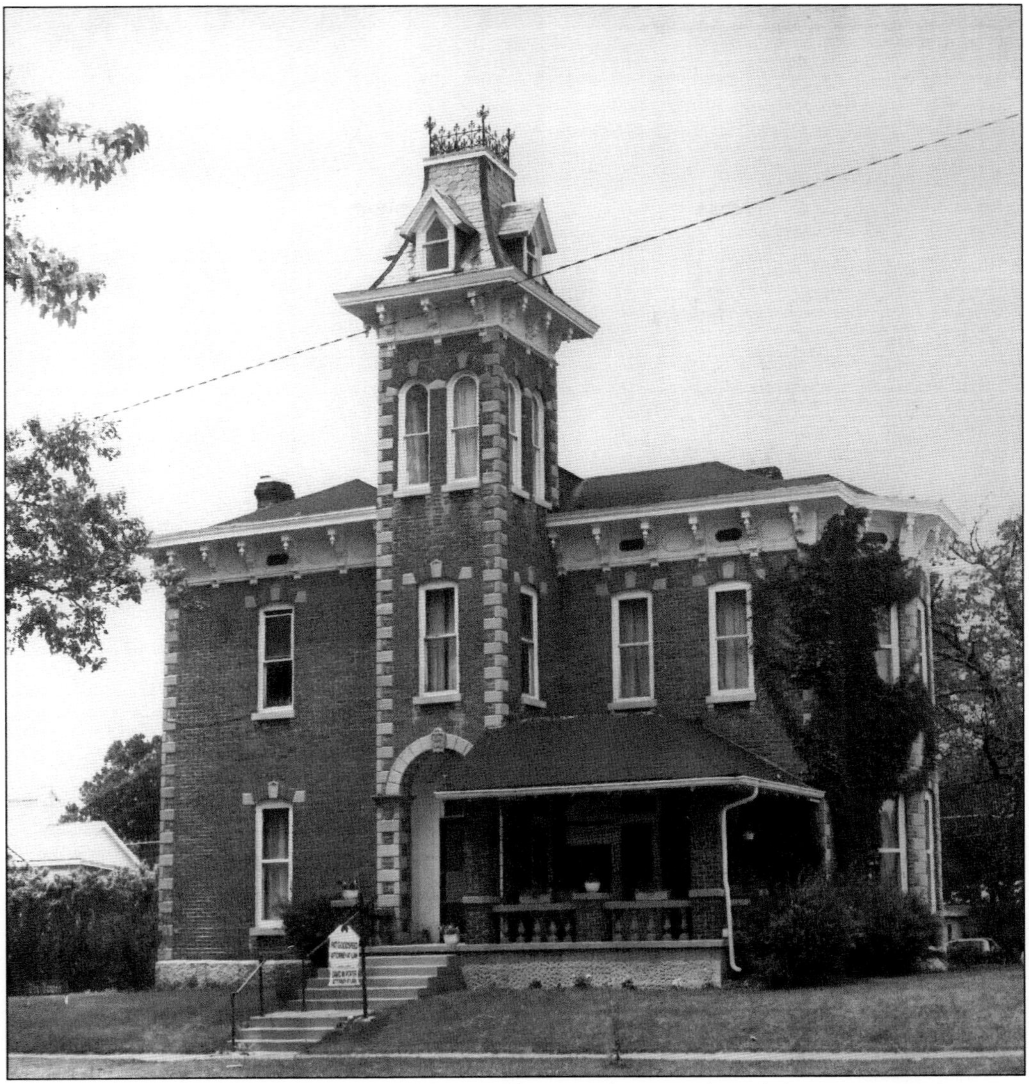

In 1863, businessman, blacksmith, and farmer Elias Hinshaw purchased this property at auction from the estate of Knightstown founder Waitstill M. Cary. Twenty years later, he constructed this Italian villa–style home, placing his initials on the keystone above the front door. Some wonder if Hinshaw added his house to an existing one- or two-room brick house in which Cary might have died. Listed on the National Register of Historic Places, Hinshaw's house has been a law office, funeral parlor, and antique shop. It is currently a private residence.

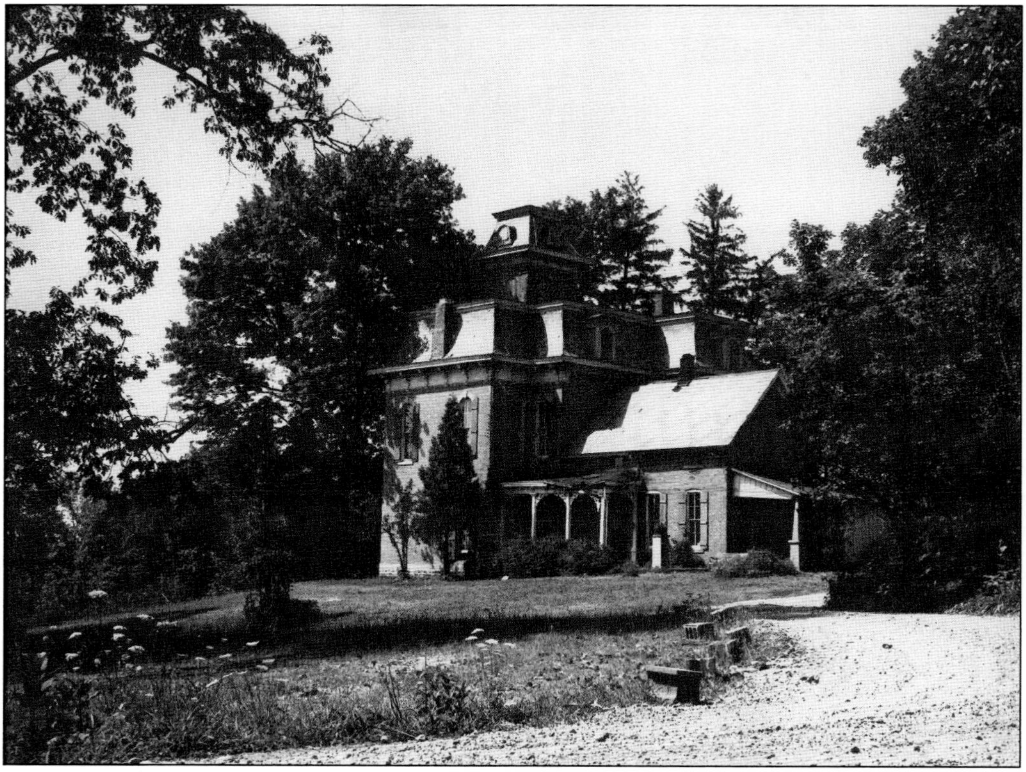

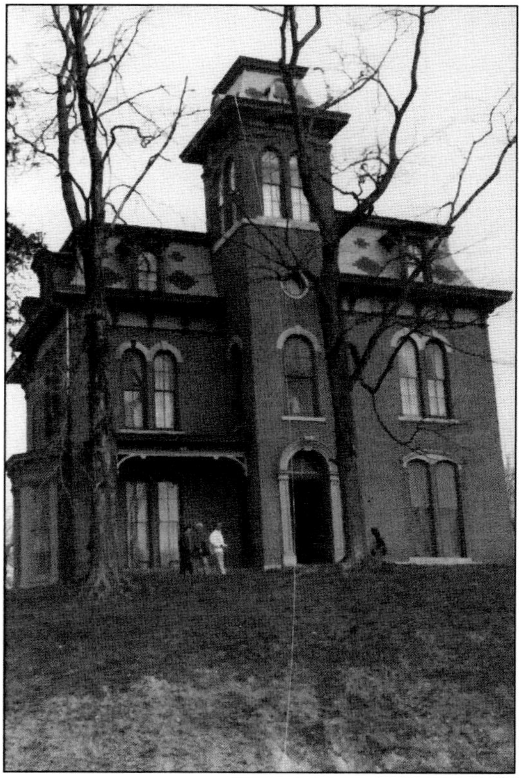

Built in 1867 for banker and attorney Charles Dayton Morgan and his family, this 17-room Second Empire home (above) is one of the best-known residences in Knightstown. The town purchased it for $2,900 in 1902 from then-owner Charles Owens to use as an isolation hospital during Knightstown's smallpox outbreak, which earned the home its nickname, the "Pest House." Also known as "Thornhill," its position atop a bluff just outside town (at left) made this redbrick house a logical location to treat smallpox patients and has added to the home's reputation as a haunted mansion. (Both courtesy of the Henry County Historical Society Museum.)

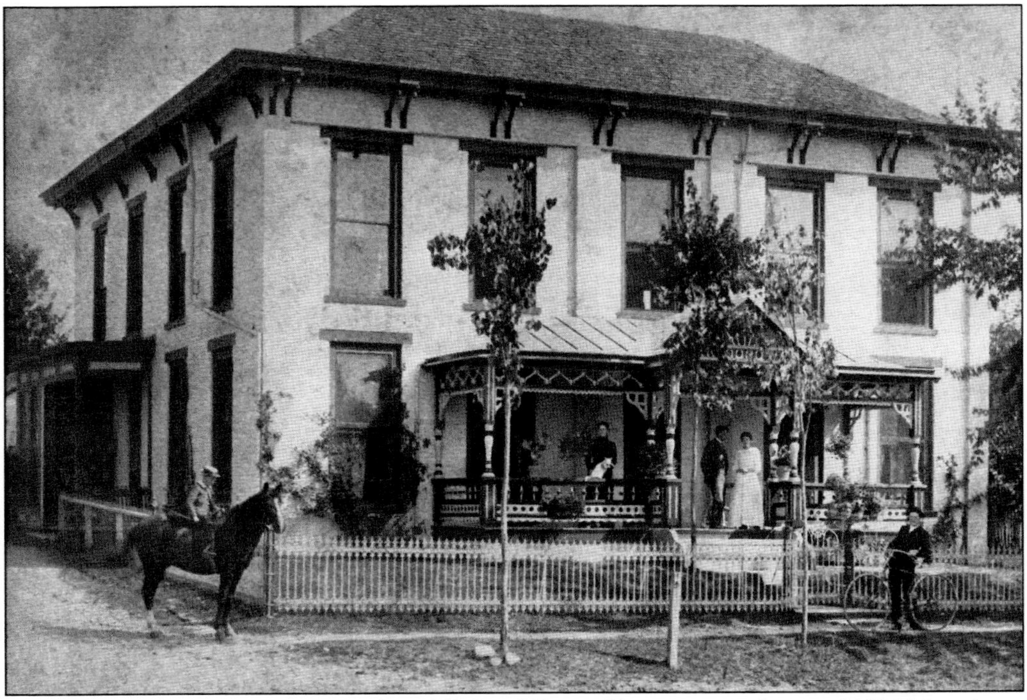

Nicknamed "The Mansion House," this 1852 Greek Revival home pictured around 1892 (above) was built by hardware merchant Harvey Bell. Bell, who also owned the entertainment establishment Bell's Hall on Knightstown's main street, often opened his home to boarders and entertainers, especially after the local hotel burned down. It is rumored that legendary P. T. Barnum circus performer General Tom Thumb was one of Bell's guests. The image shows Frank Edwards, great-grandson of Knightstown founder Waitstill Cary and grandson of Harvey Bell, with the bicycle. The house—minus the front porch—is now a private home (below).

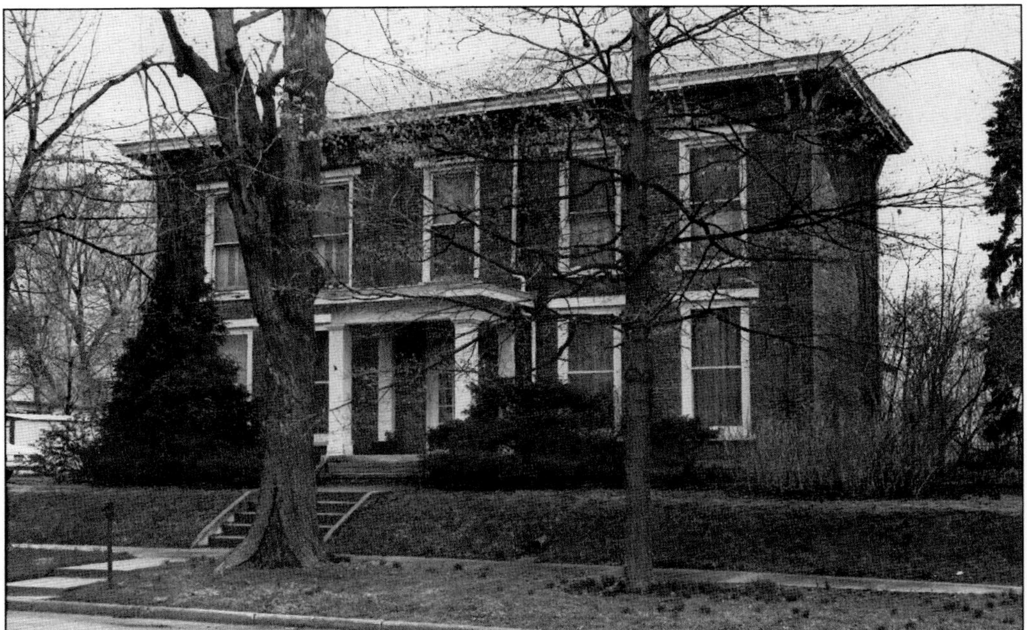

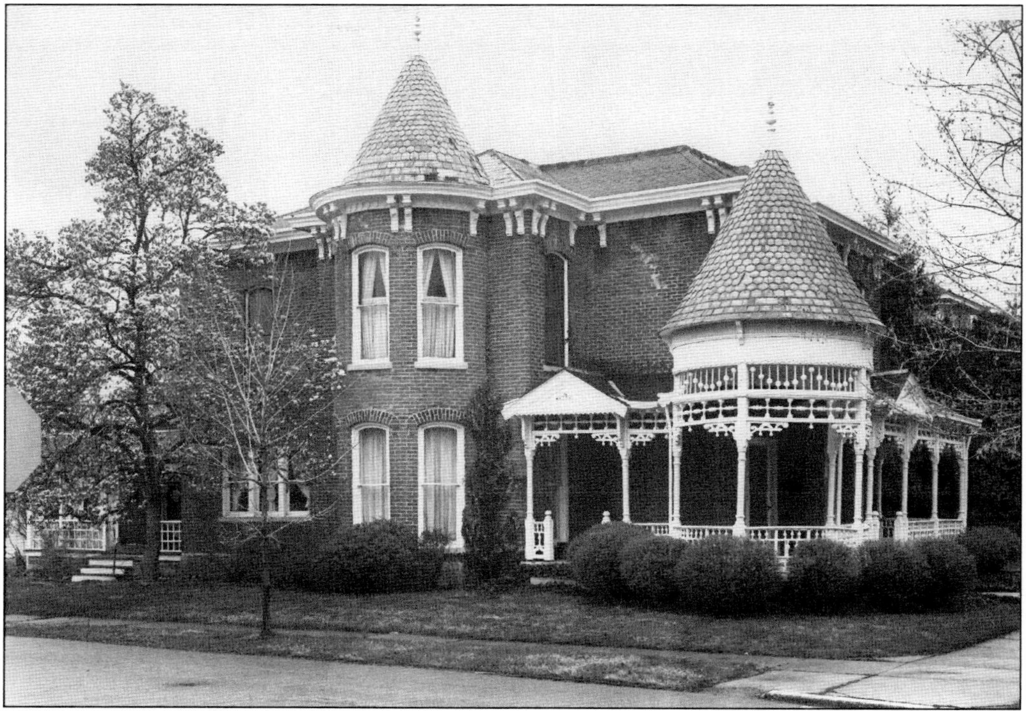

Successful attorney, state senator, and bank president Leonidas P. Newby shared his 1882 Italianate/Queen Anne home with his wife and two children. Newby was a Republican candidate for Indiana lieutenant governor in 1904, and his involvement with the Freemasons and Knights Templar earned him frequent mentions in the Indianapolis press. He was the first graduate of the Knightstown Academy in 1876.

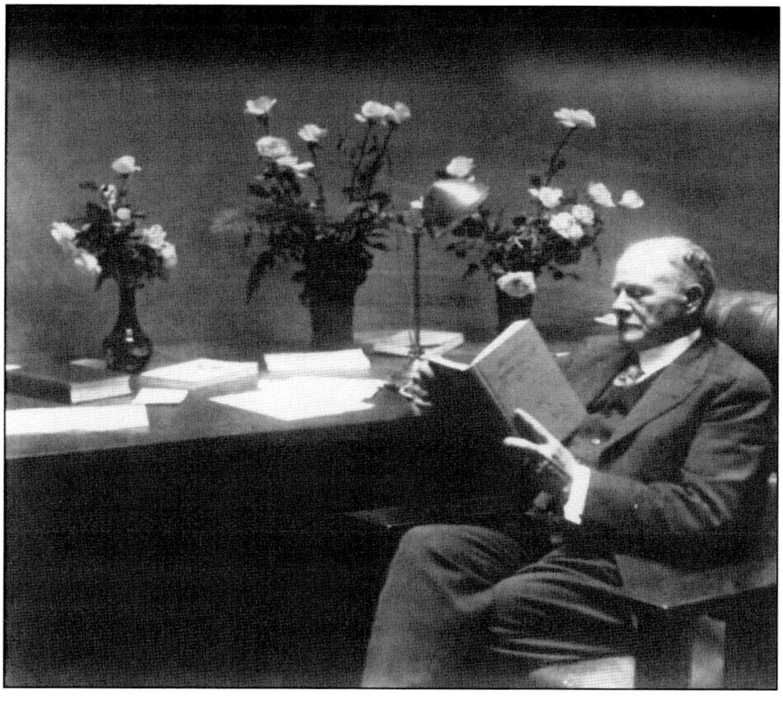

Leonidas Newby served as president of the Citizens National Bank from 1888 until 1925 and was a former attorney for the town he helped to prosperity. He also served as a state senator. Newby, or "Perry" as his friends knew him, is pictured here in his later years sitting at his desk in the bank.

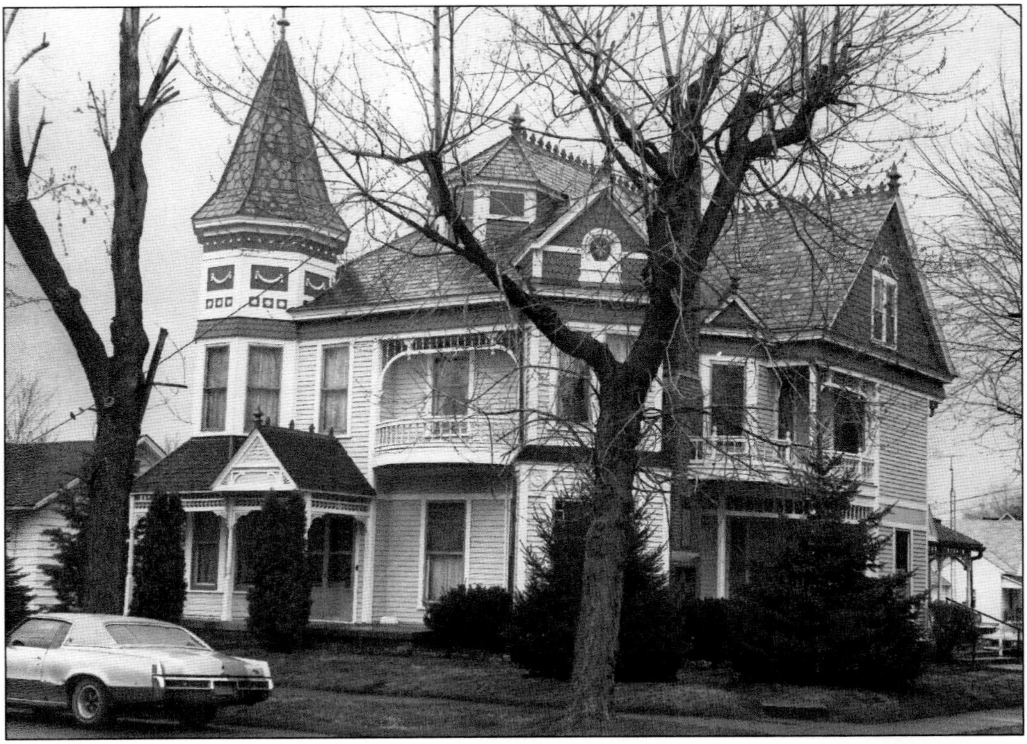

Simon Barrett built this Queen Anne home in 1890, and the exterior remains basically unaltered today. Inside the home features extensive fretwork, cherry and walnut woodwork, marble fireplaces, and a panoramic view of downtown Knightstown from the third-floor attic window. It is currently a private home and is undergoing extensive renovation.

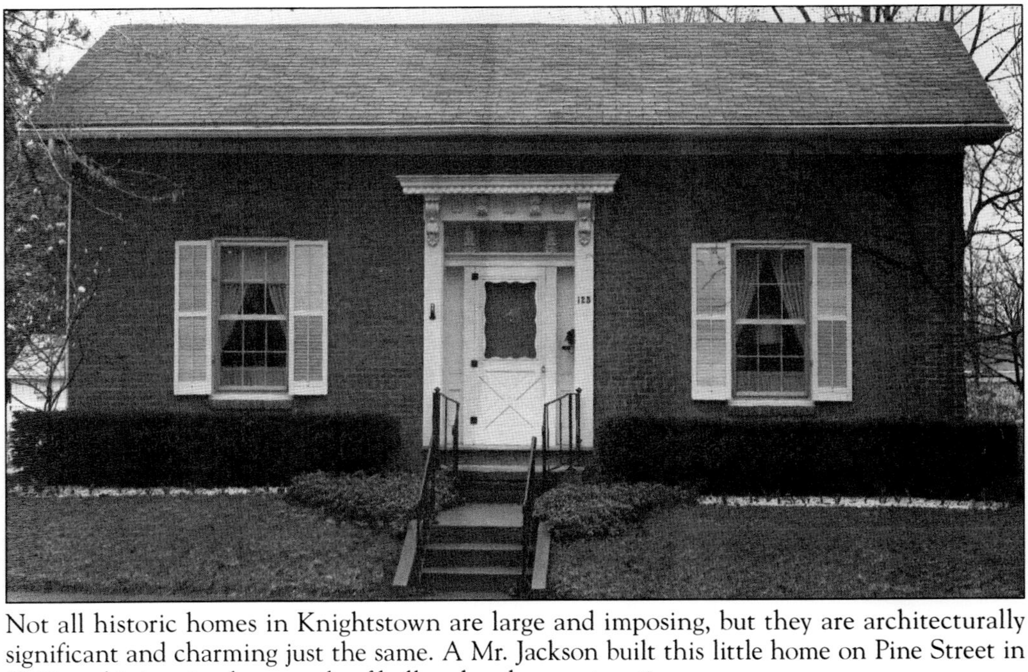

Not all historic homes in Knightstown are large and imposing, but they are architecturally significant and charming just the same. A Mr. Jackson built this little home on Pine Street in 1860, and it is a simple example of hall and parlor construction.

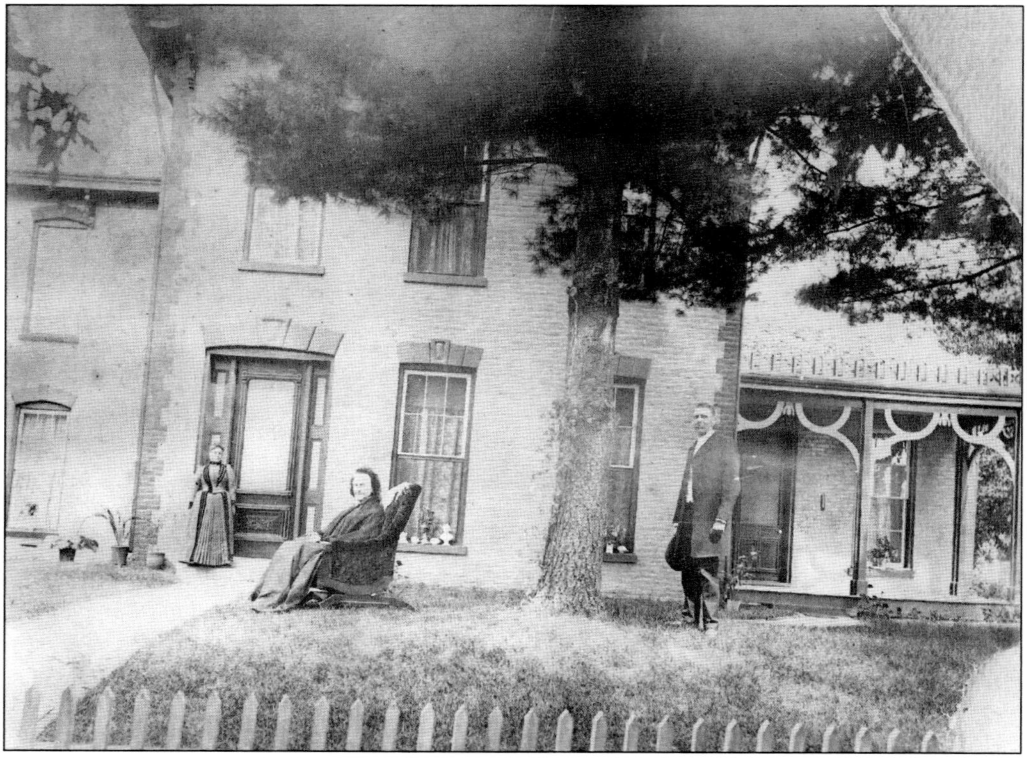

This elegant home was built in 1867 by James Mills, and early family members are pictured in the front yard (above). A north wing was added about 1890, giving the home the look that it has today (below). James Mills left a memento in the house for future owners, which the current owner was fortunate enough to find—a slip of paper with his name and the date 1867 in the newel post on the interior stairway banister.

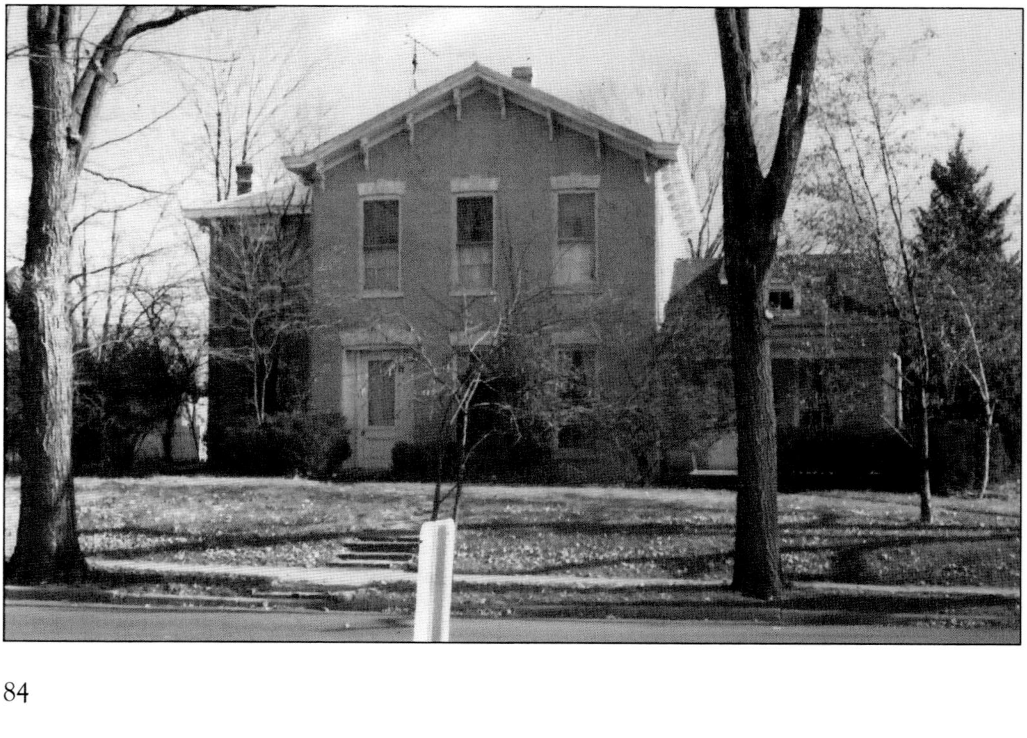

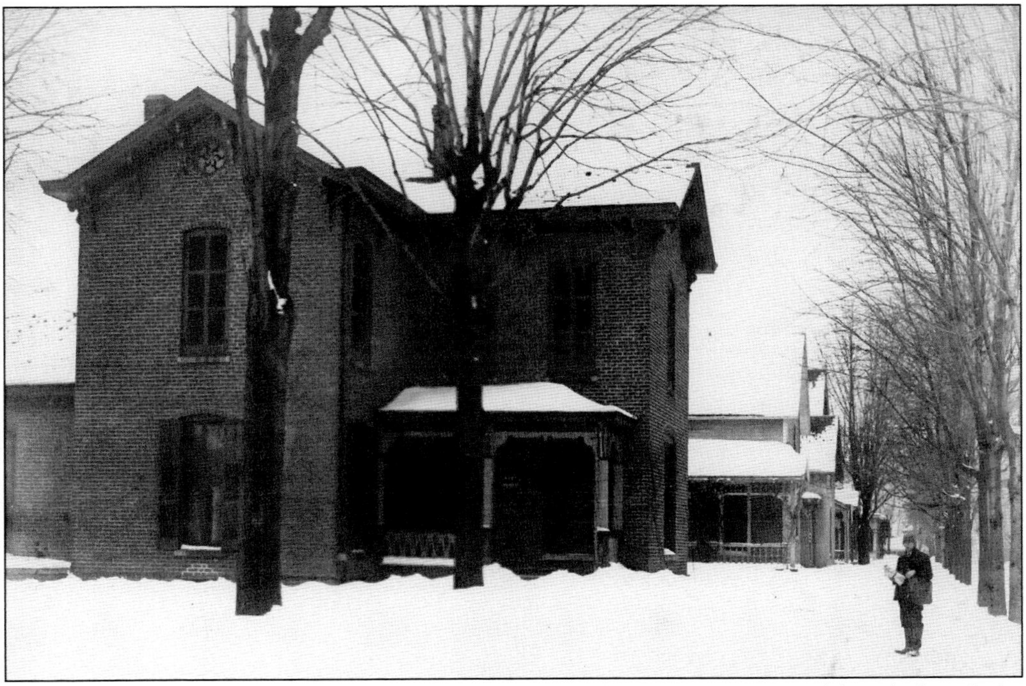

A mailman braves the snow in front of the Woods family home on Pine Street (above), thought by many to be one of the prettiest streets in town. Son Robert M. Woods was a prolific and talented photographer in his day, documenting life and architecture in Knightstown from the late 1800s until the 1940s. He photographed his sister in the backyard of the family home (below).

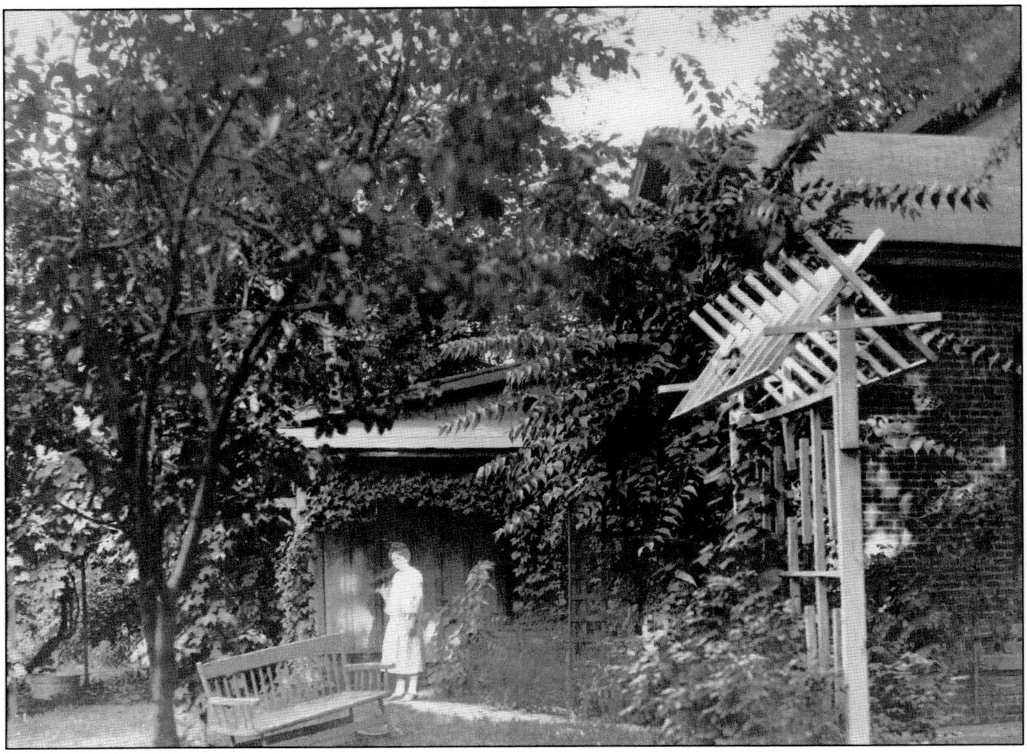

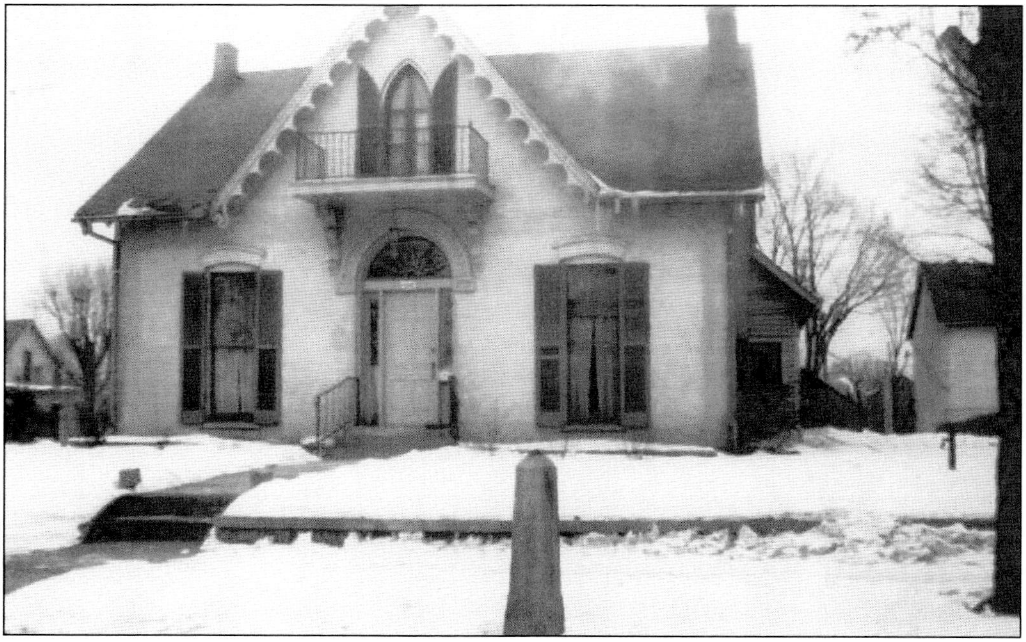

Local furniture retailer Dayton Heritage built this well-known house on Pine Street in 1866 for his bride, Susan. Heritage was known to enjoy a good game of poker, and legend states he once bragged that if there was a brick in the house that he had not paid for playing poker, he would like to see it. The home is a fine example of Gothic Revival architecture and is included in Wilbur D. Peat's book *Indiana Houses of the Nineteenth Century*. Its features and intricate details are more evident (below) in this illustration by Jack Phelps.

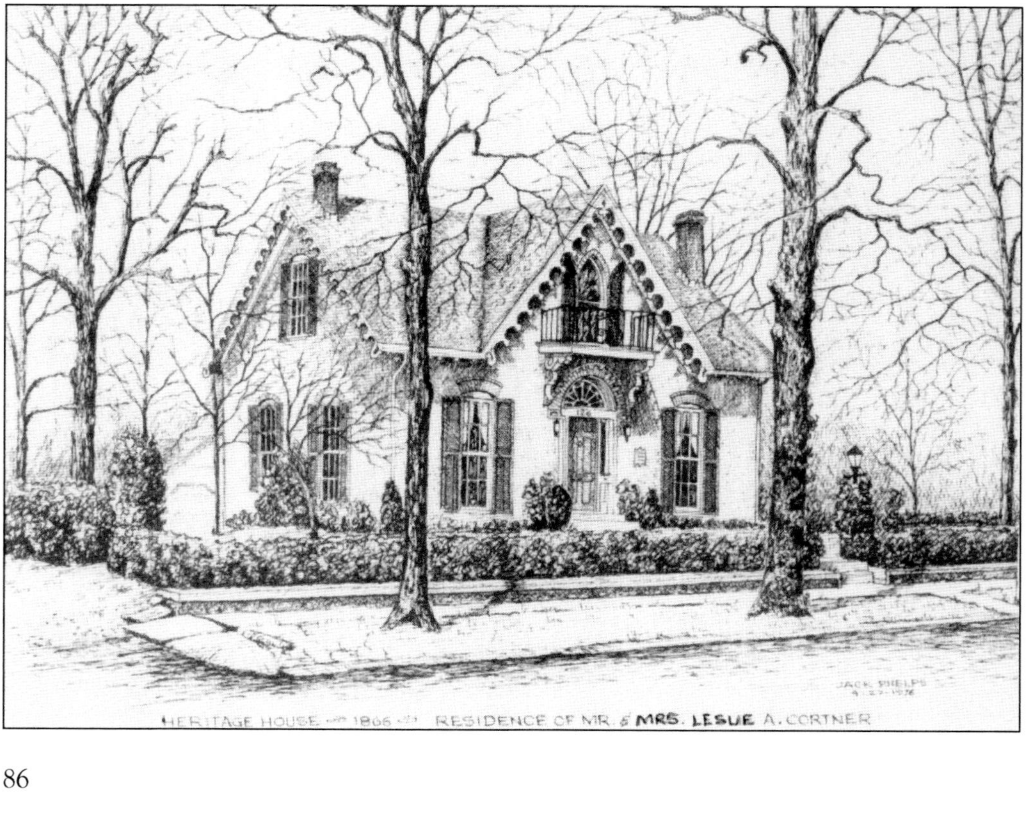

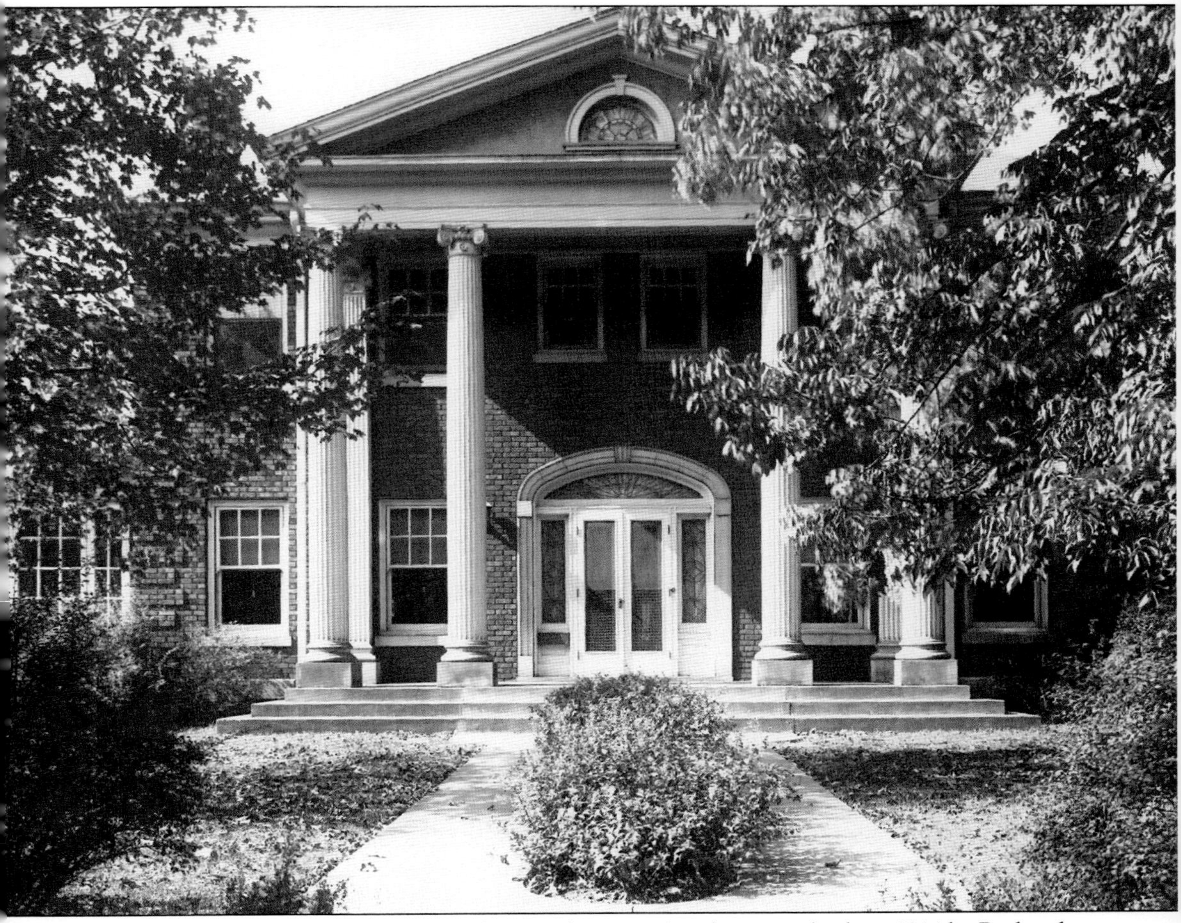

This stately home across the street from the Knightstown Academy was built in 1914 by Richard H. Schweitzer, proprietor of the Parish Alford Fence and Machine Company in Knightstown. The plant manufactured several grades of wire fencing, and it supplied much of the fencing sold and distributed by the Sears and Roebuck Company. At one time, Schweitzer's business employed nearly 100 people. Originally from Crawfordsville, Indiana, Schweitzer was involved in Knightstown banking, serving as a director of both Citizens National Bank and the First National Bank. He was a member of the Masonic Lodge and past master of Golden Rule Lodge No. 16 in Knightstown. Schweitzer and his wife, Effa, had two children.

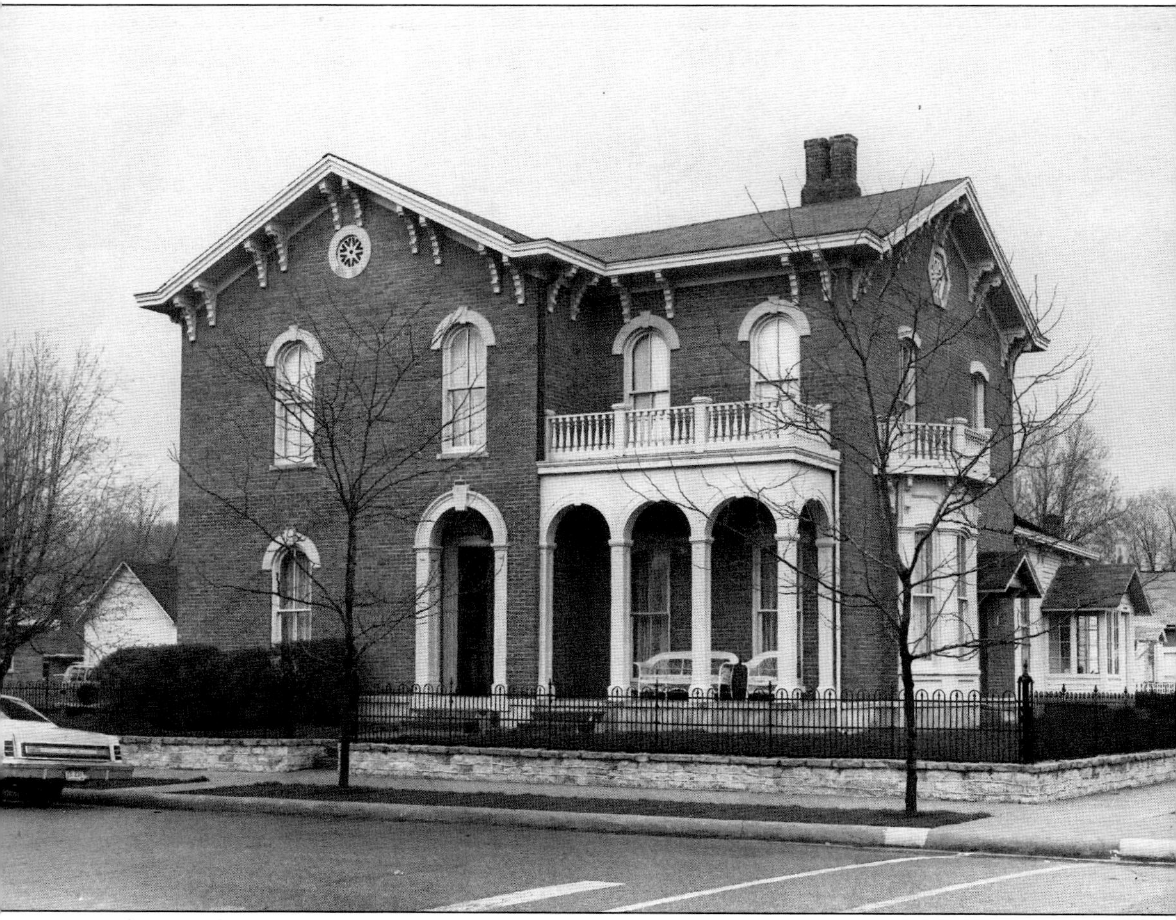

This 1874 house is known as the home of the Morgan family, but it was not built by the Morgans. Charles Dayton Morgan and his wife, Alvira Woods Morgan of "Pest House" fame, purchased this Italianate home when they moved into town after selling the house on the hill south of town.

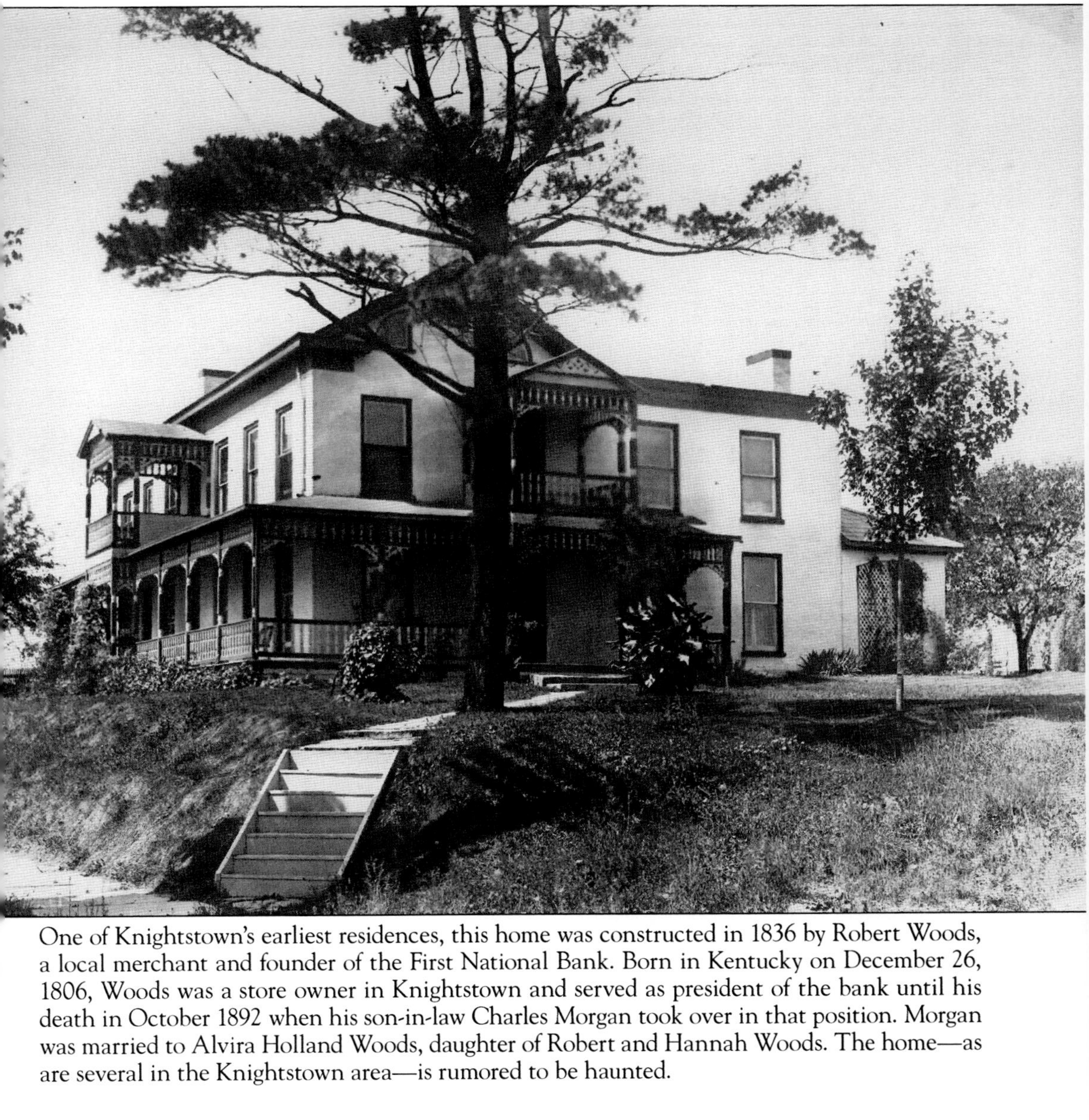

One of Knightstown's earliest residences, this home was constructed in 1836 by Robert Woods, a local merchant and founder of the First National Bank. Born in Kentucky on December 26, 1806, Woods was a store owner in Knightstown and served as president of the bank until his death in October 1892 when his son-in-law Charles Morgan took over in that position. Morgan was married to Alvira Holland Woods, daughter of Robert and Hannah Woods. The home—as are several in the Knightstown area—is rumored to be haunted.

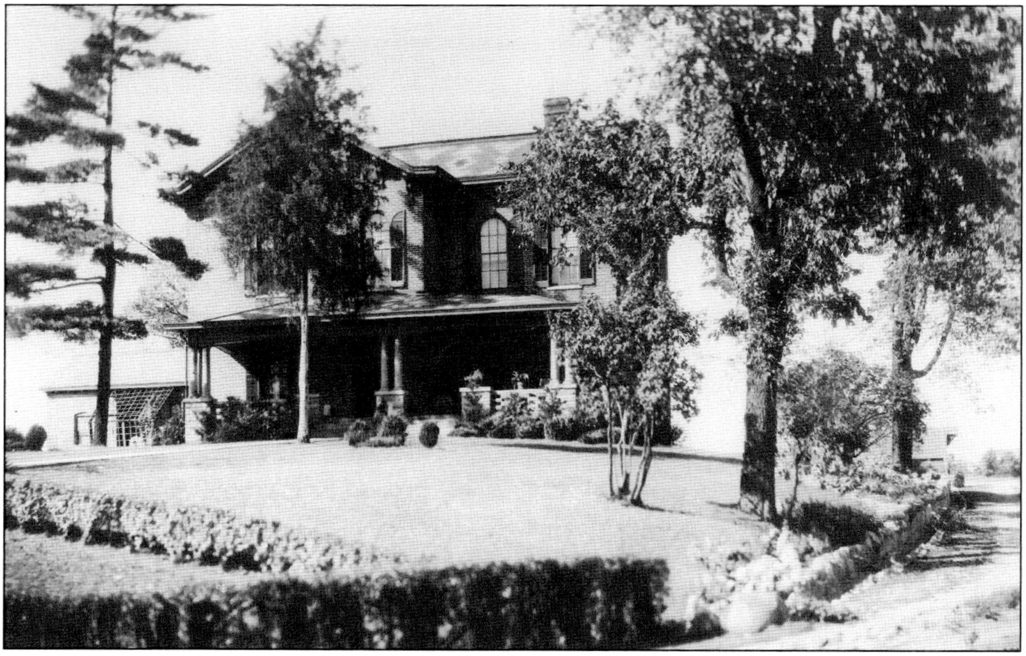

Known as "Pleasant Hill Farm," this redbrick Italianate farmhouse (above and below) was built by Ithamer W. Stuart in 1870. Remodeled in 1875 and 1910, the farm still maintains several of its original outbuildings. Stuart was a farmer and stock raiser with a limited early education. (He attended school only three months out of the year.) In 1884, Stuart owned 215 acres on the northwest edge of Knightstown. Born in 1820, Stuart married Margaret Holloway, and they were the parents of six children.

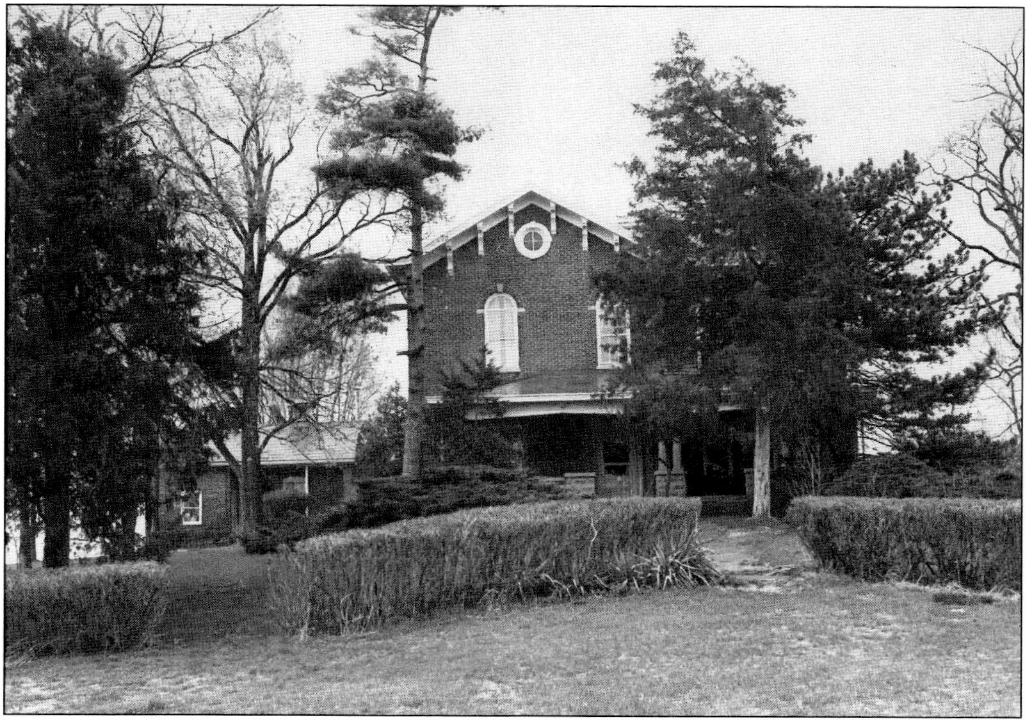

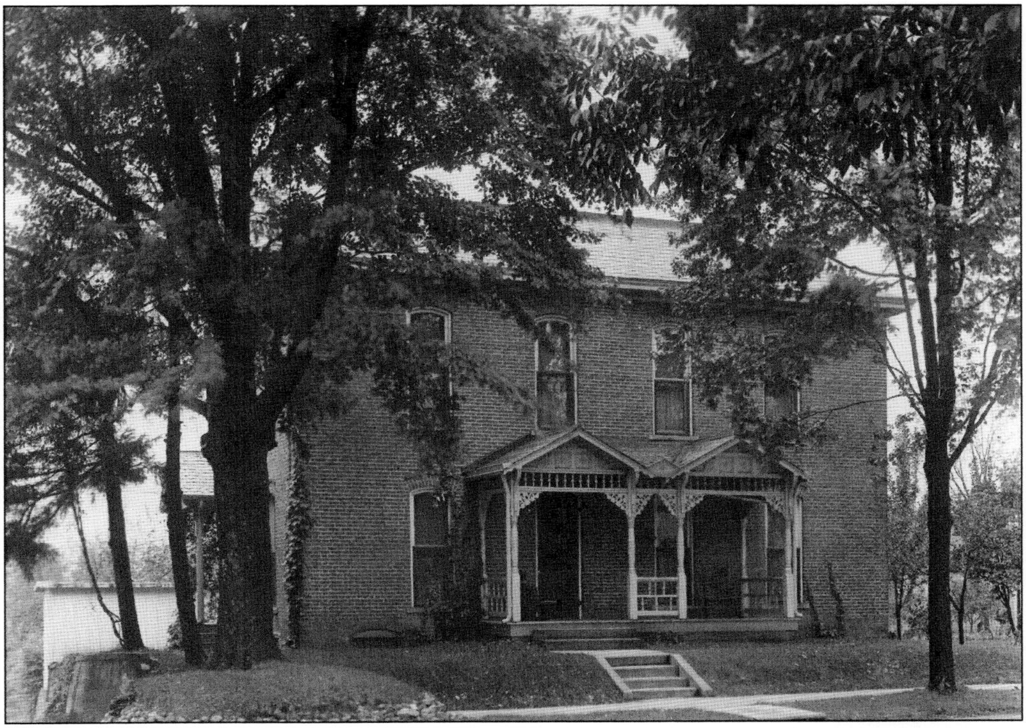

Built around 1900, this was the home (above) of Lloyd Mettel and his wife, Lucile Beeson Mettel, a teacher at Central School. A group (below) gathers on the front porch of the Mettel home for a portrait.

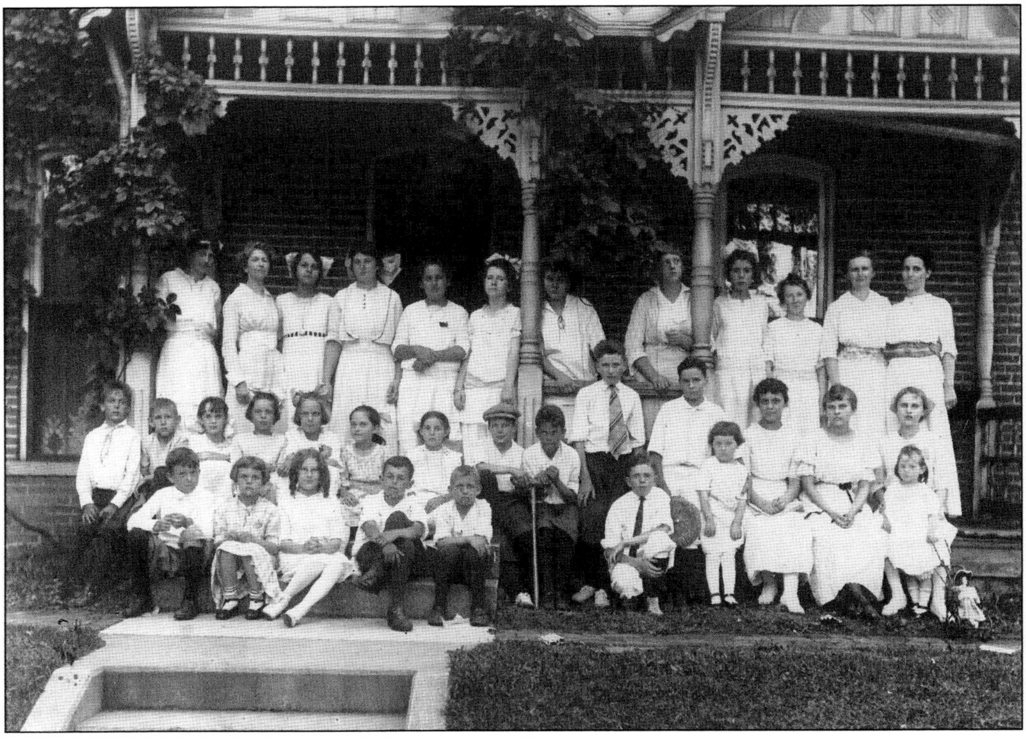

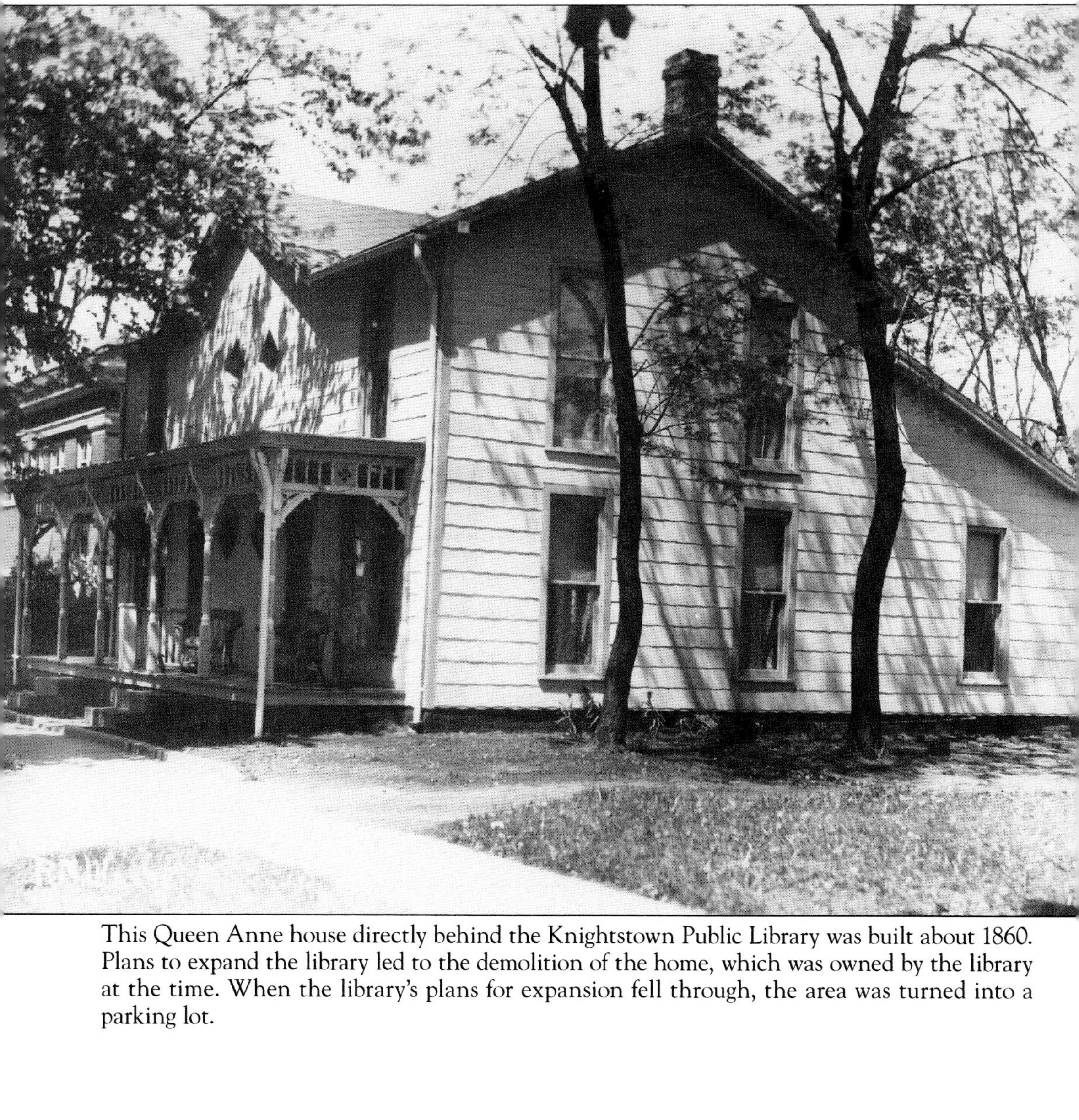

This Queen Anne house directly behind the Knightstown Public Library was built about 1860. Plans to expand the library led to the demolition of the home, which was owned by the library at the time. When the library's plans for expansion fell through, the area was turned into a parking lot.

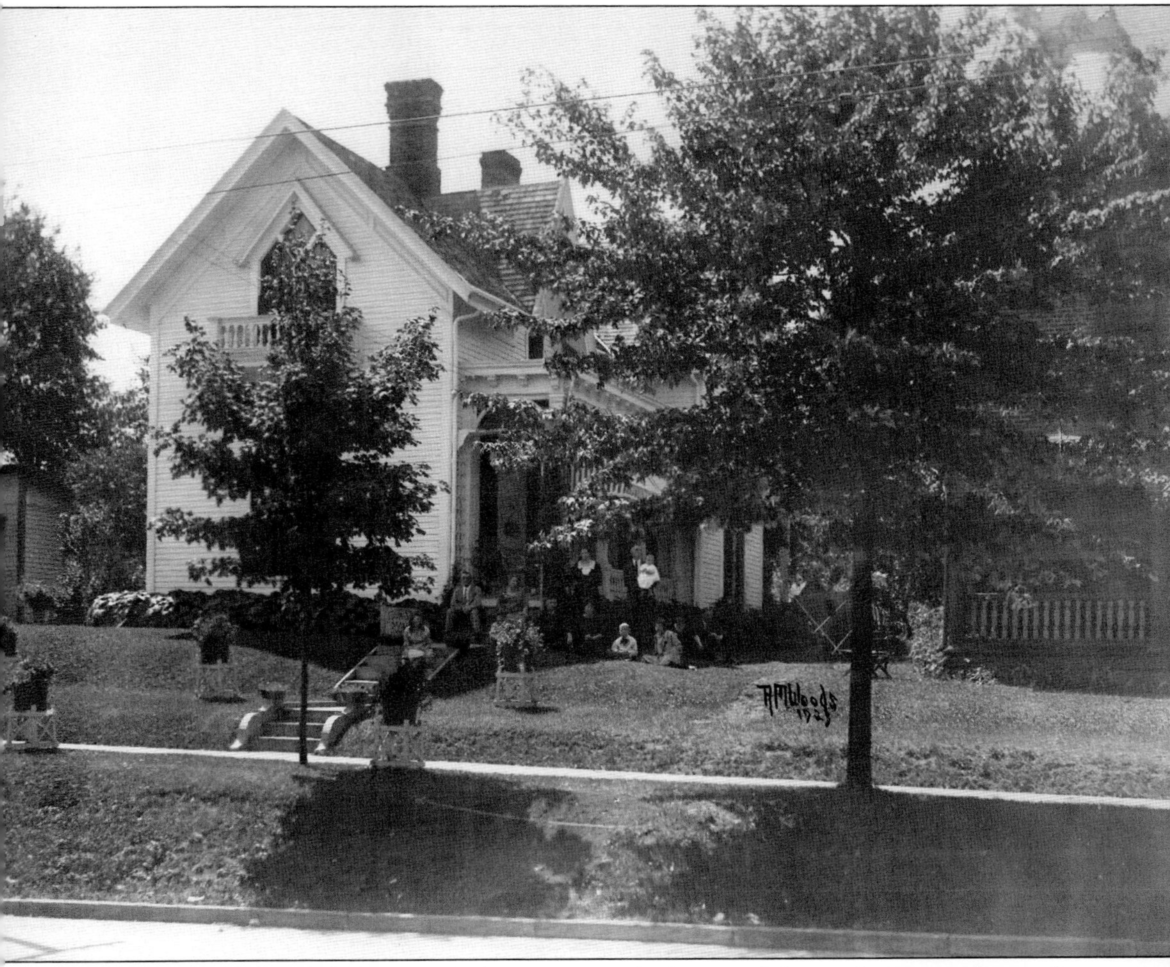

Close inspection of this 1923 photograph shows a sign in the front yard that reads, "Tourist Rooms." The house, built about 1870, is located on U.S. 40 on the east edge of downtown Knightstown. It would have been a convenient spot for tourists to stay. Work on the roadway over the years has resulted in changes to the home's front yard. Today the house appears to sit much higher, and the yard is shorter and steeper.

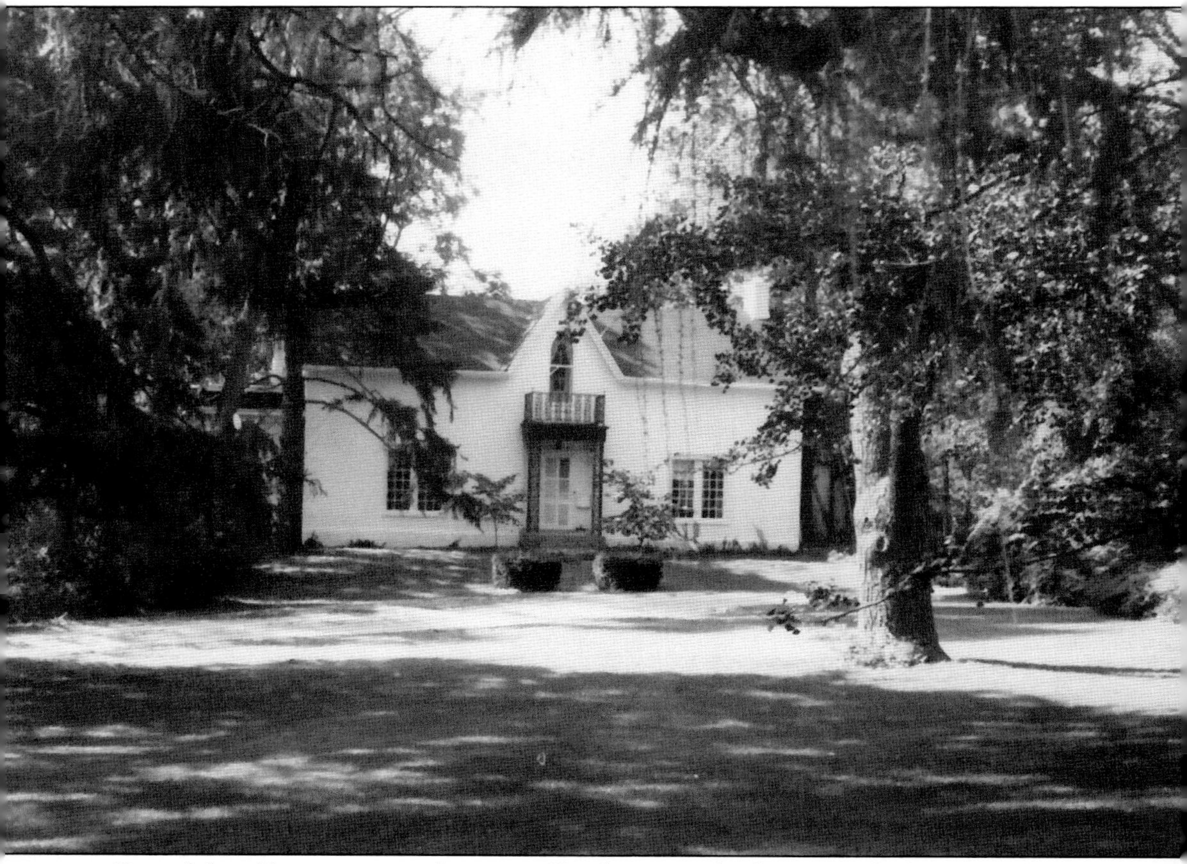

One of the oldest remaining houses in Knightstown, this home was built in 1844 by John J. Lehmanowsky, son of a Polish father and French mother. A guardsman for Napoleon Bonaparte, Lehmanowsky was condemned to death after Waterloo. He escaped and eventually settled in Knightstown. Rumor has it that Marshal Ney, a French general under Napoleon, visited Lehmanowsky at this very house. His daughter remembers a mysterious visitor speaking French one summer evening. In Knightstown, Lehmanowsky was a doctor and Lutheran minister. The original Knightstown bandstand was moved from the town square and is now in the property's backyard.

Five

School Days

Knightstown residents long have recognized the value of a good education. Early on, many Knightstown youngsters learned their lessons at local churches and in private homes. Eventually a more formal educational structure developed. Though the town was not officially incorporated until 1837, the first school building was constructed in 1832 on the corner of Jefferson and Jackson Streets. Contractor Asa Heaton built the 25-foot-by-30-foot frame building on land donated by Abraham Cary. Just a few years later, a new school building was raised on the corner of Brown and Front Streets.

It was only the beginning of what would become a long tradition of educational excellence in Knightstown. In 1850, the latest building was replaced, only to be replaced again in 1858. The final Knightstown Academy building was constructed in 1876, and it was a splendid redbrick example of Second Empire architecture that demonstrated the community's appreciation of just how much a well-rounded education is worth. The Knightstown Academy was dedicated on September 28, 1877, with more than 1,000 people in attendance.

Knightstown schools have always played a central role in neighborhood life. In many families, several generations of students have attended school in one Knightstown school building or another. It is a community where students often attend classes led by the very same teachers who also taught their parents.

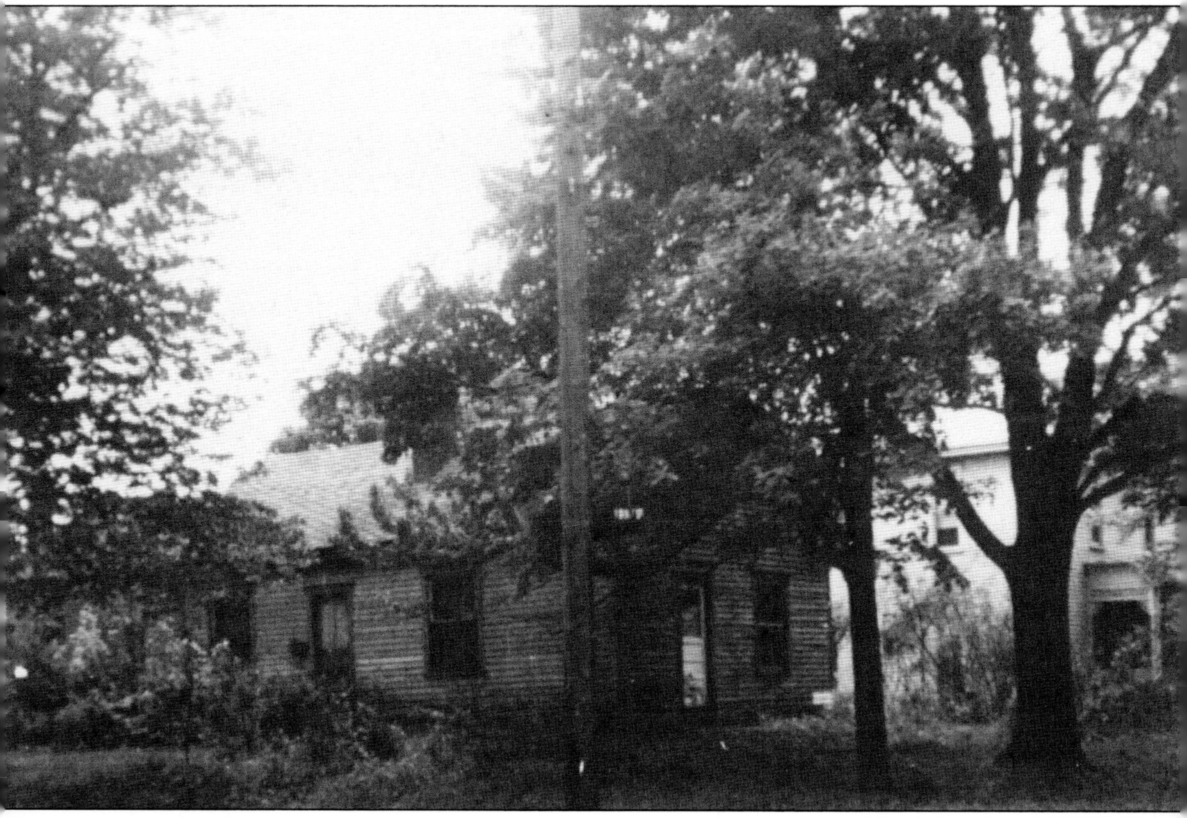

As confirmation of their belief in education, early Knightstown residents saw to it that local children had a facility in which to learn. This schoolhouse was used from 1835 until 1853. Known as "The Old Female Seminary," it was located on the southeast corner of Front and Brown Streets, not far from the Public Square. As Knightstown's population increased, the town quickly outgrew this small school building.

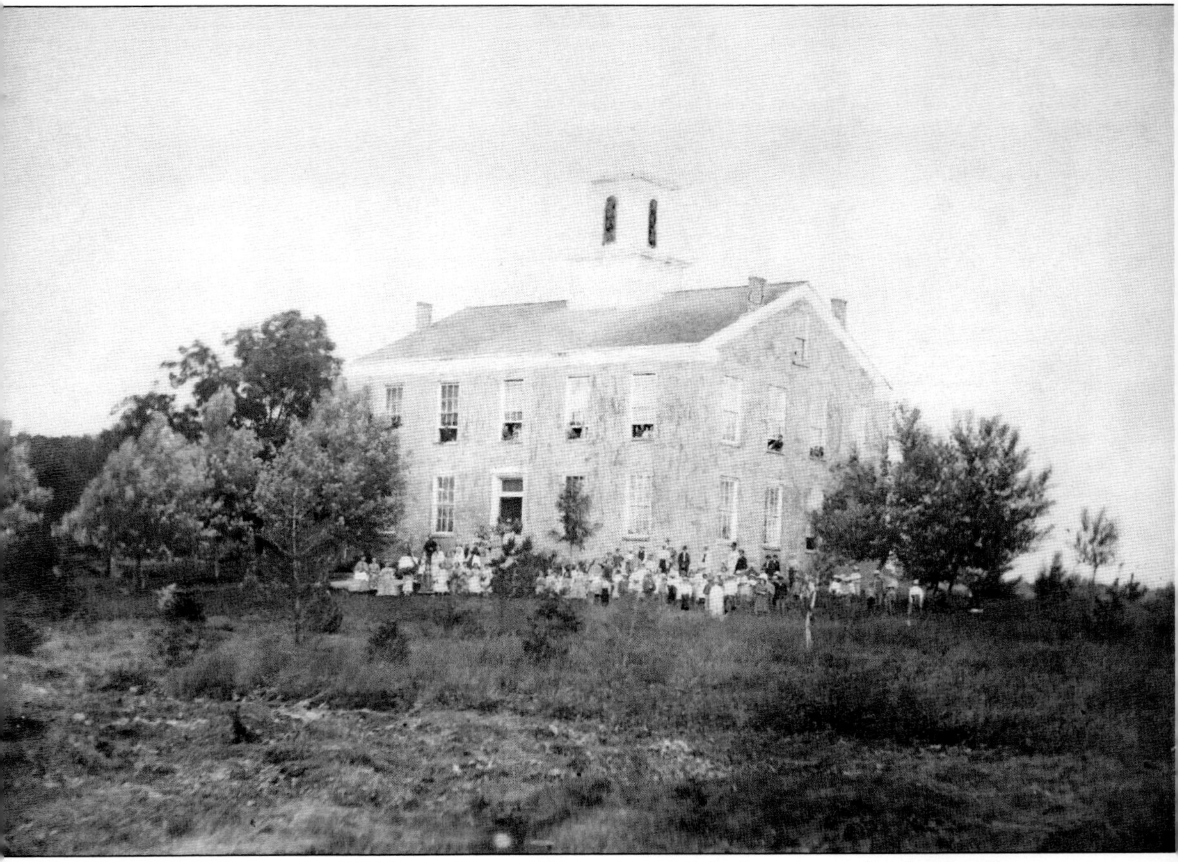

Knightstown students take time from their studies to show off their two-story brick schoolhouse; note the children in the second-floor windows. Built on or near the location of the present Knightstown Academy just north of the Public Square, the first version of the academy was finished in 1858 at a cost of $8,500.

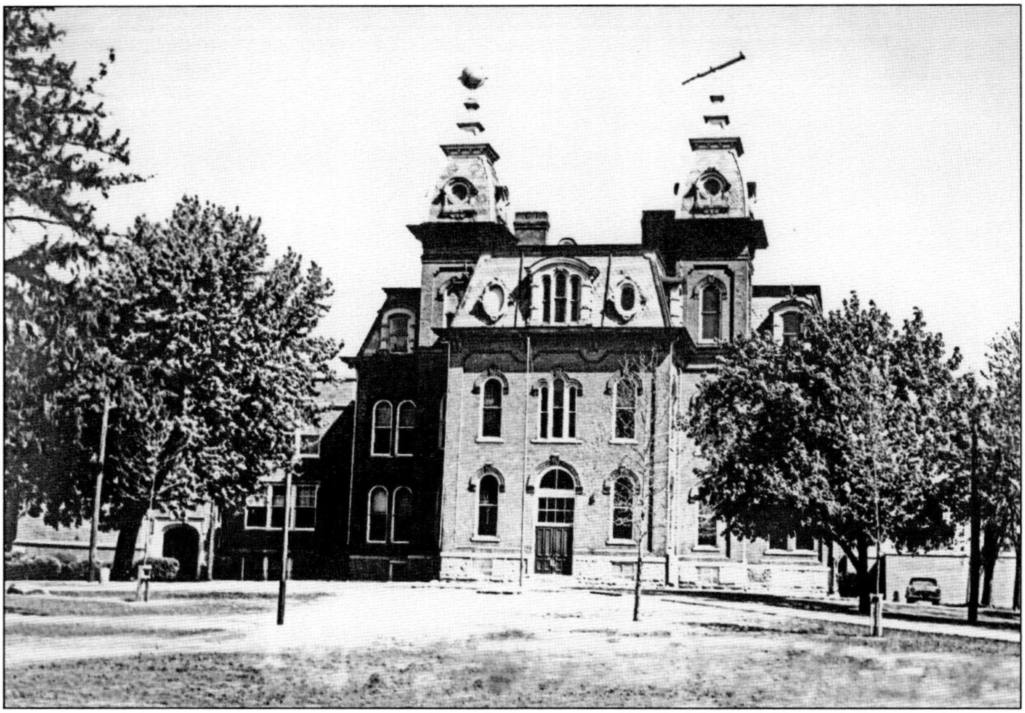

Easily recognizable by its Second Empire style and globe and telescope towers, the Knightstown Academy (above) was designed by architect John Hasecoster and constructed in 1876 at a cost of $21,501.96. Indiana education leader and Knightstown resident John I. Morrison was instrumental in the building of the academy, and he also was responsible for the inclusion of the globe and telescope atop the school's twin turrets (below).

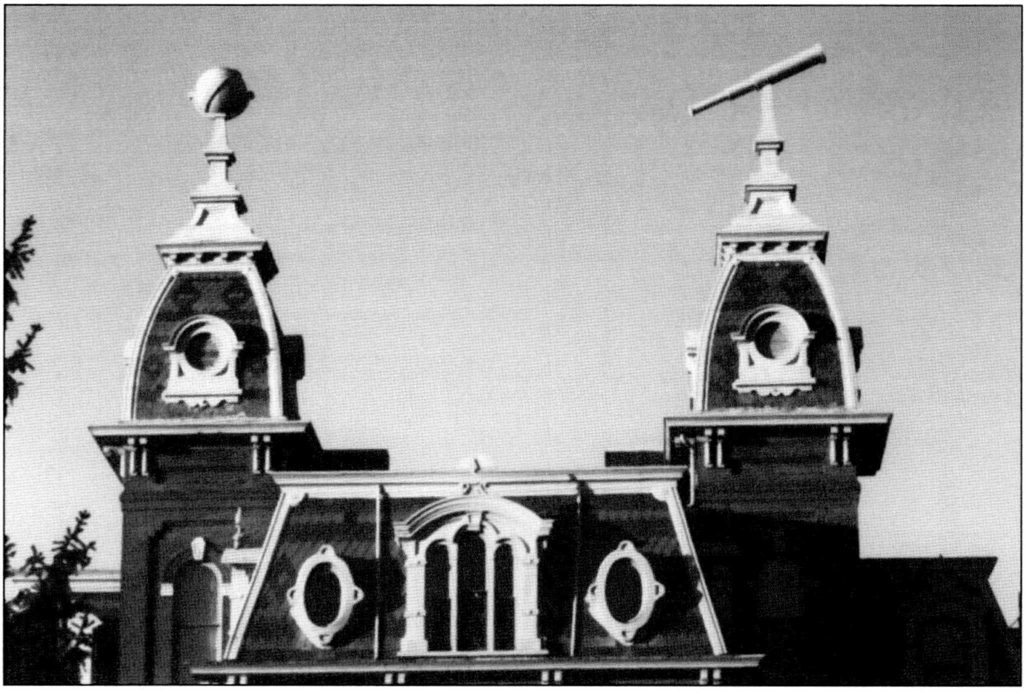

Historic Knightstown, Inc. was established by concerned citizens in the early 1980s in an effort to save the Knightstown Academy building. Partnering with the Historic Landmarks Foundation of Indiana, the organizations were able to find a new use for the structure as senior citizens' housing. Here work is done on one of the towers.

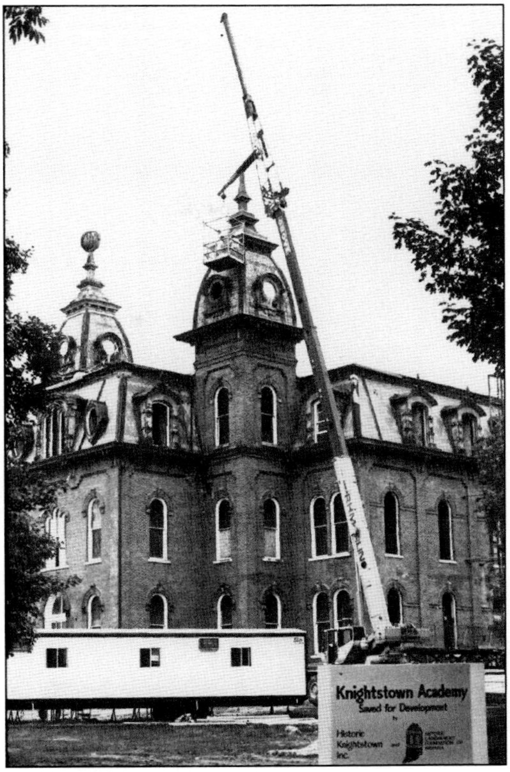

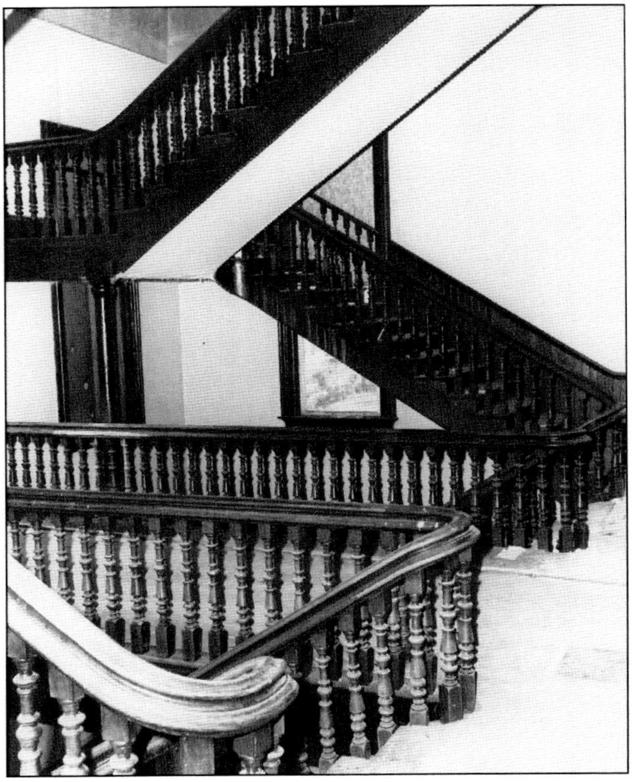

This interior staircase at the Knightstown Academy is one of many notable features in the former school building. The feet of thousands of students hit the stairs here over the course of the building's history as a place for Knightstown children to receive their education.

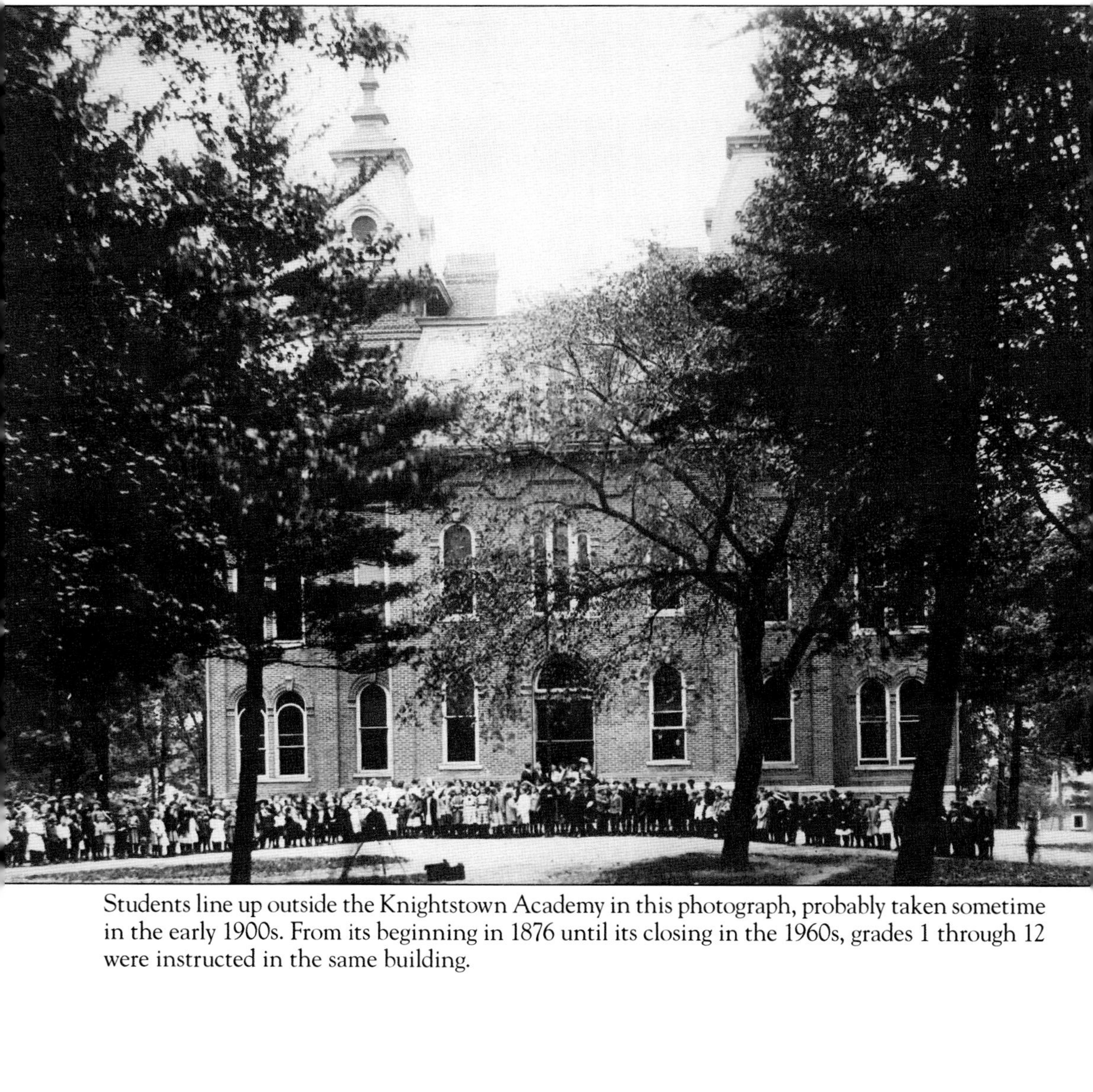

Students line up outside the Knightstown Academy in this photograph, probably taken sometime in the early 1900s. From its beginning in 1876 until its closing in the 1960s, grades 1 through 12 were instructed in the same building.

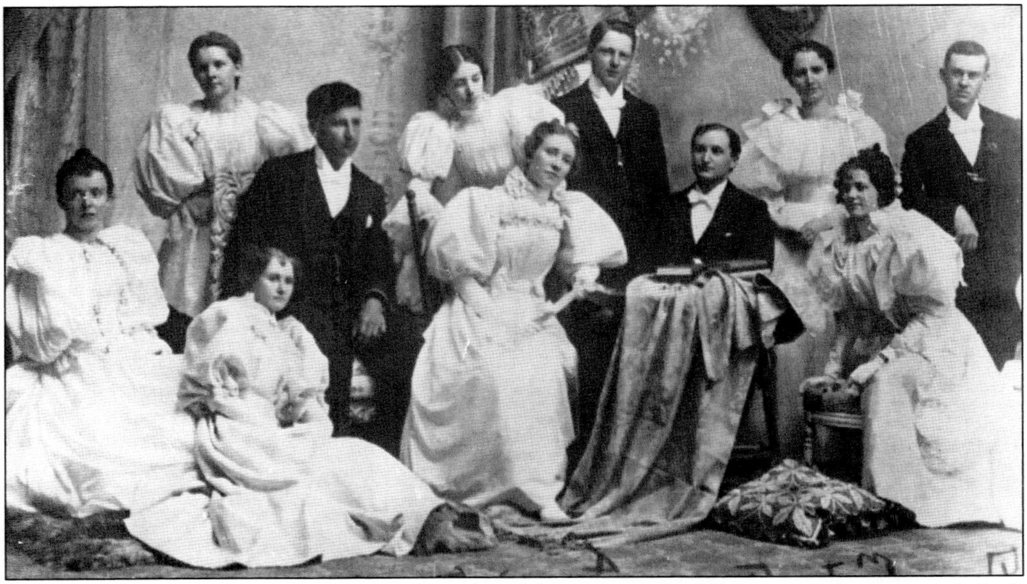

Knightstown High School's graduating class of 1895 (above) was small but nonetheless accomplished. Leonidas P. Newby, from the class of 1876, was the new school's first graduate, and the following year invitations announced commencement exercises (below). Tuition for students outside school limits in 1886–1887 was 60¢ per week for high school, 40¢ weekly for the grammar department, and 30¢ per week for the primary department. Though school days are over at the Knightstown Academy, the National Register of Historic Places landmark continues to serve the community as senior citizens' housing.

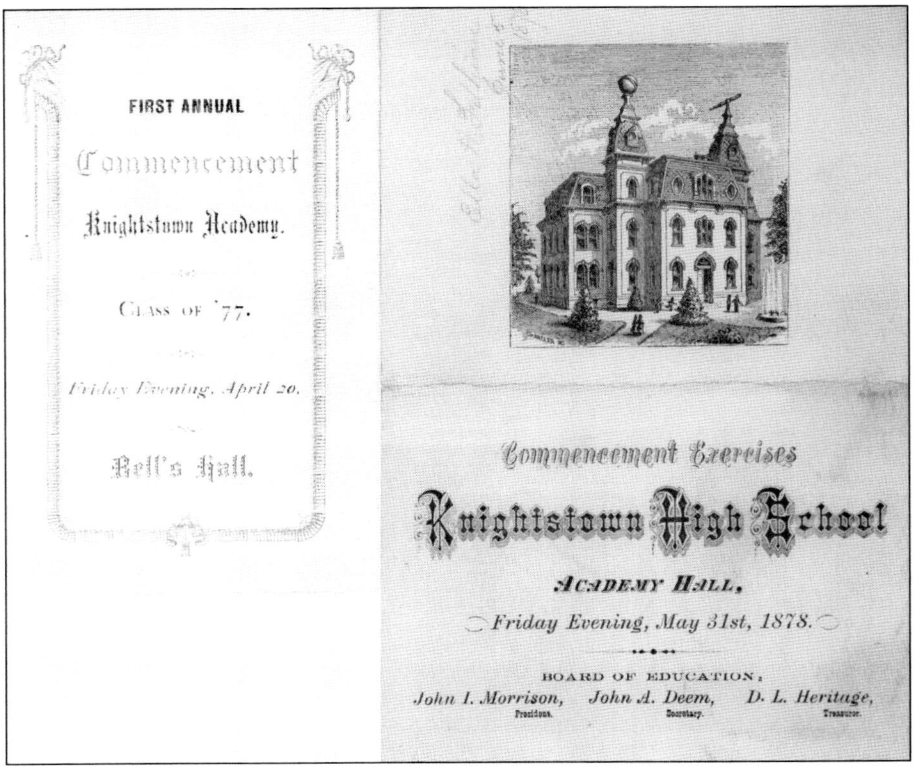

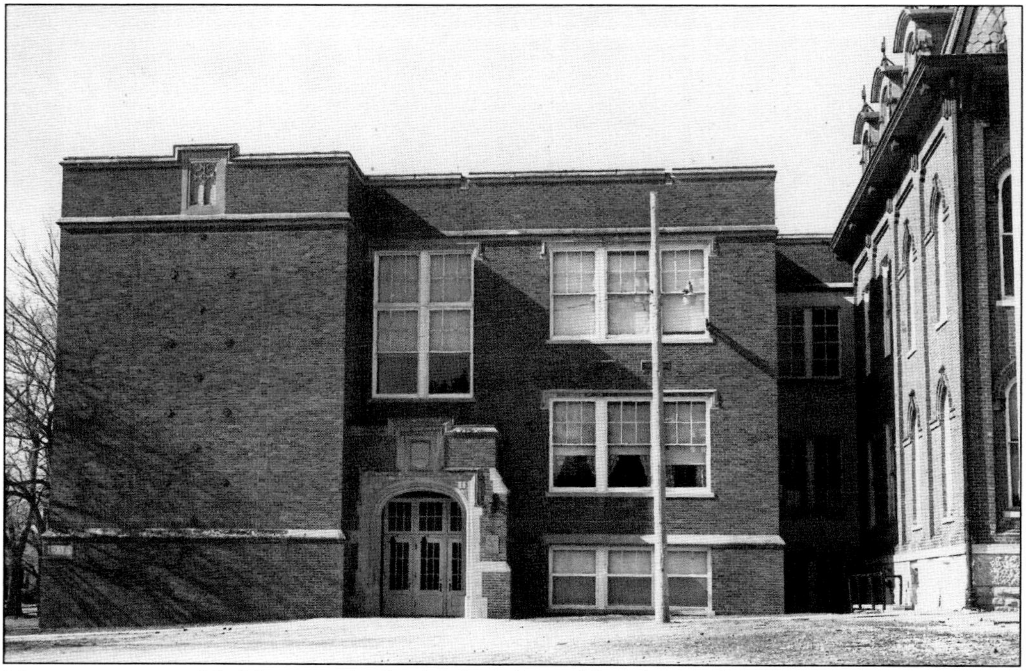

More space was added later to the back of academy (above). Knightstown's Hoosier Gym was constructed in 1922, when it became clear that school athletic teams needed somewhere else to play their games besides Bell's Hall on Main Street and the basement of the Presbyterian Church. Improvements were made to the gym (including a front lobby) using Works Progress Administration funds in 1936. The new lobby makes a fine backdrop for the Knightstown High School band (below). Knightstown High School played its last official regular season basketball game at the Hoosier Gym in 1966. Interest in the old building was revived when it was chosen as the site of a major film. Still full of charm and listed on the National Register of Historic Places, the gym was saved from demolition in 1989 and is now used as a community center.

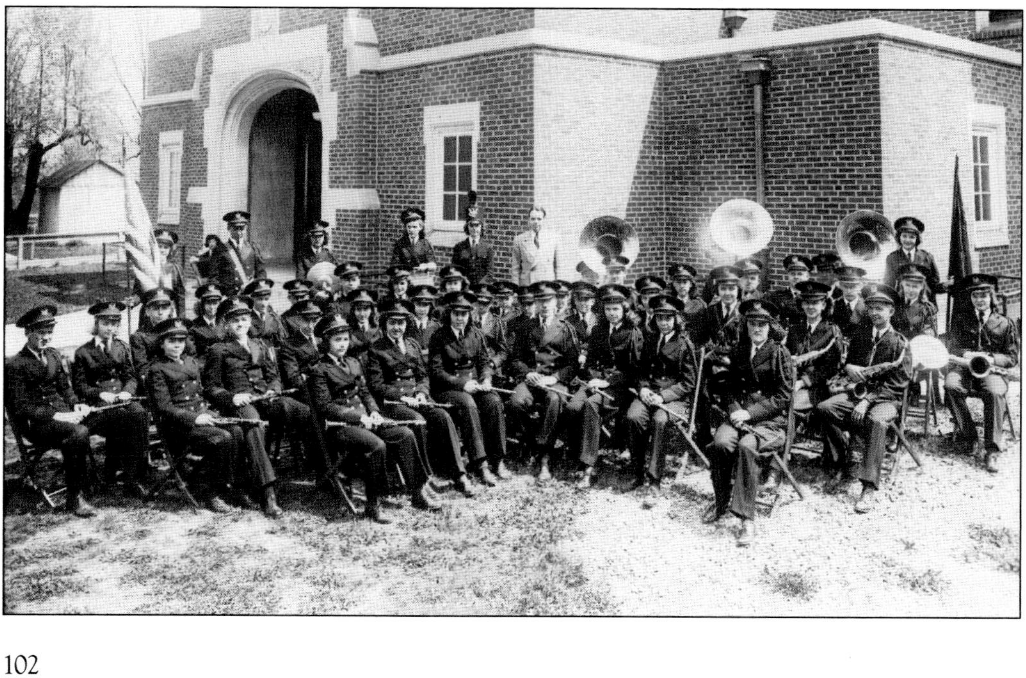

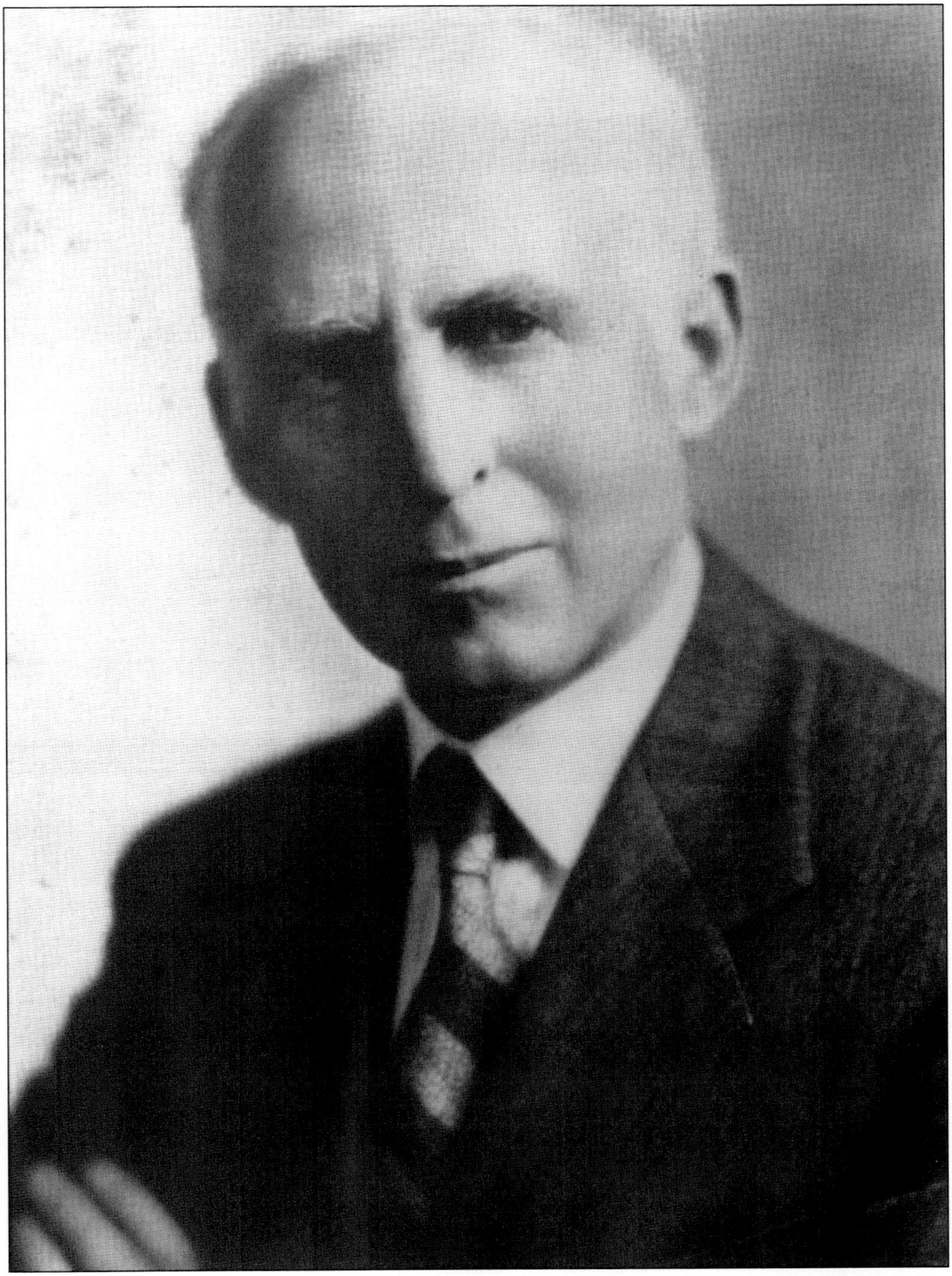

Well-known American historian Charles A. Beard was born on a farm near Knightstown in 1874 and is one of the most famous graduates of the Knightstown Academy. He graduated from Indiana's DePauw University, received his doctorate from Columbia University, and also studied at the University of Oxford in England. Many of his ideas were controversial at the time, and he was the author of numerous books and hundreds of articles. Beard died in 1948. The current Knightstown school system, the Charles A. Beard School Corporation, was named after him.

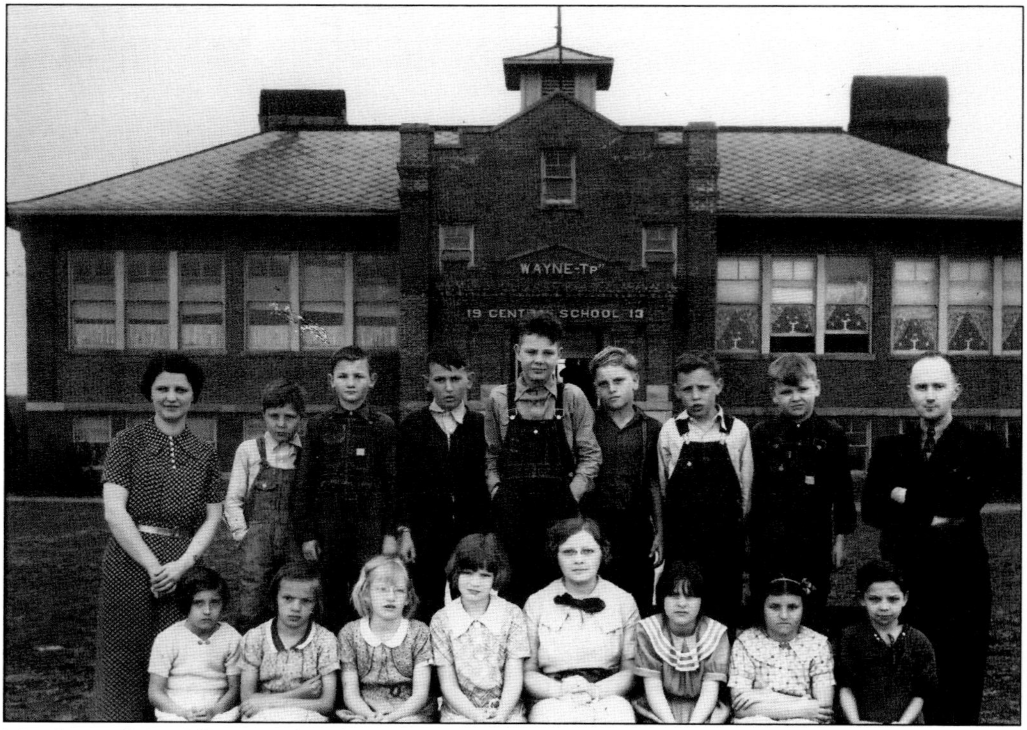

Members of Mrs. Idlewine's fourth-grade class pose in front of Wayne Township's Central School in 1934; the school principal is on the right. Only the bottom of this 1913 school building still exists, and it serves as the foundation of a later-built private home on the outskirts of Knightstown.

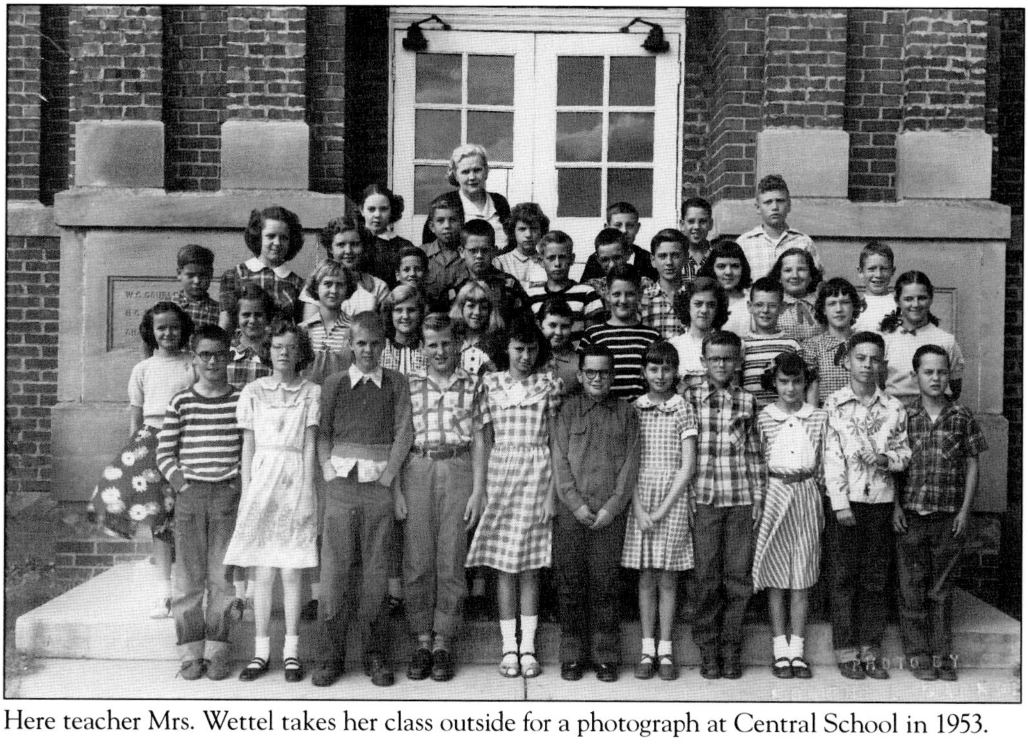

Here teacher Mrs. Wettel takes her class outside for a photograph at Central School in 1953.

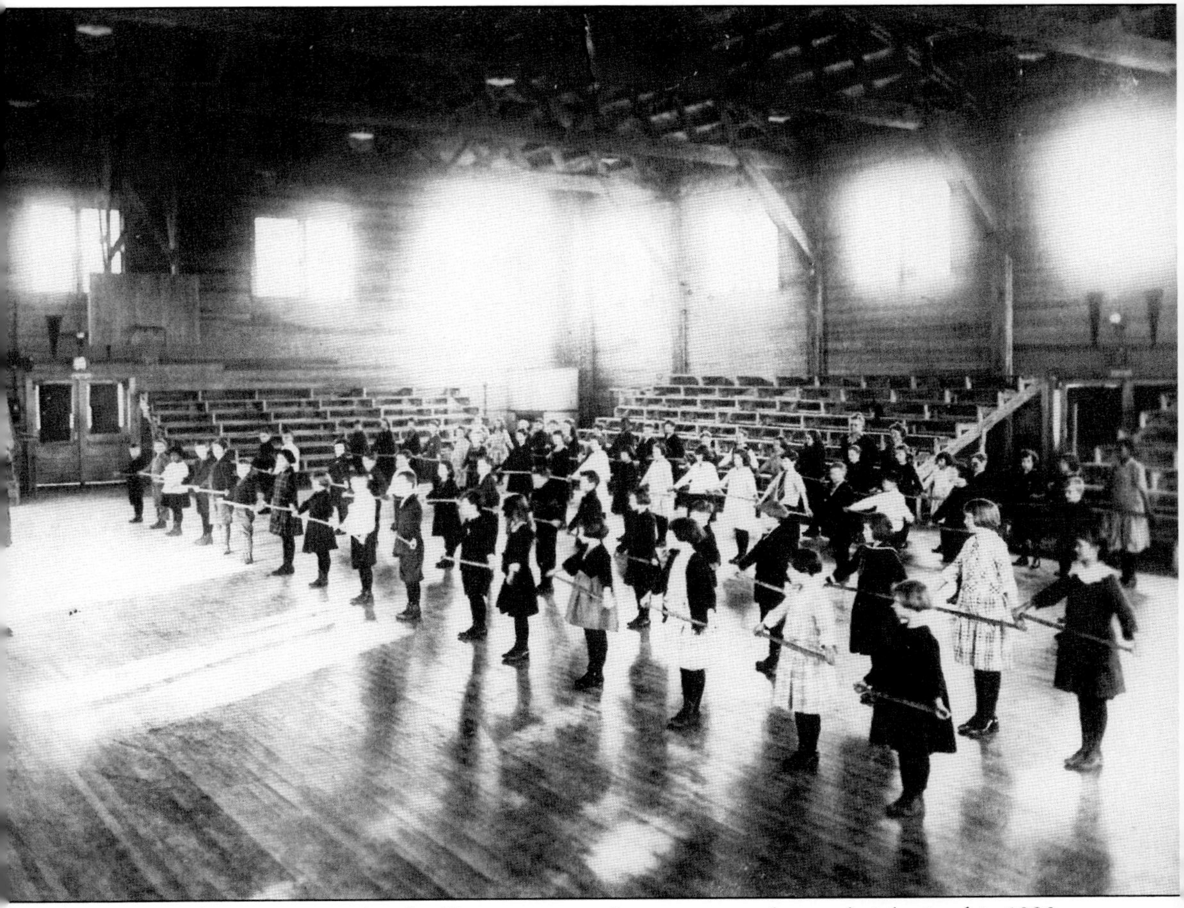

Children are learning some kind of lesson using what appear to be yardsticks in this 1920s photograph taken inside the Hoosier Gym.

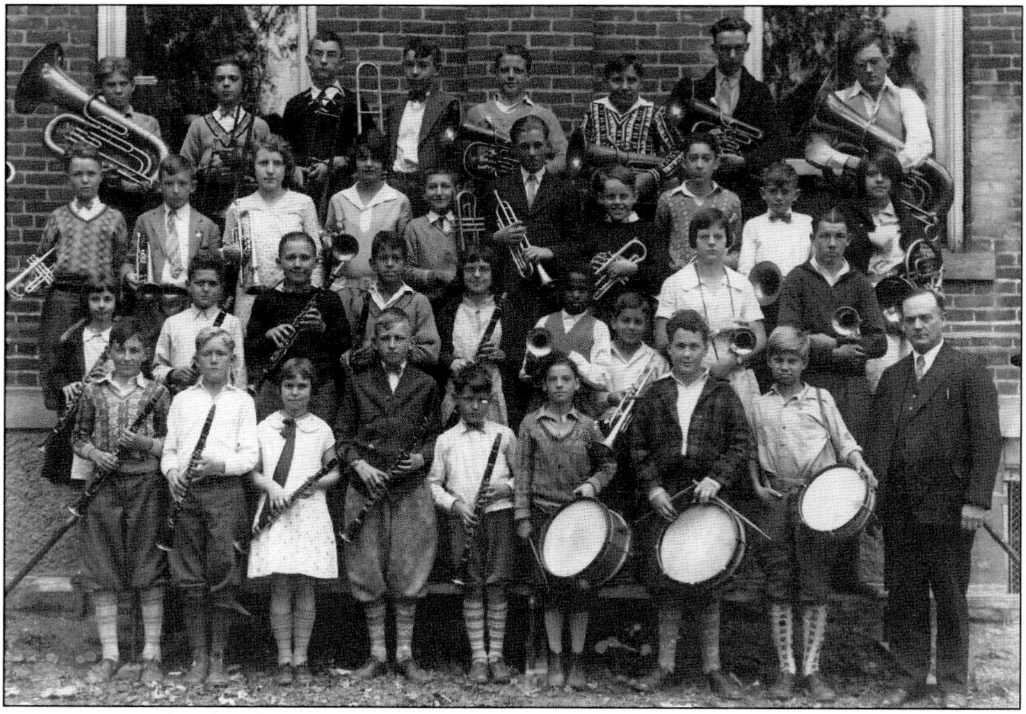

Instruments in hand and sporting a few pairs of lively patterned stockings, the 1928 Knightstown school band is eager to learn and ready to play. Popular artists of the time included Al Jolson, Louis Armstrong, and Paul Whiteman, and making music was all the rage with young people at the time.

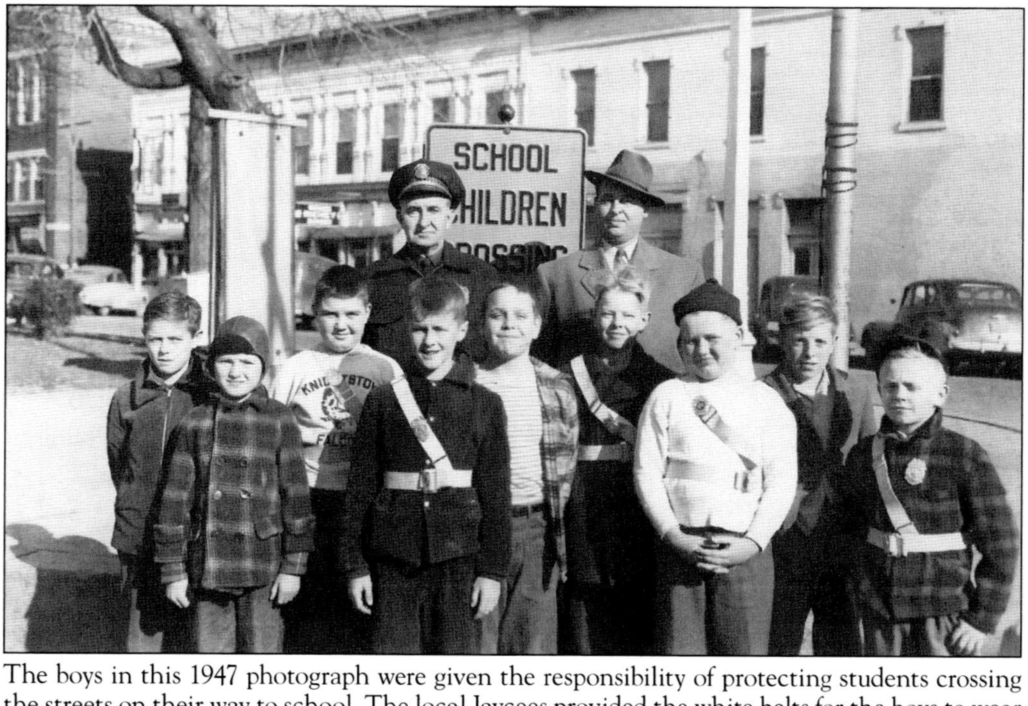

The boys in this 1947 photograph were given the responsibility of protecting students crossing the streets on their way to school. The local Jaycees provided the white belts for the boys to wear to increase their visibility and identify them as crossing guards.

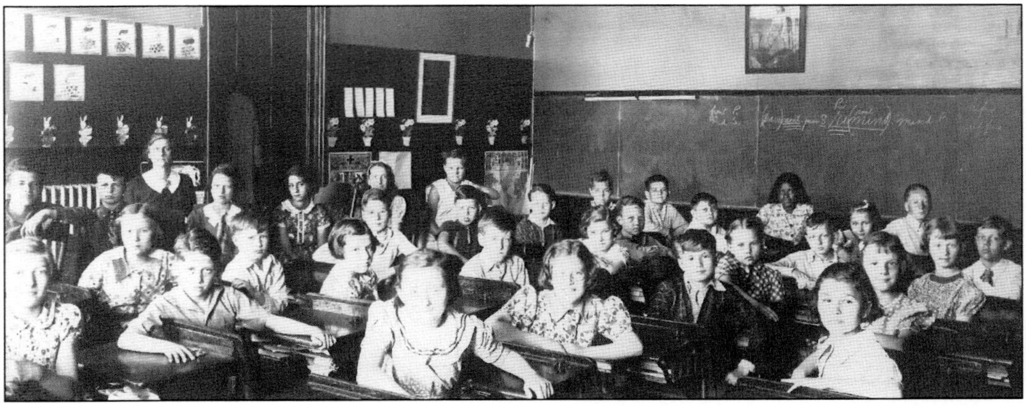

Students seated at their classroom desks turn to face the camera in this undated photograph from the Knightstown Academy.

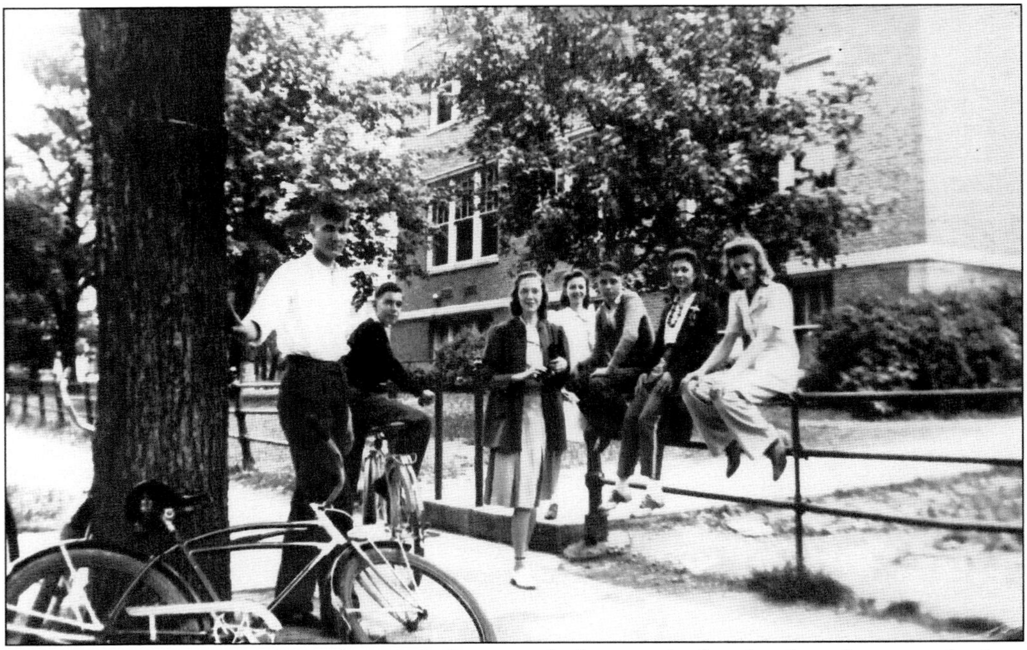

Saddle shoes were in style in this 1943 photograph showing high school students perched on the railing outside the Knightstown Academy after school. Most students walked or rode their bicycles to school at the time.

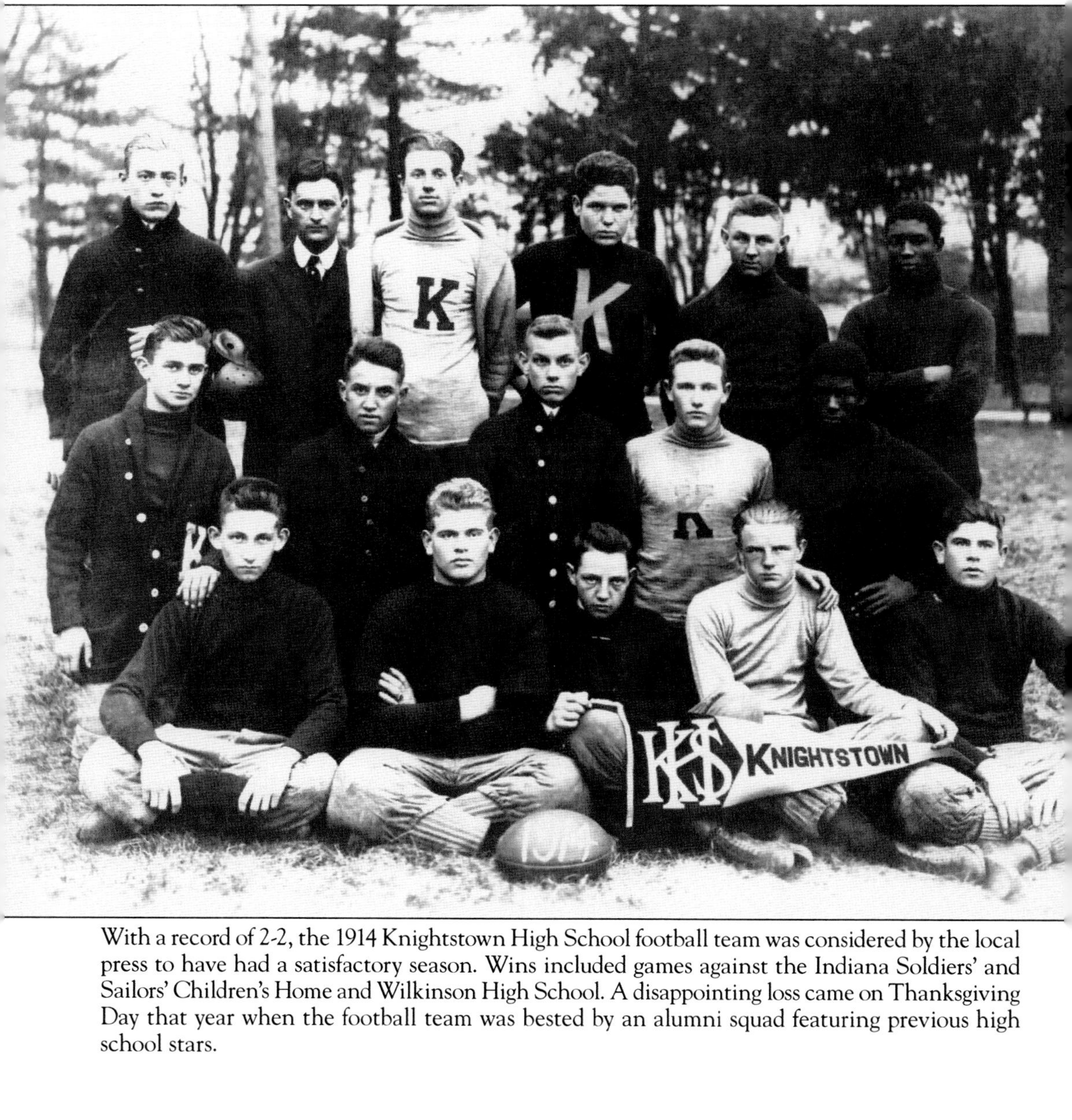

With a record of 2-2, the 1914 Knightstown High School football team was considered by the local press to have had a satisfactory season. Wins included games against the Indiana Soldiers' and Sailors' Children's Home and Wilkinson High School. A disappointing loss came on Thanksgiving Day that year when the football team was bested by an alumni squad featuring previous high school stars.

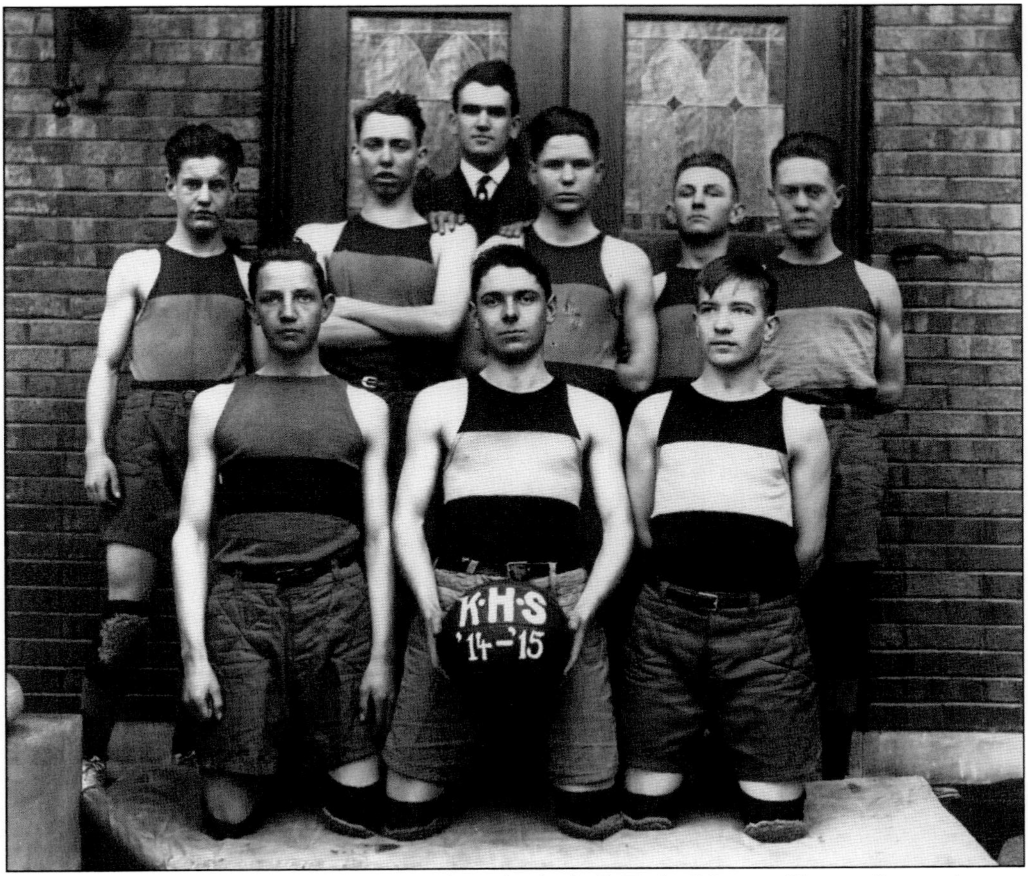

For a long time, Indiana has been crazy about basketball. Early "Hoosier Hysteria" is evident in 1914 as the Knightstown High School basketball team (above) lines up for the camera on the steps of the Hoosier Gym; notice the boys wearing the fuzzy kneepads. The players, game, and attire had changed by the 1940s (below), when team members also stood still for a team photograph.

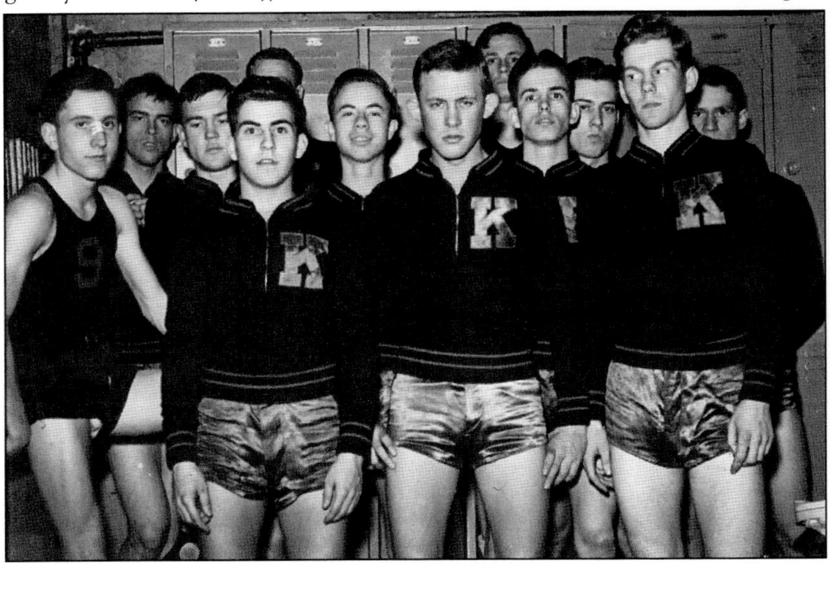

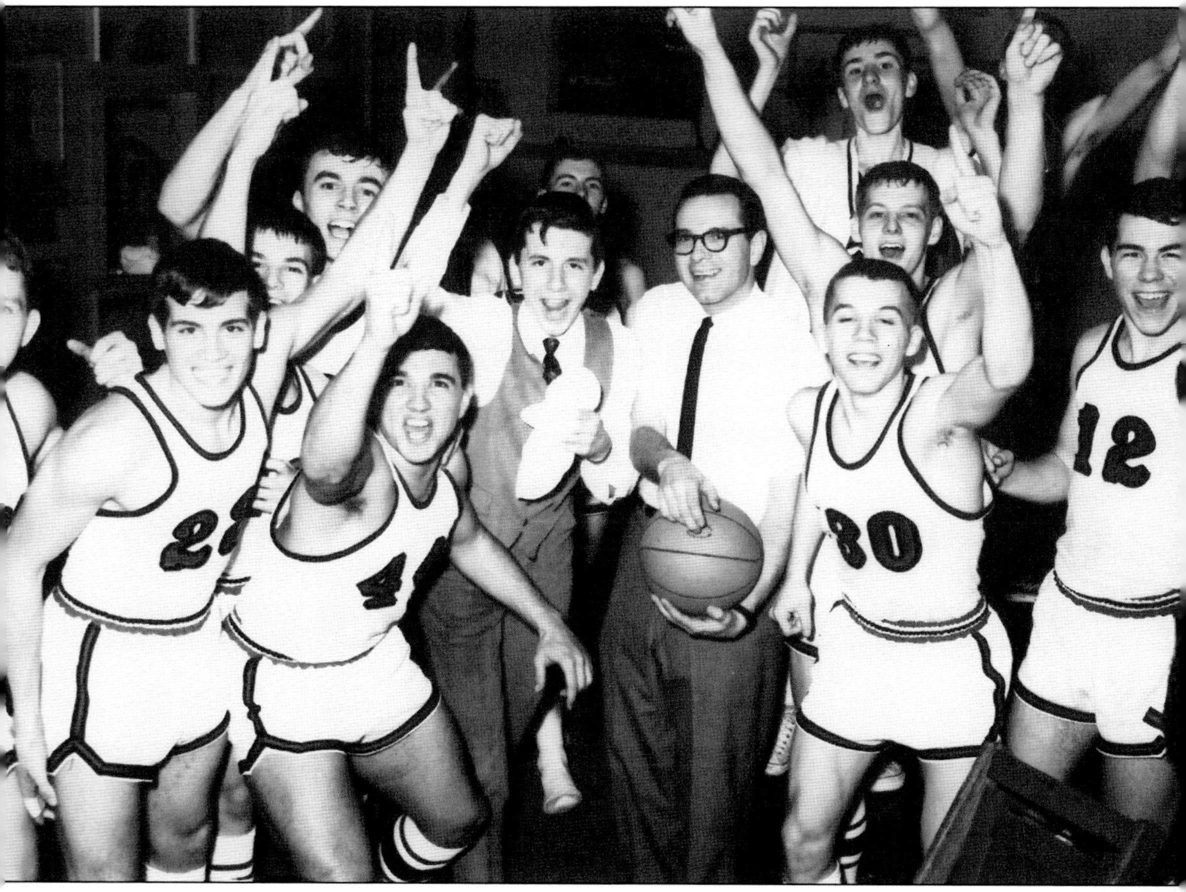

Victory is sweet as the Knightstown High School Panthers basketball team wins in the last official school game played in the Hoosier Gym in 1966. The team won the conference title against Union City.

Six

Early Churches

Church was an integral part of life for early Knightstown residents, and in many ways it was a statement of who they were—as individuals and as groups. It was considered so important, for example, that the Henry County Directory in 1874 included an individual's name, where he or she lived, when and where he or she was born, and his or her political and religious affiliation.

Though many congregations initially met in members' homes, the first church building constructed in Knightstown belonged to the Presbyterians in 1834. By 1884, Knightstown's population had reached 2,000, and the town was home to seven churches.

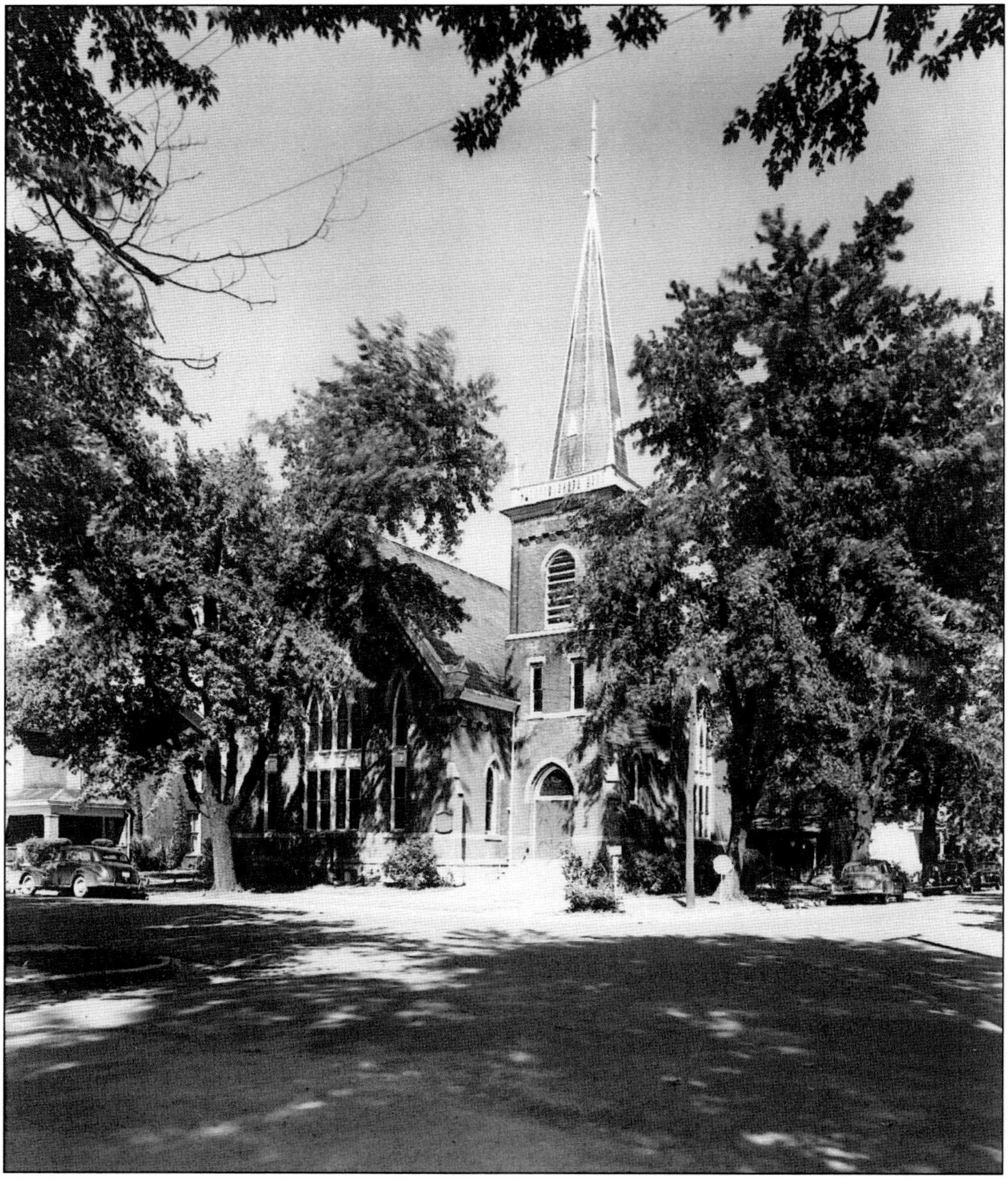

This is the Methodist Church building on the corner of Jefferson and Jackson Streets, remodeled and pictured in 1949. The tall spire was added, and this is much like how the church building appears today. The Knightstown Methodist Episcopal Church was organized in 1824, and the members worshipped in their first building in 1837.

This older view of the Methodist Church building shows the spire before it was lengthened. The original building was constructed in 1885 and underwent several remodeling efforts over the years. The value of the church property in 1874 was $8,000.

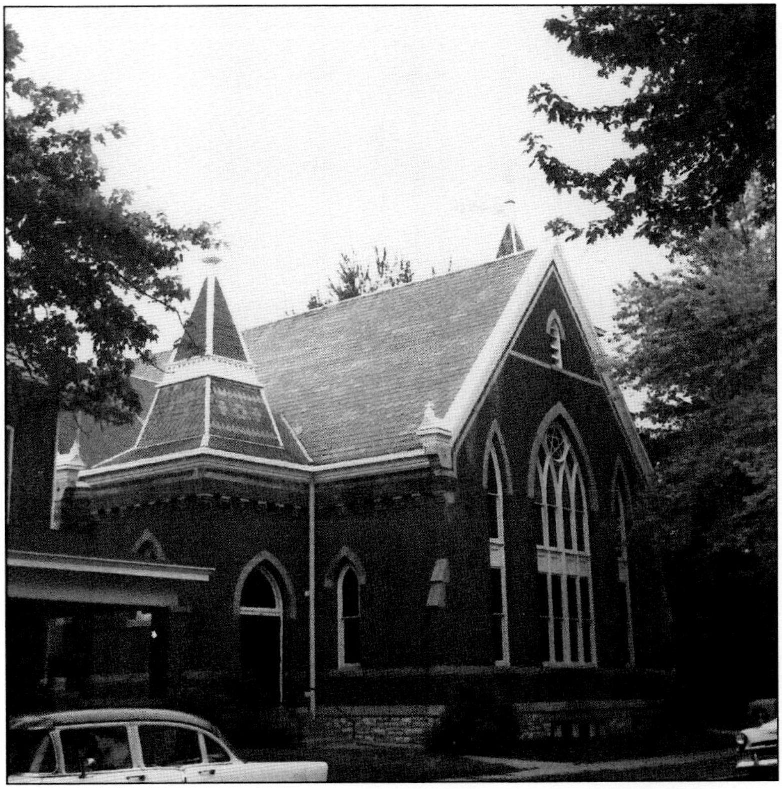

SUNDAY, SEPTEMBER 22, 1907.

MORNING SERVICES.

SUNDAY SCHOOL—9:30 o'clock.

10:30 O'CLOCK

Voluntary—"Short Pastorale in A" .... *Gustav Merkel*
Hymn 411—"Canonbury" .... *Robert Schuman*
Apostles' Creed.
PRAYER.
Hymn 407—"Fortitude" .... *David S. Smith*
Psalm for the 19th morning.
Gloria Patri.
Scripture lesson.
Offertory—"Lento Religioso" .... *Chopin*
Hymn 388—"Boylston" .... *Lowell Mason*
Sermon by the Pastor.
Hymn 393—"Arlington" .... *Thomas A. Arne*
Benediction.
Postlude.

CLASS MEETING 12 O'CLOCK.

AFTERNOON AND EVENING SERVICES

JUNIOR LEAGUE—2 o'clock.
EPWORTH LEAGUE, 6:30 o'clock ...... The Word of God Perverted.
Mrs. Mills, Leader.

7:30 O'CLOCK

Voluntary—"Andantino" .... *F. Wachs*
Song Service.
PRAYER.
Hymn 261—"Stockton" .... *John H. Stockton*
Psalm for the 19th evening.
Offertory—"Romance" .... *P. Lacome*
Hymn 272—"Woodworth" .... *William B. Bradbury*
Sermon by the Pastor.
Hymn 265—"Shawmut" .... *Lowell Mason*
Benediction.
Postlude—"March" .... *Ashford*

ANNOUNCEMENTS.

TUESDAY, 7:30 p. m.—The Prayer Band will meet in the Lecture Room of the church. Let all young people come.

THURSDAY, 7:30 p. m.—The regular Prayer Meeting invites every Christian. "Come thou with us and we will do thee good." "Don't give up the ship," was the cry of a patriot. Don't give up the prayer meeting should be echoed and re-echoed in every home and in every heart in Knightstown Methodism. Let us have a gracious meeting on next Thursday evening.

FRIDAY, 7:30 p. m.—The Sunday School Board will meet on Friday evening to discuss methods and plans of work among the children.

SATURDAY, 3 p. m.—The Standard Bearers will meet with Glenna Gillespie. All members are urged to be present.

In this copy of the Methodist Church bulletin from September 22, 1907, Sunday school services are advertised at 9:30 a.m., and the worship service is at 10:30 a.m.

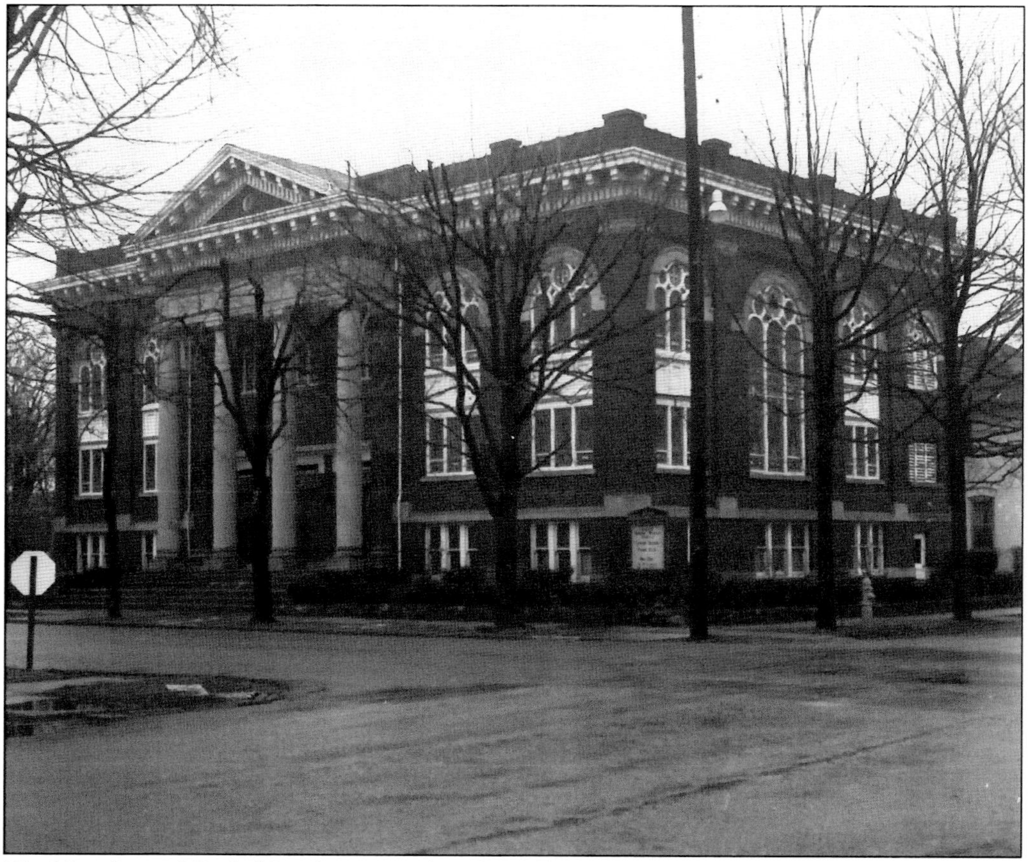

The Neoclassical Bethel Presbyterian Church building (above) is the current one located at the corner of Franklin and Jackson Streets. It was constructed in 1912 on the site of the previous church structure. The same building is depicted (below) in an illustration.

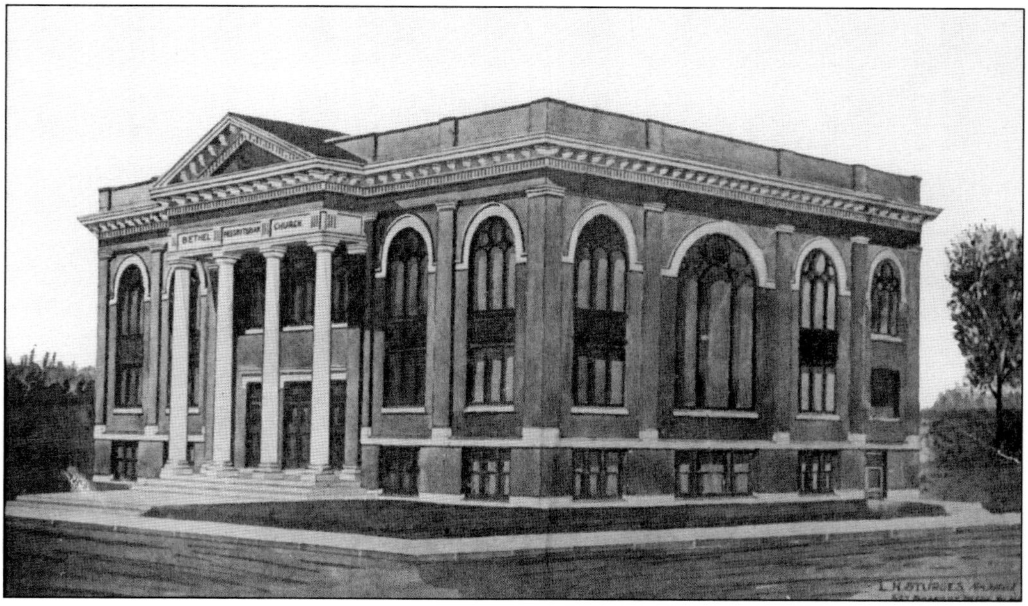

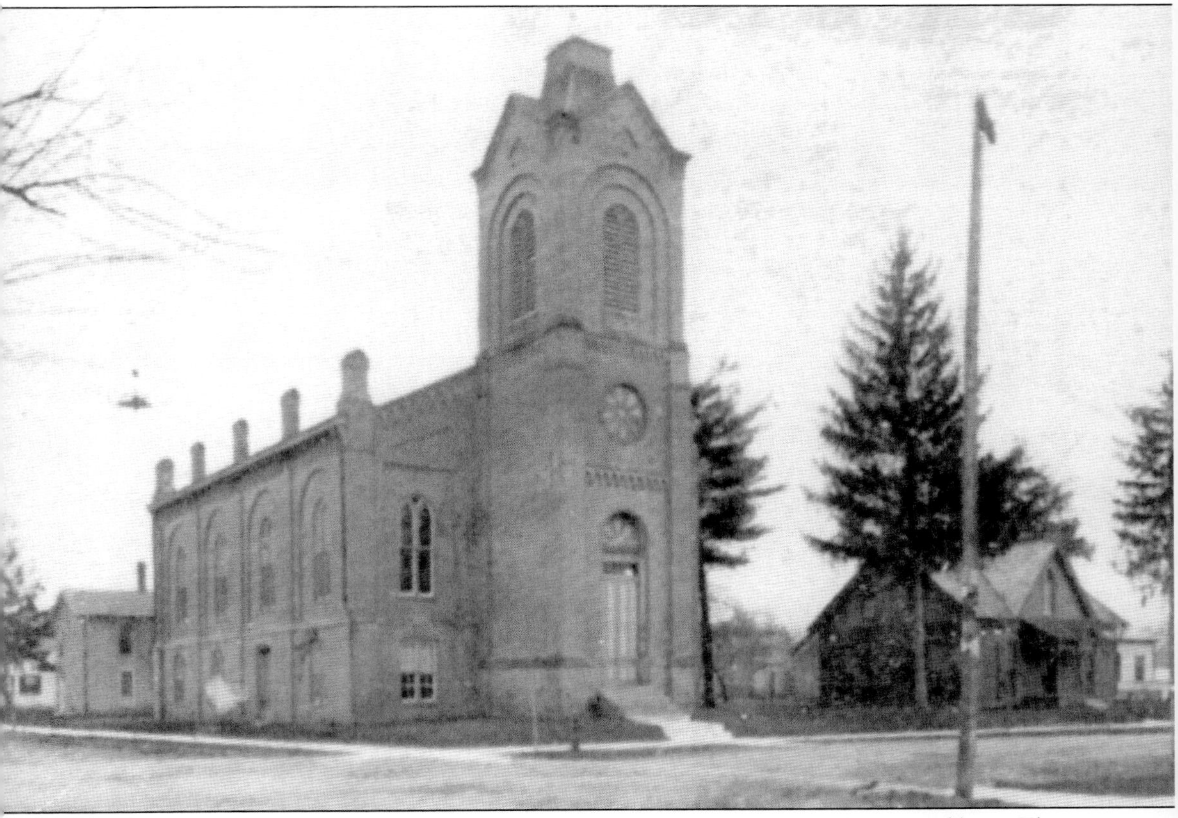

Two frame structures preceded the original brick Bethel Presbyterian Church pictured here. The Presbyterian congregation was organized in 1832 as the Bethel Church, and one of the first elders was early Knightstown businessman Harvey Bell. The brick church buildings came later.

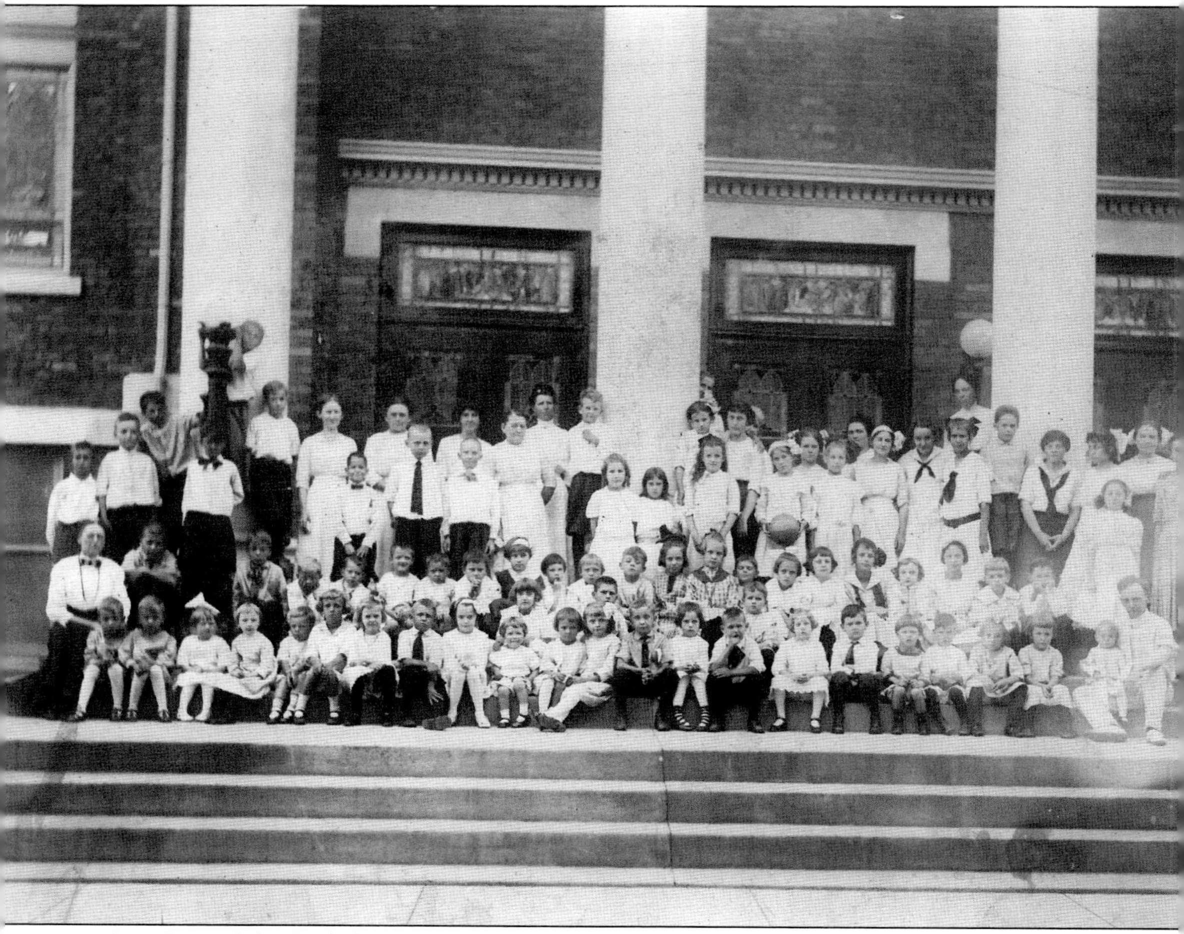

Members of the Bethel Presbyterian Church Sunday school gather on the grand front steps of the church building in this early 1900s photograph. As early as 1874, the Presbyterian Church already claimed 235 members and an average weekly attendance of 128.

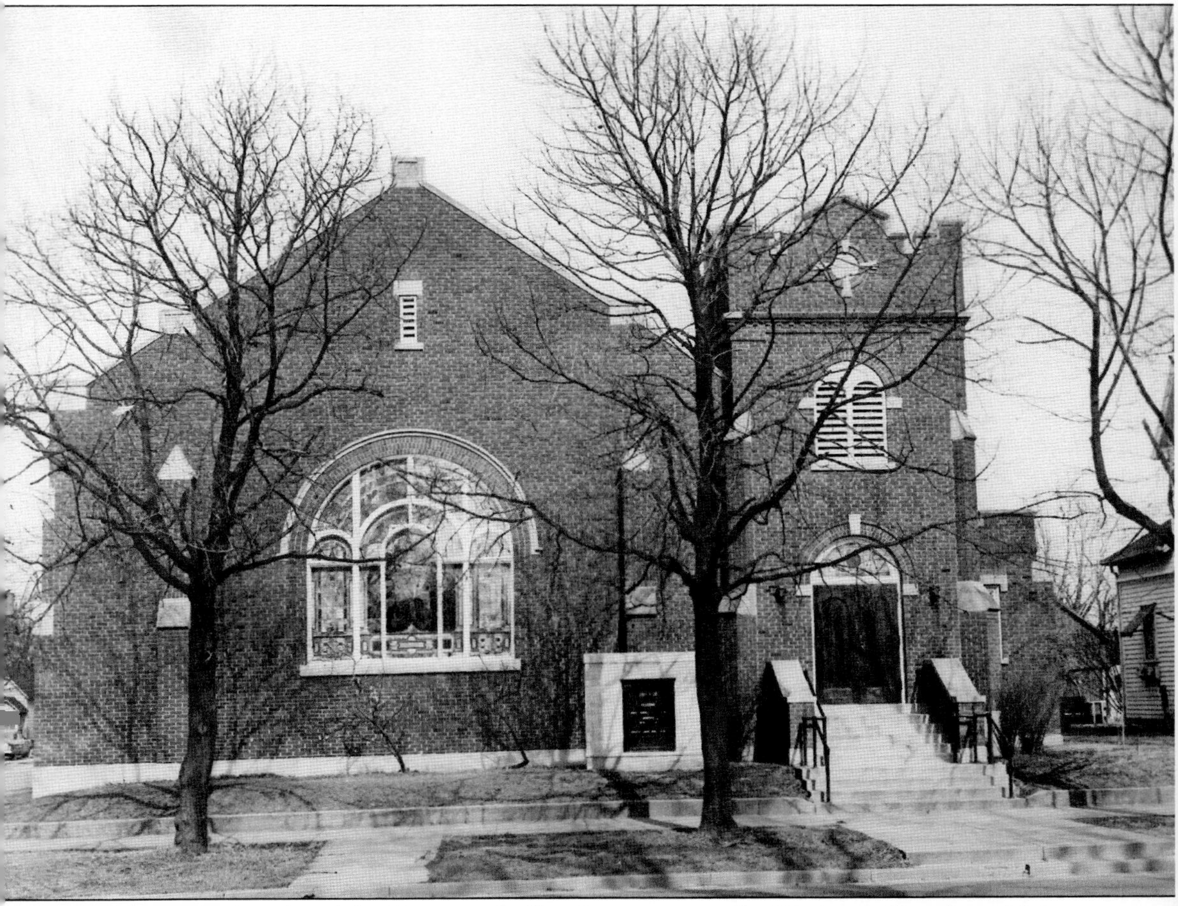

As with several other church buildings in the Knightstown area, the Christian Church on Main Street has undergone renovations over the years. The Romanesque Revival church was built in 1870, with updates made in 1882 (after the building "blew down") and in 1924. W. W. Witemer was listed as pastor of the Christian Church in 1874; membership at that time was 72. The congregation was organized in 1868.

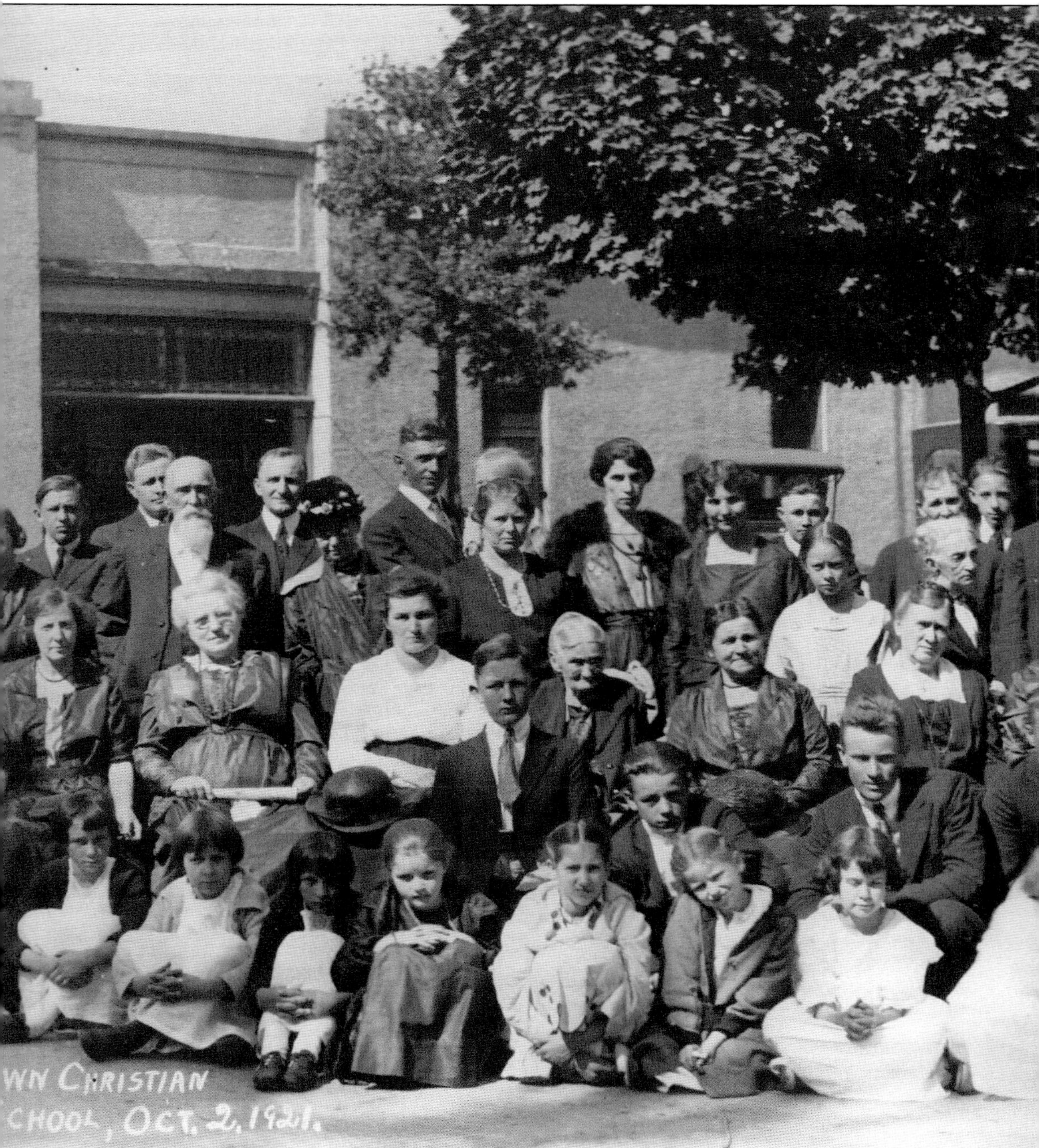

On a crisp, clear day in October 1921, members of the Christian Church headed outside for a

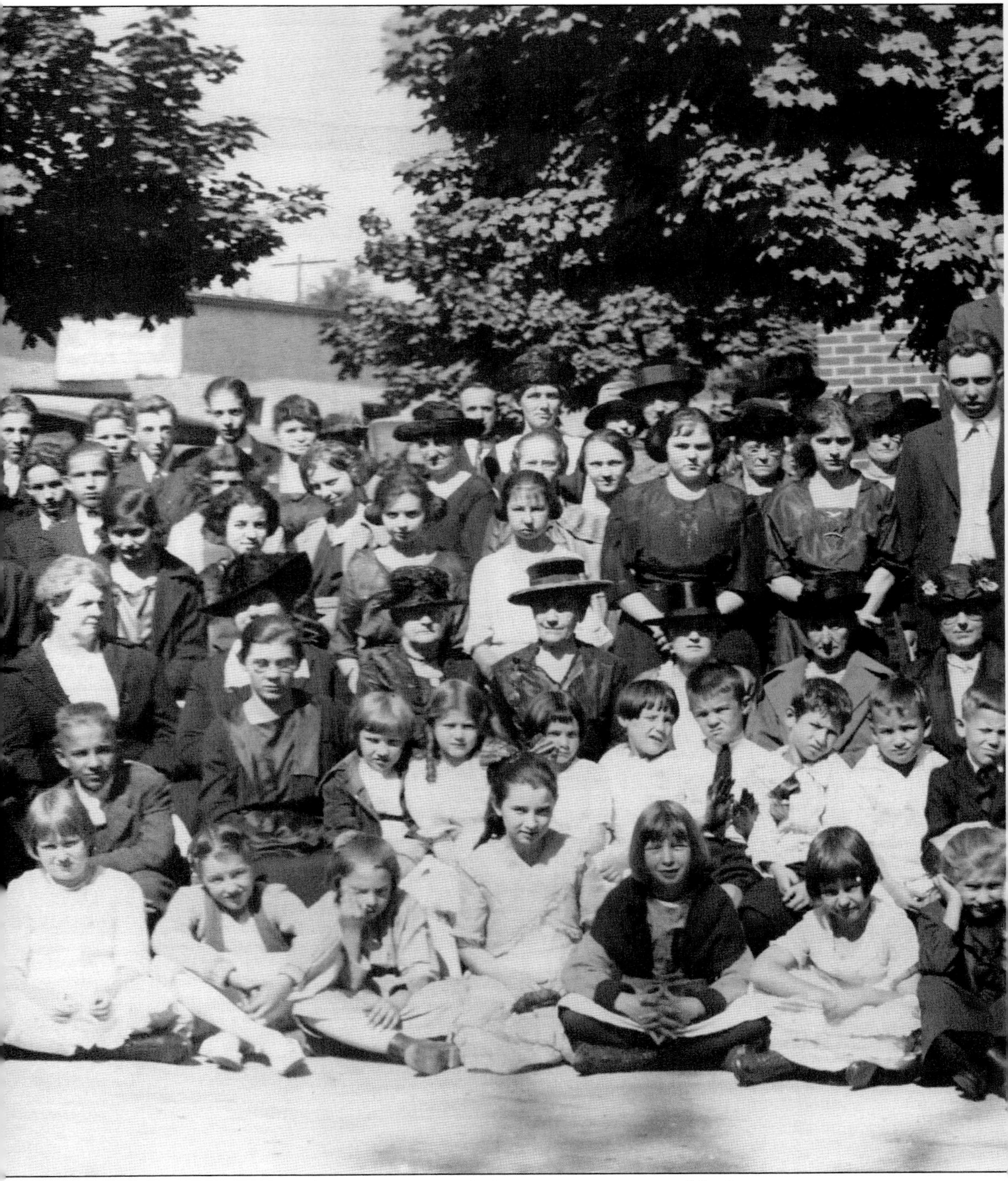

congregational photograph. The group spanned almost an entire town block.

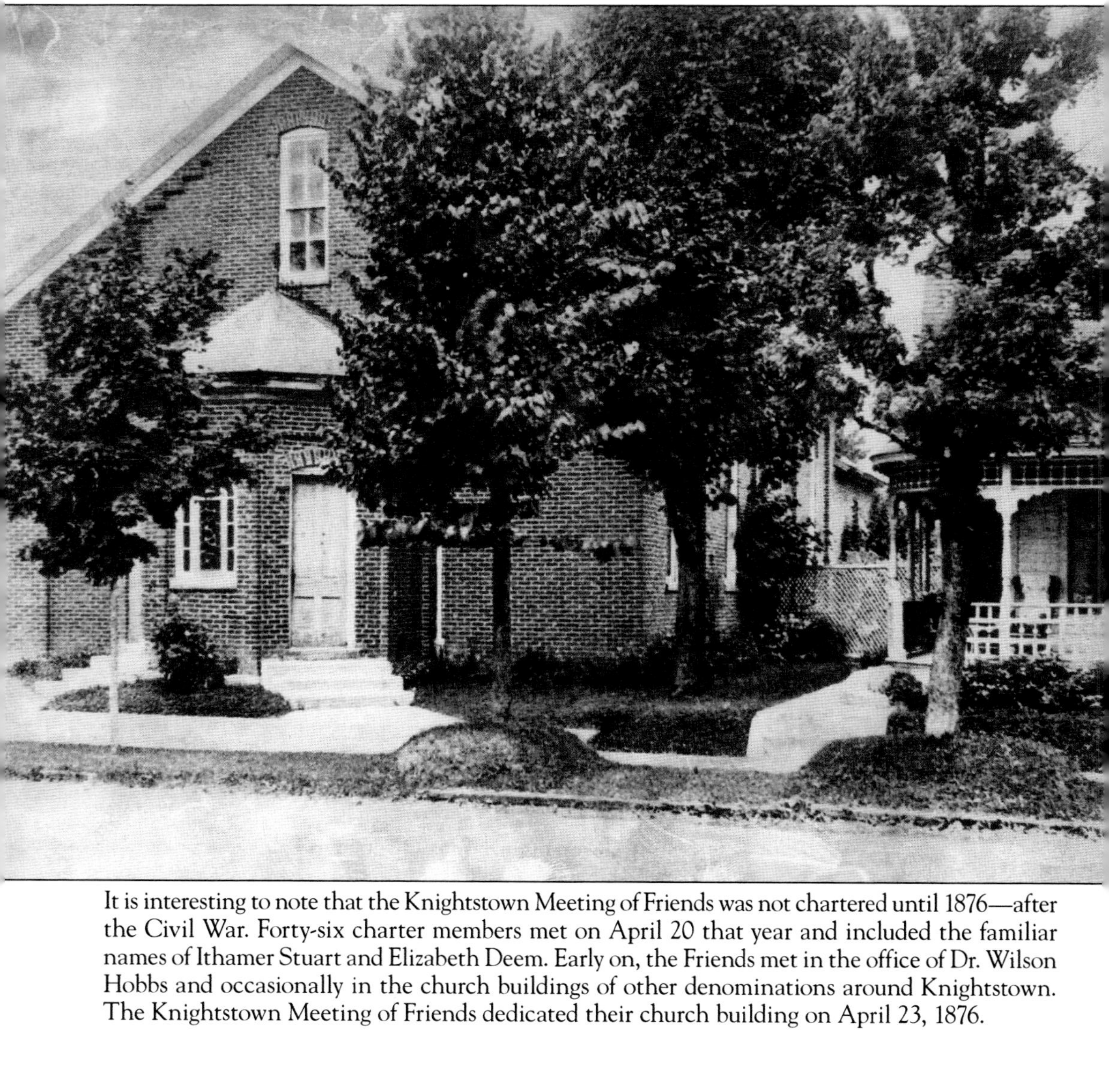

It is interesting to note that the Knightstown Meeting of Friends was not chartered until 1876—after the Civil War. Forty-six charter members met on April 20 that year and included the familiar names of Ithamer Stuart and Elizabeth Deem. Early on, the Friends met in the office of Dr. Wilson Hobbs and occasionally in the church buildings of other denominations around Knightstown. The Knightstown Meeting of Friends dedicated their church building on April 23, 1876.

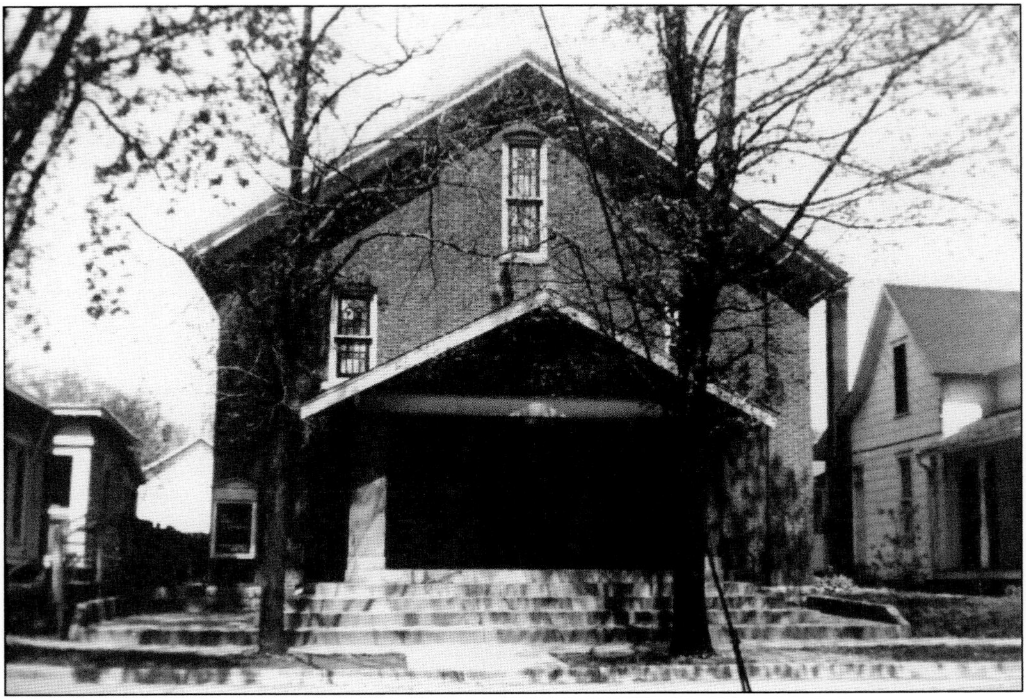

Two later views of the Friends church (above and below) show the building with several updates. In 1911, the church history notes that the building was "furnished in modern style with art glass windows, lighted with electric lights, and heated by furnace."

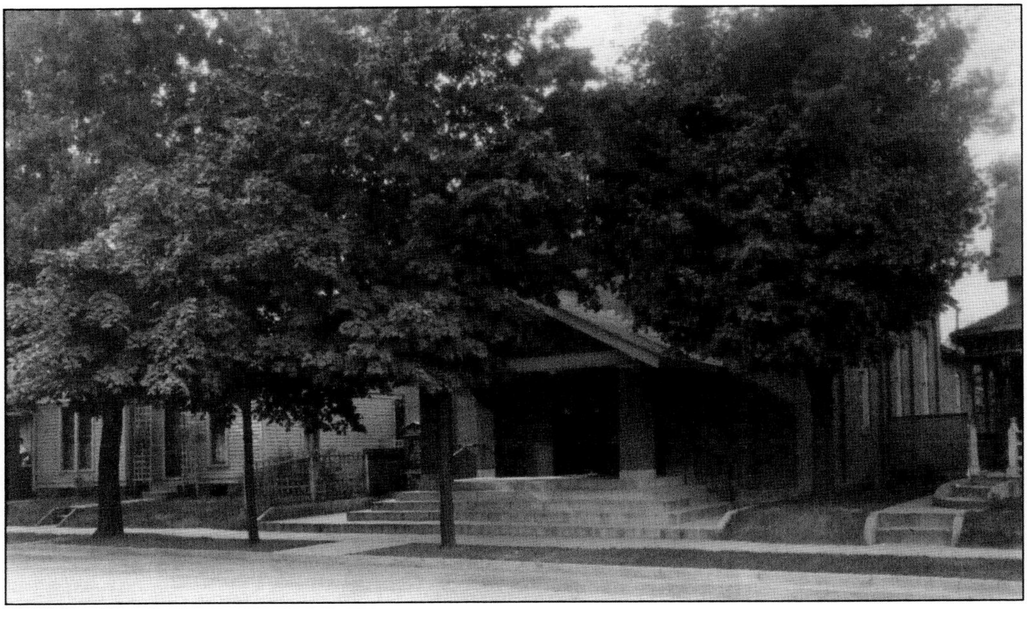

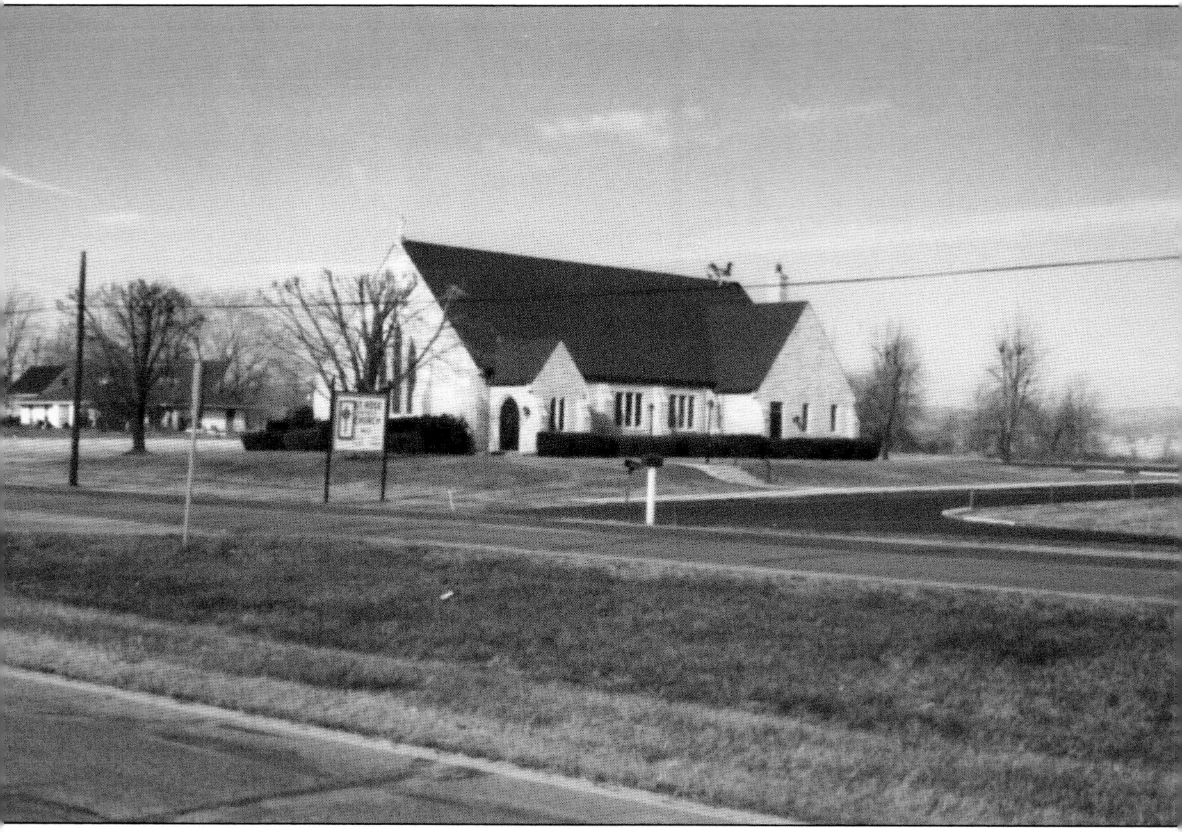

The cornerstone for the current St. Rose Catholic Church building on west U.S. 40 was laid in September 1950, and the building was dedicated in 1951. The congregation dates back to the early 1870s, however, and in 1874 the membership was listed at 150. Early on, they worshiped in a 50-foot-by-24-foot white-frame building on the corner of Adams and Pine Streets. The first Catholic marriage was recorded at St. Rose on January 23, 1873, when Gil Finton and Elizabeth Clare tied the knot.

Seven

Indiana Soldiers' and Sailors' Children's Home

The Indiana Soldiers' and Sailors' Children's Home has served Indiana since 1865, when it was established by then-governor Oliver P. Morton for Union veterans of the Civil War. Later veterans' widows and orphans also were admitted. Knightstown was officially less than 30 years old at the time, and many of the home's buildings predate historic homes within Knightstown. Waitstill M. Cary, however, didn't live to see construction of the children's home; he died two years earlier in 1863.

Anchored by the 1886 administration building, the nearly 250-acre Indiana Soldiers' and Sailors' Children's Home complex has been a fixture in the Knightstown community (even though it is located in Rush County) and has served thousands of children. More than 10,000 children were admitted to the home between 1867 and 1980. It is currently used by the Indiana National Guard. "The Home" closed its doors in early 2009, when it was shut down by the state.

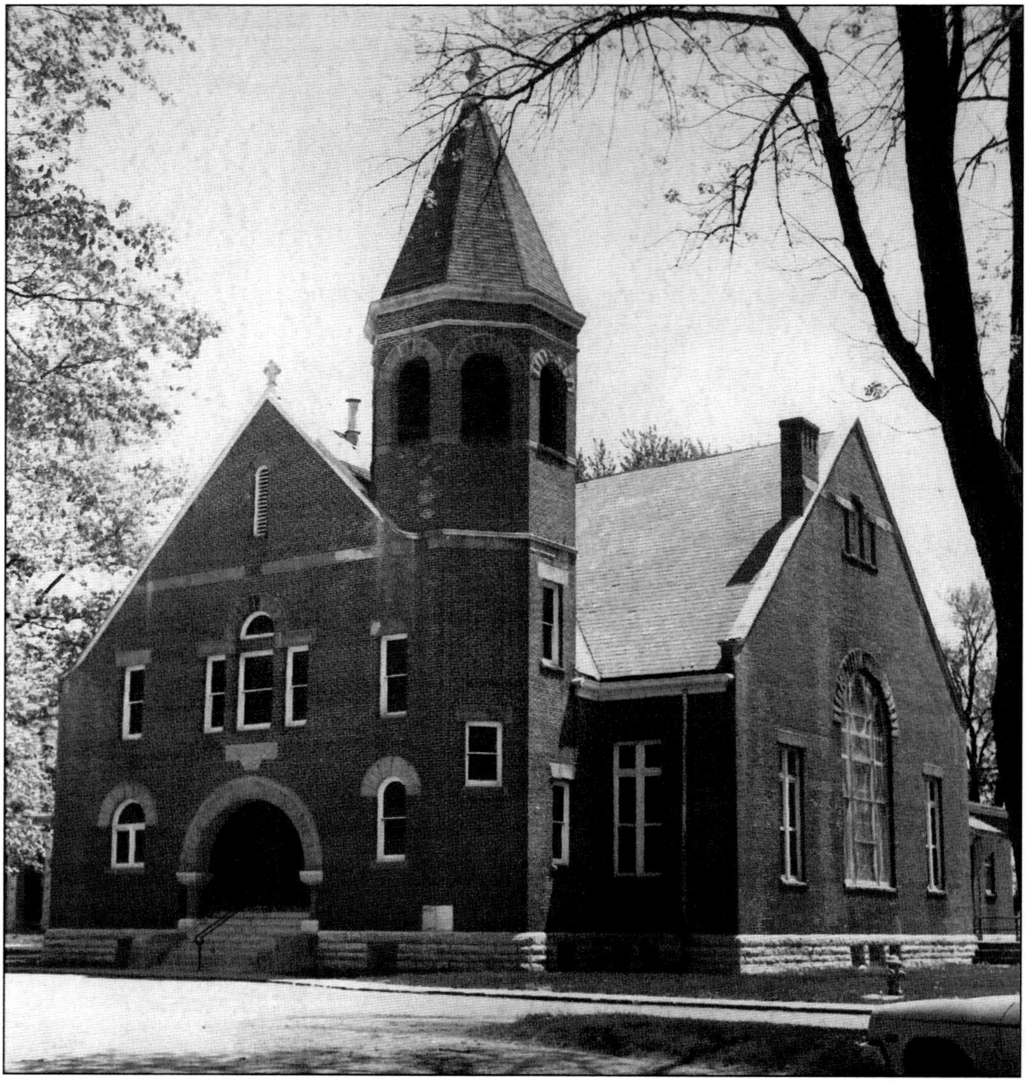

For almost 120 years, Lincoln Hall hosted church services at the Indiana Soldiers' and Sailors' Children's Home. Designed by Architect John Hasecoster, who also designed the 1876 Knightstown Academy, the redbrick chapel is well known for its stained-glass windows featuring—what else—a soldier and a sailor.

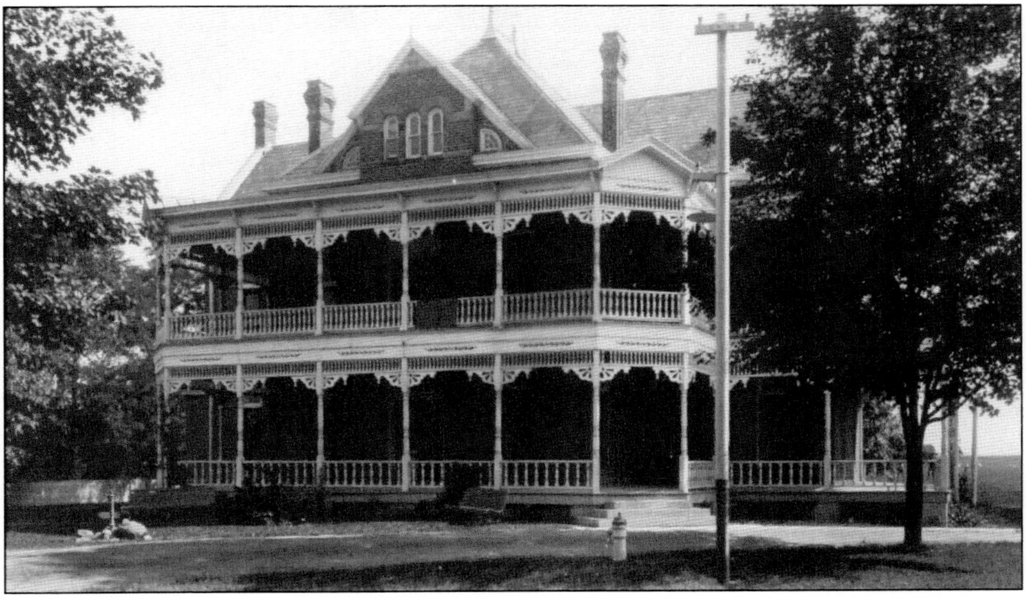

No longer standing, the ornate hospital building (above) on the grounds of the Indiana Soldiers' and Sailors' Children's Home was replaced with a newer version to keep up with advances in medicine and the needs of the children residing at the home. Constructed in 1886, the home's administration building (below) looms large over the campus.

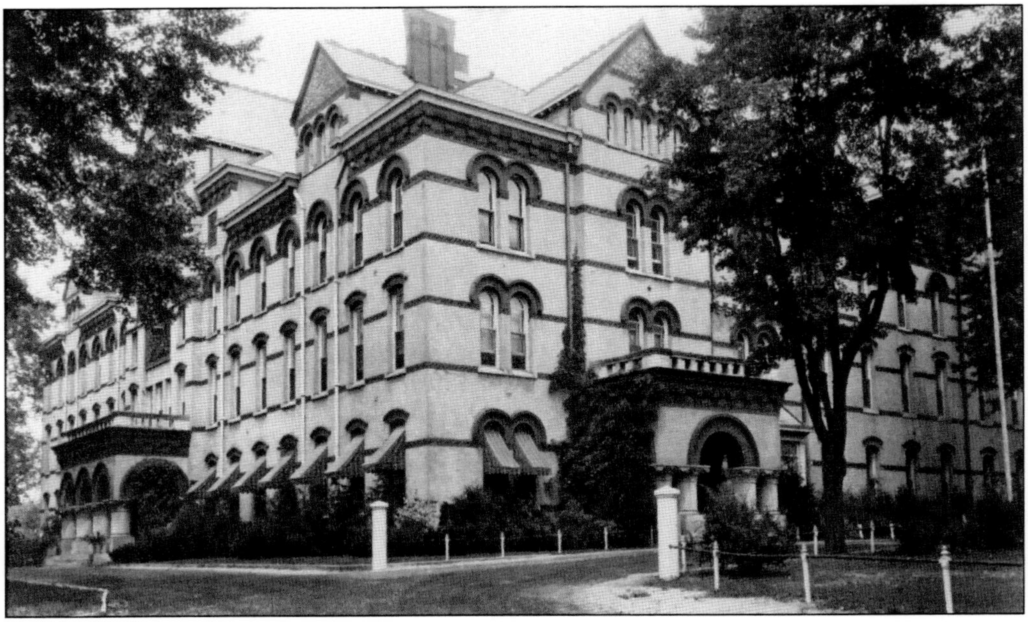

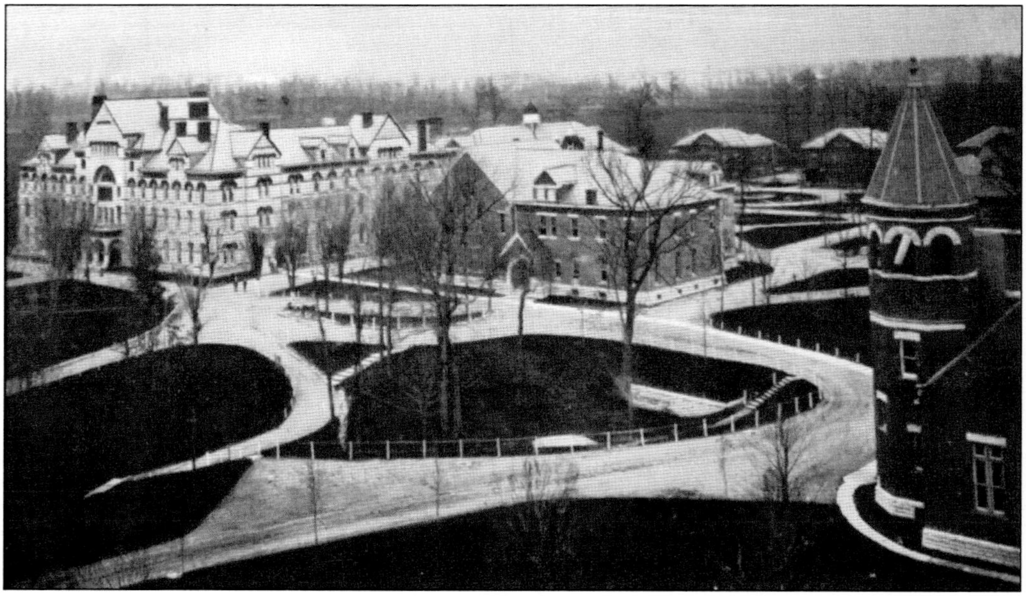

From above, the home's administration building can be seen to the left in this photograph, Lincoln Hall is to the right, and the student cottages are visible in the background. Below ground, a system of underground tunnels runs between the campus buildings. (Courtesy of the Henry County Historical Society Museum.)

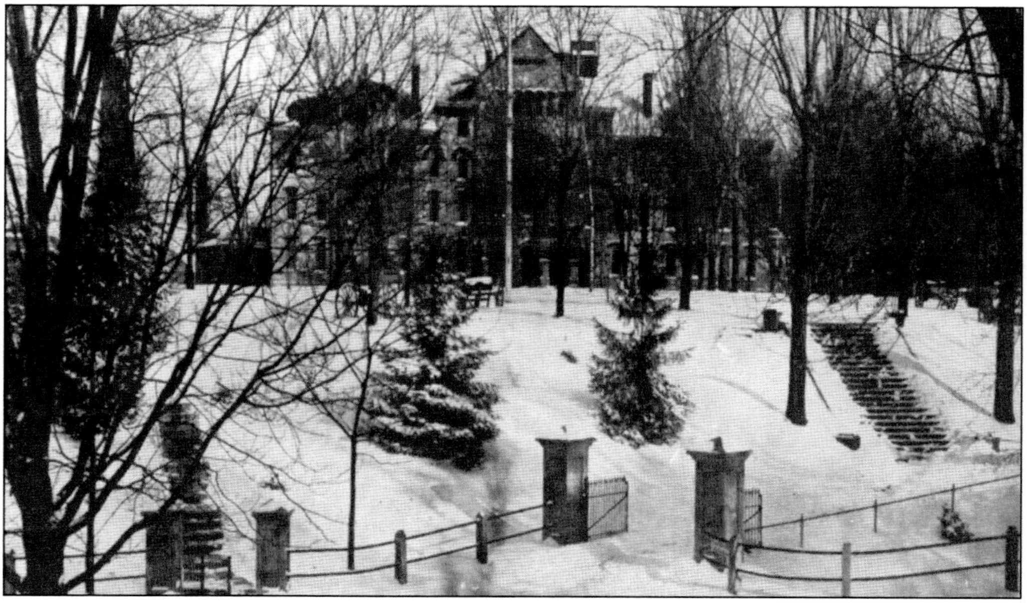

The gate is open in this undated photograph of the Indiana Soldiers' and Sailors' Children's Home, but the trip up the hill to the administration building might be treacherous in the snow. (Courtesy of the Henry County Historical Society Museum.)

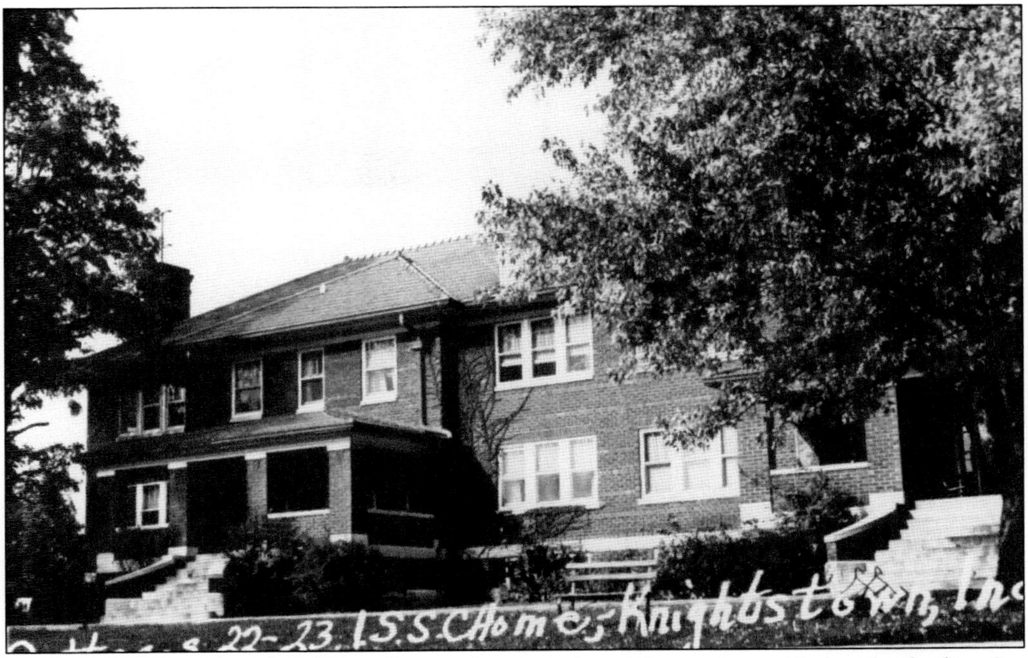

These cottages on the school grounds were home to the students who resided at the facility. Set up like dorm rooms with separate accommodations for boys and girls, the cottages were staffed by house parents who supervised the students and provided guidance and care. (Courtesy of the Henry County Historical Society Museum.)

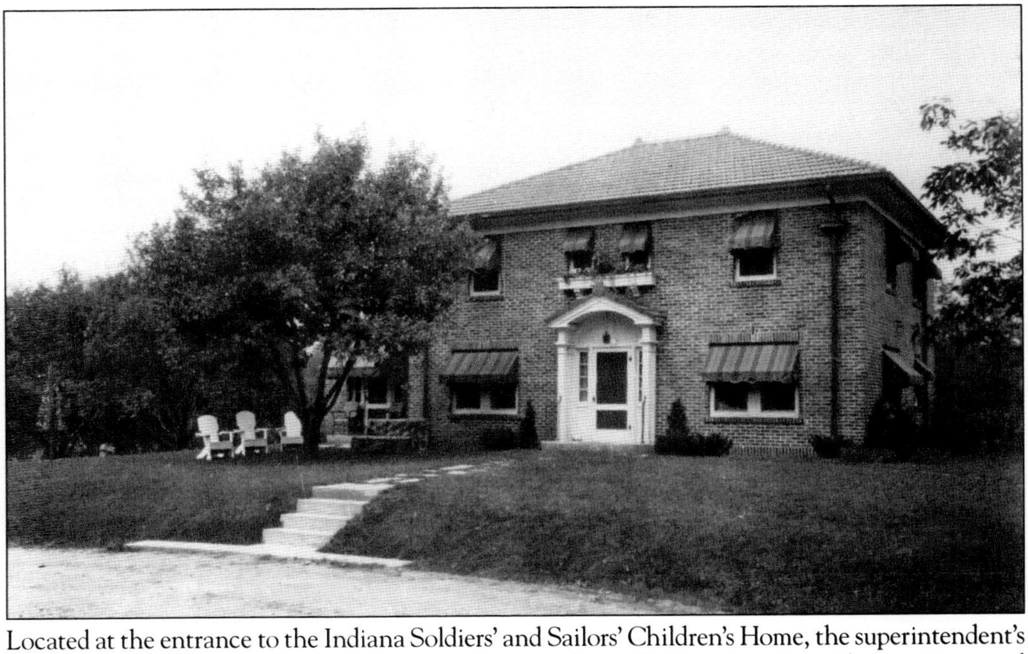

Located at the entrance to the Indiana Soldiers' and Sailors' Children's Home, the superintendent's house kept the head of the school close to campus and provided a welcoming sight to visitors and residents. One popular past superintendent offered special suppers at the superintendent's home as a big reward to deserving students.